T0008168

Dear Reader,

As a registered dietitian, I regularly work with people who have high blood pressure and want to make dietary changes rather than add on more medications. If you've picked up this book, you may feel the same! It can be challenging to **change your habits**, including dietary habits and food behaviors, but even making small changes can lead to big results. Start with adding one fruit and vegetable into your daily food intake and go from there! Over time, healthy modifications like this can positively impact your body and overall health.

With the DASH diet, there's a **wonderful balance** with foods from all food groups. The focus of DASH is on what foods we can add into our daily routine, rather than drastically cutting out entire food groups. This makes DASH a great, sustainable way of eating!

This cookbook means so much to me because I know the incredibly positive impacts dietary changes can have on health. As I gathered information and recipes for this book, I remembered encouraging clients to make **essential nutrition changes** to lead healthier lives. Knowledge is key, and in this book, you'll learn evidence-based, reliable nutrition guidance on lowering blood pressure through dietary choices. Since having access to a registered dietitian isn't feasible for everyone, I hope this book will be a helpful guide to trying the DASH diet and figuring out a meal prep routine that works best for you!

Karman

Welcome to the Everything® Series!

These handy, accessible books give you all you need to tackle a difficult project, gain a new hobby, comprehend a fascinating topic, prepare for an exam, or even brush up on something you learned back in school but have since forgotten.

You can choose to read an Everything® book from cover to cover or just pick out the information you want from our four useful boxes: Questions, Facts, Alerts, and Essentials. We give you everything you need to know on the subject, but throw in a lot of fun stuff along the way too.

question	fact
Answers to common questions.	Important snippets of information.

alert	essential
Urgent warnings.	Quick handy tips.

We now have more than 600 Everything® books in print, spanning such wide-ranging categories as cooking, health, parenting, personal finance, wedding planning, word puzzles, and so much more. When you're done reading them all, you can finally say you know Everything®!

PUBLISHER Karen Cooper

MANAGING EDITOR Lisa Laing

ASSOCIATE COPY DIRECTOR Casey Ebert

PRODUCTION EDITOR Jo-Anne Duhamel

ACQUISITIONS EDITORS Rachael Thatcher and Lisa Laing

DEVELOPMENT EDITORS Jennifer Kristal and Brett Palana-Shanahan

EVERYTHING® SERIES COVER DESIGNER Erin Alexander

THE

EVERYTHING®

DASH DIET
MEAL PREP
COOKBOOK

KARMAN MEYER, RDN

**200 EASY, MAKE-AHEAD RECIPES TO HELP YOU
LOSE WEIGHT AND IMPROVE YOUR HEALTH**

ADAMS MEDIA

NEW YORK   LONDON   TORONTO   SYDNEY   NEW DELHI

To my endlessly supportive husband for standing by my side—even in the kitchen.

Adams Media
An Imprint of Simon & Schuster, Inc.
100 Technology Center Drive
Stoughton, Massachusetts 02072

Copyright © 2023 by Simon & Schuster, Inc.

All rights reserved, including the right to reproduce this book or portions thereof in any form whatsoever. For information address Adams Media Subsidiary Rights Department, 1230 Avenue of the Americas, New York, NY 10020.

An Everything® Series Book.

Everything® and everything.com® are registered trademarks of Simon & Schuster, Inc.

First Adams Media trade paperback edition January 2023

ADAMS MEDIA and colophon are trademarks of Simon & Schuster.

For information about special discounts for bulk purchases, please contact Simon & Schuster Special Sales at 1-866-506-1949 or business@simonandschuster.com.

The Simon & Schuster Speakers Bureau can bring authors to your live event. For more information or to book an event contact the Simon & Schuster Speakers Bureau at 1-866-248-3049 or visit our website at www.simonspeakers.com.

Interior layout by Kellie Emery
Photographs by James Stefiuk

Manufactured in the United States of America

10 9 8 7 6 5 4 3 2

Library of Congress Cataloging-in-Publication Data
Names: Meyer, Karman, author.
Title: The everything® DASH diet meal prep cookbook / Karman Meyer, RDN.
Description: First Adams Media trade paperback edition. | Stoughton, Massachusetts: Adams Media, 2023. | Series: Everything® series | Includes index.
Identifiers: LCCN 2022035046 | ISBN 9781507220078 (pb) | ISBN 9781507220085 (ebook)
Subjects: LCSH: Hypertension--Diet therapy--Popular works. | Hypertension--Diet therapy--Recipes. | Reducing diets--Recipes. | Make-ahead cooking. | LCGFT: Cookbooks
Classification: LCC RC685.H8 M484 2023 | DDC 616.1/320654--dc23/eng/20220805
LC record available at https://lccn.loc.gov/2022035046

ISBN 978-1-5072-2007-8
ISBN 978-1-5072-2008-5 (ebook)

Many of the designations used by manufacturers and sellers to distinguish their products are claimed as trademarks. Where those designations appear in this book and Simon & Schuster, Inc., was aware of a trademark claim, the designations have been printed with initial capital letters.

This book is intended as general information only, and should not be used to diagnose or treat any health condition. In light of the complex, individual, and specific nature of health problems, this book is not intended to replace professional medical advice. The ideas, procedures, and suggestions in this book are intended to supplement, not replace, the advice of a trained medical professional. Consult your physician before adopting any of the suggestions in this book, as well as about any condition that may require diagnosis or medical attention. The author and publisher disclaim any liability arising directly or indirectly from the use of this book.

Always follow safety and commonsense cooking protocols while using kitchen utensils, operating ovens and stoves, and handling uncooked food. If children are assisting in the preparation of any recipe, they should always be supervised by an adult.

Contains material adapted from the following titles published by Adams Media, an Imprint of Simon & Schuster, Inc.: *The Everything® Easy DASH Diet Cookbook* by Christy Ellingsworth and Murdoc Khaleghi, MD, copyright © 2021, ISBN 978-1-5072-1521-0; and *Eat to Sleep* by Karman Meyer, RD, LDN, copyright © 2019, ISBN 978-1-5072-1028-4.

Contents

INTRODUCTION 10

CHAPTER 1: THE DASH DIET 13

What Is the DASH Diet? 14

How DASH Helps with Hypertension 15

How DASH Helps with Weight Loss 16

Foods to Choose on the DASH Diet 16

Foods to Limit on the DASH Diet 17

Making the DASH Diet Fit Your Lifestyle 18

CHAPTER 2: BASICS OF MEAL PREPPING 19

Save Time with Meal Prepping 20

Steps to Successful Meal Prep 20

Helpful Tools for Meal Prepping 21

Grocery Shopping Tips 22

Prepared Meal Storage 23

CHAPTER 3: STAPLE MEAL PREP COMPONENTS 25

Whole Roasted Chicken 26

Homemade Chicken Stock 28

Basic Low-Sodium Broth 29

Rice-Quinoa Blend 30

Brown Rice 31

Quinoa 32

Homemade Cauliflower Rice 33

Overnight Oats 34

Sautéed Asparagus and Mushrooms 34

Roasted Sweet Potatoes 35

Roasted Red Potatoes, Carrots, and Brussels Sprouts 37

Roasted Broccoli and Cauliflower 38

Curry-Roasted Butternut Squash 39

Spicy and Tangy Barbecue Sauce 39

Spicy Lime, Cilantro, and Garlic Marinade 40

Basil Pesto 40

Salt-Free Mayonnaise 41

Asian-Inspired Low-Sodium Marinade 42

Salt-Free Chili Seasoning 42

CHAPTER 4: BREAKFAST 43

Blueberry Banana Oat Muffins 44

Vegetable Egg Muffins 45

Honey-Sweetened Fruit and Ricotta Toast 46

Pistachio Cranberry Granola 48

Breakfast Quinoa Salad 49

Butternut Squash and Fajita Vegetable Frittata 51

Pumpkin Seed and Chia Granola 53

Raspberry Almond Overnight Oats 54

Grapefruit and Orange Yogurt Parfait 54

Swiss Cheese and Chive Mini Quiches 55

Asparagus, Swiss, and Ricotta Frittata 56

Maple Turkey Sausage 57

Scrambled Tofu with Mushrooms and Zucchini 58

Oven-Baked Apple Pancake 59

Whole-Wheat Cinnamon Pancakes with Banana 61

Orange Cornmeal Pancakes 62

Sweet Potato Breakfast Pie 63

Sunday Morning Waffles 64

Whole-Grain Spiced Pear Waffles 65

ABC Muffins 66

Whole-Wheat Strawberry Corn Muffins 67

Maple, Oatmeal, and Applesauce Muffins 68

CHAPTER 5: SALADS AND SIDES 69

Kale and Roasted Beet Salad 70

Fresh Corn, Pepper, and Avocado Salad 72

Spring Pea Salad 74

Tuscan Kale Salad 75

Grapefruit Salmon Salad 77

Green Beans with Pecans, Cranberries, and Parmesan 79

Sautéed Cabbage, Kale, and Bacon 80

Garlic Rosemary Potato Salad 81

Southwestern Beet Slaw 82

Salade Niçoise 83

Tart Apple Salad with Fennel and Honey Yogurt Dressing 84

Italian Vinaigrette 84

Thai-Inspired Pasta Salad 85

Whole-Wheat Couscous Salad with Citrus and Cilantro 86

Simple Autumn Salad 87

Tabbouleh Salad 88

Arugula with Pears and Red Wine Vinaigrette 90

Zucchini Cakes 91

Lemon Parmesan Rice with Fresh Parsley 92

Israeli Couscous with Sautéed Spinach, Bell Pepper, and Onion 93

Wheat Berry Pilaf with Roasted Vegetables 95

Sautéed Spinach with Shallots and Garlic 96

Whole-Wheat Couscous with Plums, Ginger, and Allspice 97

Garlic Rosemary Mashed Potatoes 98

Sun-Dried Tomato Couscous with Pine Nuts, Garlic, and Basil 99

Perfect Corn Bread 100

CHAPTER 6: BEEF AND PORK ENTRÉES 101

Sheet Pan Pork Roast and Vegetables 102

Easy Deconstructed Wonton Soup 103

Beef Tenderloin and Roasted Vegetables 104

Red Lentil Soup with Bacon 106

30-Minute Ground Beef Pizza 107

Whole-Grain Pasta with Meat Sauce 108

Beef with Pea Pods 109

Pressure Cooker Beef Bourguignon 110

Pressure Cooker Harvest Stew 111

Asian-Inspired Mini Meatloaves with Salt-Free Hoisin Glaze 113

Seared Sirloin Steaks with Garlicky Greens 114

Whole-Grain Rotini with Pork, Pumpkin, and Sage 115

Ginger and Garlic Pork Stir-Fry 116

Pork Chops with Sautéed Apples and Shallots 117

CHAPTER 7: CHICKEN AND TURKEY ENTRÉES 119

Italian Chicken Kebabs 120

Greek Chicken and Cauliflower Rice Bowl 122

Asian Turkey Lettuce Wraps 123

Cheesy Potato Chowder 124

Classic Chicken Noodle Soup 125

Chicken, Black Bean, and Vegetable Soft Tacos 127

Chicken, Corn, and Black Bean Chili 128

Grilled Tequila Chicken with Sautéed Peppers and Onion 129

Saucy Barbecued Chicken with Rice 130

Spicy Yogurt-Marinated Chicken Tenders 131

Chicken Curry with Creamy Tomato Sauce 132

Oven-Baked Chicken Tenders 134

Chicken with Rice, Lemon, and Kale 135

Honey Mustard Chicken Breasts 136

Tropical Chicken Salad Wraps 137

Broccoli, Ground Turkey, and Pesto Pizza 139

Ground Turkey Meatloaf Minis 140

Turkey and Brown Rice–Stuffed Peppers 141

Seasoned Turkey Burgers with Sautéed Mushrooms and Swiss 142

CHAPTER 8: SEAFOOD ENTRÉES 143

Shrimp and Bok Choy Noodle Soup 144

Sheet Pan Salmon 145

Zesty Tuna Lettuce Wraps 146

Sesame Shrimp Stir-Fry 148

Baked Tuna Cakes 149

Healthy Fish and Chips 150

Roasted Steelhead Trout with Grapefruit Sauce 152

Ahi Tuna with Grape Tomato Salsa   155

Spicy Tilapia with Pineapple Relish   156

Salmon Cakes   157

Shrimp Creole   158

Open-Faced Tuna Melts   159

Tuna Pasta Salad with Broccoli and Sun-
   Dried Tomatoes   160

**CHAPTER 9: VEGAN/VEGETARIAN
ENTRÉES**   161

Tofu Vegetable Potpie   162

Black-Eyed Pea Burrito Bowl   164

Crispy Tofu Stir-Fry   165

Southwest Loaded Sweet Potatoes   166

Portobello Mushroom Parmigiana   168

Mushroom Soup with Orzo   169

Roasted Cauliflower Steaks with Creamy
   Chimichurri   170

Apple Butternut Soup   172

Sesame Tofu with Sautéed Green
   Beans   173

Falafel with Tzatziki   175

Whole-Grain Penne with Lemony Roasted
   Asparagus   177

Pesto Rice with Portobello Mushrooms   178

Spicy Chickpea Tacos with Arugula   179

10-Minute Thai Noodles   180

Vegetable Baked Ziti   181

Linguine with Plum Tomatoes, Mushrooms,
   and Tempeh   182

Coconut Cauliflower Curry   183

Kale-Stuffed Manicotti   184

Black Bean Burgers   186

Sweet Potato and Black Bean Burritos   187

Vegetable Sushi   188

CHAPTER 10: FREEZER MEALS   189

Spicy Lime Chicken   190

Chili-Rubbed Seared Salmon   191

Turkey Meatballs   192

Mediterranean Turkey Burgers   193

Vegetarian Lasagna   195

Greek Lemon Chicken Orzo Soup   197

Black Bean Vegetable Soup   198

White Bean and Vegetable Soup   199

Tandoori Masala Chicken   200

Chili-Spiced Ground Beef   202

Slow Cooker Squash and Chickpea
   Curry   203

Vegetable Burgers   204

Baked Pumpkin Oatmeal   205

Lemon Blueberry Quinoa Breakfast
   Bars   207

Breakfast Burritos   208

CHAPTER 11: SNACKS   209

Summer Fruit Salsa with Cinnamon Pita
   Chips   210

Cranberry Almond Energy Bites   211

Avocado "Hummus"   212

Healthier 7-Layer Dip   213

Blueberry Cottage Cheese Parfait   214

Zucchini Sticks 215

Homemade Soft Pretzels 216

Crunchy Coated Nuts 218

"Cheesy" Seasoned Popcorn 219

Seasoned Sesame Kale Chips 220

Sweet Potato Crisps 221

Chewy Granola Bars 222

Whole-Grain Crackers with Rosemary, Garlic, and Parmesan 223

Roasted Red Pepper Hummus 225

Holy Guacamole 226

Garlic Lovers' Hummus 227

Pineapple Salsa 227

Roasted Tomato Salsa 228

CHAPTER 12: DESSERTS 229

Zucchini Oatmeal Cookies 230

Coconut Chia Pudding 231

Lemon White Chocolate Popcorn 232

Cinnamon Peanut Butter Cookies 233

Vegan Lemon Drops 234

Cinnamon Apple Pear Sauce 236

Roasted Plantain Boats 237

Banana Walnut Scones 238

Gingersnaps 240

Carrot Cake Cookies 241

Coconut Chocolate Chip Blondies 243

Mini Cornmeal Rhubarb Crisps 244

Mango Crumble 245

Vegan Chocolate Cupcakes 246

Pound Cake Minis 247

Jumbo Pumpkin Chocolate Chip Muffins 248

Crumb-Topped Mango Muffins 249

Peach Cobbler 250

Lemon Coconut Scones 252

CHAPTER 13: BEVERAGES/ SMOOTHIES 253

Chocolate Strawberry Power Smoothie 254

Thin Mint Cocoa 254

Chocolate Banana Smoothie 255

Almond Butter Jelly Smoothie 255

Mango Coconut Water Slush 256

Watermelon Refresher 256

Mango Mint Smoothie 257

Wild Blueberry Edamame Smoothie 257

Green Mango Smoothie 259

Gingered Wheatgrass Tea 260

Ruby Red Grapefruit Spritzer 260

Orange Banana Smoothie 261

Maple Iced Mocha 261

Piña Colada Smoothies 262

APPENDIX: TWO-WEEK MEAL PLAN 264

STANDARD US/METRIC MEASUREMENT CONVERSIONS 268

INDEX 269

Introduction

The DASH diet was designed as a powerful tool to help manage blood pressure. But in addition to that, the DASH diet has *many* other health benefits, including improving cholesterol levels, decreasing the risk of many types of cancer, and even decreasing the chance of kidney stones. Overall, it's a healthy and customizable eating pattern that can work for anyone!

When you combine the DASH diet with meal prepping, you'll find that eating for your health has never been easier. By prepping key meal components ahead of time, having extra meals left over in the freezer, and keeping a few pantry essentials on hand, you can easily pull together a nutritious meal that falls in line with your DASH-style eating pattern. Getting comfortable with meal prepping can take some time, but with a little practice and dedication, you can be a meal prep pro!

In *The Everything® DASH Diet Meal Prep Cookbook*, you'll find two hundred DASH diet–friendly and flavorful recipes created with meal prepping in mind. From power-packed breakfasts like Swiss Cheese and Chive Mini Quiches and Maple Turkey Sausage to delicious dinners like Healthy Fish and Chips and Saucy Barbecued Chicken with Rice and tempting snacks like Chewy Granola Bars and "Cheesy" Seasoned Popcorn, there is something delicious for every meal! And just because you are on the DASH diet doesn't mean you have to give up desserts: Dig into Coconut Chocolate Chip Blondies and Carrot Cake Cookies for a sweet way to end the day.

To help you as you are beginning this lifestyle, you'll find some steps to successful meal prep, smart grocery shopping tips, and best practices for storing ingredients and prepared meals in either the refrigerator or the freezer. In addition, you'll find information on the essentials of the

DASH diet and meal prepping, the benefits of the DASH diet and how it can help manage hypertension, all the delicious foods that you can enjoy, the ones you should avoid, and a few tips to make the DASH diet work for your lifestyle. And don't forget to check out the Two-Week Meal Plan in the Appendix that will help you get you started on your journey.

The most important thing you should remember, though, is that eating well and meal prepping is not an all-or-nothing deal. If you have a week where meal prep doesn't happen because things in life are just too hectic, don't beat yourself up. Try again next week and start with small steps toward meal prepping rather than commit to a full week of made-ahead meals. The same goes for following the DASH diet eating pattern. There will undoubtedly be meals or occasions where you go outside of the DASH diet recommendations, but every meal you eat is a new opportunity to make different choices.

An essential part of cooking healthy meals at home is to do some level of meal prepping to make the process easier. In fact, meal prepping can guarantee your success in making the DASH diet a simple part of your life.

CHAPTER 1
The DASH Diet

"DASH" stands for "Dietary Approaches to Stop Hypertension." While the word "diet" is attached to DASH, the DASH diet is not meant to be temporary. DASH is designed to be a practical, ongoing eating pattern to keep you healthy for the long term! In fact, the DASH diet has become one of the most popular dietary lifestyles today. In this chapter, you'll learn how the DASH diet can help with hypertension, which foods to limit and which foods to enjoy more of, and how you can make DASH fit into your daily routine.

What Is the DASH Diet?

Although the DASH diet was created with a focus on hypertension, other positive impacts of this diet have been discovered within the last decade. The DASH diet can help lower blood pressure, improve cholesterol levels, decrease the risk of many types of cancer, and even decrease the chance of kidney stones. Overall, it's a healthy eating pattern that works for many individuals.

Unlike many other dietary plans, the DASH diet has wide-ranging health benefits that have been backed by numerous studies, such as those from the National Institutes of Health. The DASH eating pattern is designed to reduce sodium, limit certain fats, and increase consumption of fruits, vegetables, and whole grains. Nutrients that are of primary focus on the DASH diet include sodium, cholesterol, saturated fat, protein, potassium, calcium, magnesium, and fiber. This chapter will discuss each of these nutrients at greater length.

One distinguishing feature of the DASH diet is that it provides a range of the optimal amounts of different food types to eat. Without knowing ranges for the number of servings a day, it is easy to eat in excess. Eating food beyond what your body needs will lead to the food being stored as fat and may contribute to obesity. The DASH diet suggests the following amounts for a 2,000-calorie-a-day diet:

- **Whole grains:** 6–8 daily servings (1 serving = 1 slice bread, 1 ounce dry cereal, or ½ cup cooked cereal, rice, or pasta)
- **Lean meats or fish:** 2 daily servings or fewer (1 serving = 3 ounces cooked meat or fish or 1 jumbo cooked egg)
- **Vegetables:** 4–5 daily servings (1 serving = 1 cup raw leafy green vegetables, ½ cup raw or cooked vegetables, or ½ cup vegetable juice)
- **Fruits:** 4–5 daily servings (1 serving = 1 medium fruit; ½ cup fresh, frozen, or canned fruit; ¼ cup dried fruit; or ½ cup fruit juice)
- **Lean dairy products:** 2–3 daily servings (1 serving = 1 cup milk, 1 cup yogurt, or 1½ ounces cheese)
- **Fats and oils:** 2–3 daily servings or fewer (1 serving = 1 tablespoon low-fat mayonnaise, 1 teaspoon vegetable oil, or 2 tablespoons light salad dressing)
- **Nuts, seeds, or legumes:** 4–5 weekly servings (1 serving = ⅓ cup or 1½ ounces nuts, 1 tablespoon or ½ ounce seeds, or ½ cup cooked beans)
- **Sweets and added sugars:** 5 weekly servings or fewer (1 serving = 1 tablespoon sugar, 1 tablespoon jelly or jam, or 1 cup lemonade)

These servings vary based on caloric needs, but the proportions of food to calories should stay relatively the same. For example, if you are very active and burn about 3,000 calories per day, you may want to increase whole grains to 9–12 servings, fruits and vegetables to 6–8 servings each, and so on. Similarly, if you are inactive, you may want to reduce these amounts somewhat. However, if you're not currently physically active but you can be, it's best to increase your activity and the number of calories you use rather than reduce your food intake. There are so many health benefits to being physically active!

How DASH Helps with Hypertension

Hypertension, also referred to as *high blood pressure*, was the initial focus of the DASH diet because it is known to be one of the leading killers of Americans. Hypertension is considered the "silent killer" because the effects of high blood pressure often aren't felt for years and can lead to a heart attack, a stroke, or end-stage renal disease. It's also the most preventable contributor to cardiovascular disease! Currently, about 45 percent of adults in the United States have hypertension. Before you learn how the DASH diet can help manage blood pressure, you first need to review basics about blood pressure and important health-related numbers to keep in mind.

Blood pressure is the pressure your blood exerts on blood vessels, which is also the pressure used by your heart to push blood through your body. The higher your blood pressure, the more damage that occurs to your blood vessels. These damaged areas eventually form plaques that can cause a heart attack or stroke. The damage can build up over many years, which,

again, is why high blood pressure is known as a silent killer. With a high blood pressure reading, your heart must work harder and therefore becomes predisposed to failing.

alert

On a global level, a suboptimal diet is responsible for one in five deaths. That's greater than any other risk factor, including tobacco use. Cardiovascular disease is the leading cause of diet-related deaths, followed by cancer and type 2 diabetes.

There are two key numbers to consider when it comes to understanding blood pressure. The first number, which tells you the pressure being exerted by your heart and blood when your heart is actively pumping, is referred to as *systolic blood pressure*. The other number, a measurement of pressure exerted when your heart is not actively pumping, is called *diastolic blood pressure*. Blood pressure is measured in millimeters of mercury, or mmHg, and is displayed by showing the systolic blood pressure over the diastolic blood pressure. People who have a systolic blood pressure at or above 130 mmHg and a diastolic blood pressure at or above 80 mmHg, as well as those who are already taking antihypertensive medications, are considered hypertensive. By managing and reducing high blood pressure before it negatively affects your body, you can successfully reduce your risk for a heart attack, a stroke, and chronic kidney disease. The even better news here is that no matter how long you may have had high blood pressure, you can still reduce your risk by acting on it now. It's not too late to make a change in your health when it comes to reducing blood pressure!

The standard DASH diet is lower in sodium than the typical American diet, limiting sodium to about 2,300 milligrams (mg) per day. To give you an idea of what 2,300 mg of sodium would be if you measured it using regular table salt, it would be about 1 teaspoon. The average daily intake of sodium in the American diet is closer to 3,400 mg or more per day. One study found that participants who followed the DASH diet without altering their sodium intake lowered their blood pressure within weeks, while those who reduced sodium intake from 3,400 mg to 2,300 mg or less per day had even greater reductions in blood pressure. There is a lower-sodium version of the DASH diet, limiting sodium to 1,500 mg per day, that your doctor or registered dietitian may recommend if necessary.

How DASH Helps with Weight Loss

While the primary goal of a DASH diet is often to reduce sodium intake to help manage hypertension, weight loss is often an unintentional but welcomed secondary benefit. When switching from a standard American diet to the DASH diet, there's a significant increase in fiber-rich, lower-calorie foods like fruits and vegetables, which increase satiety, making you feel fuller longer and preventing overeating or snacking between meals. This in and of itself can help with weight management. There's also a focus on choosing lean meats, eating fewer refined carbohydrates, eating healthy fats, and consuming fewer processed foods, all of which can play a part in weight loss over time.

fact

Diet quality in the United States has declined from 2001 to 2018 based on American Heart Association and Healthy Eating Index scores. Approximately 122 million Americans have cardiovascular disease, which causes 2,300 deaths per day.

The weight loss experienced with the DASH diet may not be as significant or drastic as with some other diets, but it is often more sustainable and longer-lasting. A review published in 2016 in *Obesity Reviews* found that the DASH diet, compared with other low-energy diets, was statistically significant for weight loss, and people were able to keep the weight off after a year of following the DASH diet.

Foods to Choose on the DASH Diet

Earlier, this chapter shared important nutrients that have a positive impact on high blood pressure and are prevalent in the DASH diet: potassium, magnesium, calcium, protein, and fiber.

The DASH eating plan focuses on eating plenty of fruits and vegetables. Many of the foods that fall into those two categories will also be good sources of potassium, fiber, and even magnesium. Some green leafy vegetables even provide calcium! Filling your plate with a variety of vegetables and fruits will help you get the essential nutrients you need to help manage your blood pressure.

It's okay to use frozen fruits and vegetables as part of your DASH diet plan, and they're often the better choice nutritionally! Frozen produce is picked at the peak of ripeness and flash frozen, so it maintains its nutrient content rather than degrading. Another benefit is that frozen produce is available year-round. Canned fruits and vegetables are also acceptable to use, but look for fruits canned in 100 percent fruit juice and vegetables that have either "reduced sodium" or "no salt added" on the label.

essential

Following a plant-forward dietary pattern, such as the DASH diet, has been associated with positive health outcomes, including reduced risk of cardiovascular disease. This is primarily because there's an increased intake of fruits, vegetables, and whole grains.

In addition to eating fruits and vegetables each day, having foods that are naturally rich in calcium and potassium, such as low-fat or fat-free dairy, will be beneficial. It's recommended to have 2–3 servings of dairy daily. Other good sources of calcium include sardines, dark leafy greens, soybeans, fortified cereals, and enriched breads and grains. For magnesium, turn to nuts, seeds, avocado, and beans.

Foods to Limit on the DASH Diet

While there are many foods you can enjoy on the DASH diet, you should limit foods containing sodium, cholesterol, saturated fat, and alcohol.

Sodium is the primary ingredient in the most common form of salt. When you eat salt, sodium gets absorbed into your bloodstream. This increases the concentration of sodium in your blood compared to other tissues in your body. Through osmosis, fluid in tissues flows back into the bloodstream. The greater volume of fluid in your bloodstream exerts more pressure on your heart and blood vessels, causing higher blood pressure. Therefore, ingesting more salt increases your blood pressure.

By cooking more at home and reducing your intake of highly processed foods and restaurant meals, you can see significant improvements in blood pressure. Adding salt to foods cooked at home generally accounts for only about 11 percent of the total sodium in American diets. The rest of it comes from eating out and from consumption of highly processed foods such as deli meats, hot dogs, cured meats, canned soups, frozen entrées, and frozen pizza.

Saturated fat can raise cholesterol levels, which increases the risk of heart disease. Found in many animal-based foods, such as meat, full-fat dairy products, butter, and eggs, saturated fat is typically solid at room temperature. The American Heart Association recommends less than 5–6 percent of calories come from saturated fat. In a 2,000-calorie diet, that means only 120 calories should come from saturated fat—about 13 grams of saturated fat per day.

Like saturated fats, cholesterol is found mostly in animal-based foods. You should limit your cholesterol consumption to no more than 300 mg per day. You can reduce cholesterol and saturated fat intake by eating 2 servings of lean protein a day and limiting full-fat dairy foods, butter, and use of tropical oils such as coconut oil and palm oil.

Making the DASH Diet Fit Your Lifestyle

Through the DASH diet, you can reduce your risk of many devastating diseases while reaching an ideal weight and giving yourself more energy. The most important aspect of the DASH diet is eating more of certain types of foods and decreasing certain other types. Following these basic principles will have a major impact on your health! In situations where you must avoid a certain food group due to an allergy or intolerance, you need to understand which beneficial nutrients the food contains and how you can compensate for it. Here is a simplified overview of the important nutrients in the different DASH-recommended foods:

- **Whole grains:** Energy (carbohydrates) and fiber
- **Fruits and vegetables:** Potassium, magnesium, fiber, and sometimes calcium (leafy greens)
- **Low-fat dairy products:** Protein, calcium, and potassium
- **Lean meats and fish:** Protein, magnesium, and essential fatty acids
- **Nuts:** Energy (carbohydrates and essential fatty acids), magnesium, potassium, and fiber

For example, to make DASH fit your lifestyle, if you don't enjoy leafy green vegetables, you can still eat a variety of other fruits and vegetables to get potassium, magnesium, and fiber, but you can also make sure that your calcium needs are met through other foods, such as low-fat dairy.

The DASH diet is not intended to be a temporary change but rather a sustainable lifestyle, and therefore it needs to be personalized to you. Gradually implement some of the changes rather than making drastic changes in your eating routine and lifestyle. The DASH diet can be very forgiving, and small steps can lead to big results over time. You have taken the first step to learn about the DASH diet, and the rest of this book will provide you with other practical information and flavorful, nutritious recipes to help you put your new knowledge into practice.

CHAPTER 2

Basics of Meal Prepping

Meal prepping will look different for everyone. There's no one right way to do it. Prepping should be about what works best for you and your routine. You also don't need to spend an entire Saturday or Sunday to be successful at meal prep. With as little as 30 minutes of prepping, you can get a head start on meals for the upcoming week. This chapter will review steps to successful meal prep, tips for grocery shopping, and ways to safely store your ingredients and your prepared meals.

Save Time with Meal Prepping

Prepping meals ahead does require some up-front investment of time and energy, but it's well worth it. If you've considered meal prepping before or given it a try, some of the following benefits may resonate with you. Meal prepping helps you:

- Stay on track with your dietary goals
- Create variety in your meals so you don't rotate through the same five meals every week
- Be less apt to eat impulsively, especially at snack time
- Resist buying fast food, takeout, or processed convenience foods
- Save money by buying in bulk
- Save time by prepping ingredients for multiple meals at once
- Feel less stressed about what to make

Steps to Successful Meal Prep

You don't need to be a master chef or a meal prep professional to succeed with meal prepping at home. With a few basic principles and components, you'll be able to prep ingredients and recipes in advance without much additional effort. There are two primary ways to go about organizing your meal prep:

1. **The "extra portions" method:** This is where you make full meals, such as soups, salads, and casseroles, and store portions to use later.

2. **The "free-form" method:** In this strategy, you will batch-cook individual foods such as grains, roasted vegetables, and proteins. These can be mixed and matched for versatile meals on the fly. Use your imagination to combine one protein, one grain, and as many vegetables as you'd like into a complete meal. This type of meal is commonly referred to as a *power bowl* because it's a balanced meal all in one bowl!

If you're new to meal prepping, the extra-portions method is a good place to begin. Once you're more comfortable with prepping meals, you can advance to the free-form method. The recipes in *The Everything® DASH Diet Meal Prep Cookbook* have purposely been chosen for crossover ingredients that can be used in different recipes, whether you're using the extra-portions or free-form method. For example, after making Homemade Cauliflower Rice (see recipe in Chapter 3), you'll have it on hand to use for the Greek Chicken and Cauliflower Rice Bowl (see recipe in Chapter 7). You can also use the Homemade Cauliflower Rice to mix into other grains you've prepared or use it on its own to build a delicious power bowl!

Once you're ready to give the free-form method a try, you can create a healthy, balanced meal that falls within the DASH guidelines by striving to include the following at each meal: a fruit; 1–2 vegetable servings; a lean meat, fish, egg, or beans; and a whole grain. Getting in the mindset of building your plate with these essential food groups will help you get those important nutrients in every day. This mindset will also assist you in figuring out what to prioritize when it comes to meal prep.

alert

You may be excited to start meal prepping, but try to plan only one week of prepped ingredients and meals at a time as you get into the routine. That will help you avoid overwhelm and prevent food waste.

Low-sodium prepackaged items that can work well with the free-form method and make meal prep easier include:

- Prepped vegetables (shredded carrots, chopped greens, diced onion, etc.)
- Ready-made salad mix
- Prepped fruits such as pineapple and strawberries
- Rotisserie chicken
- Microwaveable grains
- Frozen smoothie packs
- Granola

Helpful Tools for Meal Prepping

To work efficiently and happily when meal prepping, it's best to have some of these kitchen tools:

- **Food processor:** This machine is helpful for chopping leafy greens like kale and for making cauliflower rice in a matter of seconds. It's also handy for making hummus, homemade bread crumbs, nut butter, and pesto.
- **Knives:** A good set of quality knives will make chopping and other prep work much easier. Keep knives sharp and learn basic knife skills to save time in the kitchen.
- **Blender:** Not only can you use it to make smoothies, but you can also make soups, salad dressings, sauces, and frozen desserts.
- **Slow cooker or pressure cooker:** These appliances can be a real help when it comes to meal prepping. The slow cooker is great for cooking soups, stews, and large pieces of meat, while a pressure cooker can cook just about anything! The pressure cooker will save you some time since it cooks items quicker than a slow cooker.
- **Skillets and pans:** A set of pans and baking sheets of different sizes is necessary for cooking at home. With nonstick pans, you can often use less oil than with other types of pans.
- **Garlic press:** Garlic is a great way to add flavor to food. Save time on chopping by using a garlic press instead.

Remember, you can start small. Only prepare a few items each week. Once you have that down, try adding a few more staple meal components or recipes to the weekly meal prep routine.

essential

Label containers with the name of the dish and the date it was made before storing them in the refrigerator or freezer. This will help you keep track of what's what and how long items have been in there. Keep it simple with masking tape and a permanent marker, or purchase labels online.

Grocery Shopping Tips

In order to meal prep, you must obtain groceries from the store or get them delivered. However, there will be some ingredients you'll want to keep stocked at home all the time so you can easily create a meal. Recommended items to keep in stock are:

- Lentils and dried or canned beans (no-salt-added variety)
- Canned vegetables with no salt added, such as diced tomatoes
- Fruits canned in 100 percent fruit juice, such as pineapple, pears, or peaches
- Whole grains such as brown rice, quinoa, oats, and whole-grain pasta
- Canned tuna and chicken
- Dried herbs and spices
- Fresh garlic
- Olive oil
- Nuts, seeds, and dried fruits
- Frozen foods such as vegetables, fruits, and frozen seafood

It's good to have a checklist for pantry staples if you're new to meal prepping. By going through the checklist before stepping out the door, you can ensure these staples are always on hand. Once you've determined the items you already have stocked in the pantry and freezer, you can start making your grocery list.

fact

It's often thought that canned vegetables and meats should be avoided due to sodium content, but there are low-sodium options. To reduce the sodium content even more, rinse beans, vegetables, and even canned meats under water to reduce sodium by 40 percent!

You may prefer to group items into categories based on what section of the grocery store they can be found in. For example, listing produce first, followed by meat/seafood, then grains, beans, and shelf-stable items. Lastly, list any frozen items and dairy foods to buy. This saves time as you make your way through the grocery store, and it can help you save money when you stick to the list.

If your grocery store has a nice bulk bin section, take advantage of it by stocking up on pantry items like grains, beans, and lentils. Buying in bulk can help you save money and time. Most items found in the bulk bin section will last 1–3 months in an airtight container in the pantry, but you can extend the shelf life by freezing items, especially nuts, seeds, and whole grains. Before stocking food, label the packages with the item name and date purchased (and date frozen, if different).

Prepared Meal Storage

Keeping your prepped meals in the refrigerator and freezer is easy! You simply need the right storage containers. Follow these tips to ensure the best quality and food safety:

- Invest in airtight, heavy-duty plastic or glass containers that are stackable. It's good to have a variety of sizes.
- Keep quart- and gallon-sized freezer-safe plastic bags on hand. These are great for storing prepared soups, shredded cooked meats, prepped vegetables, and other prepped ingredients. Be sure to squeeze out as much air as possible before sealing.
- Label containers that you're storing in the refrigerator and freezer so you don't lose track of what's what and when it was made. Masking tape and a permanent marker work well.
- Transfer cooked food directly from your pan into labeled airtight containers and store in the refrigerator.
- When freezing prepared ingredients and recipes, cool cooked products in the refrigerator before putting them in the freezer. Make sure there is about ¾" of space between the food and the top of the container to allow for any expansion that may occur.
- Certain cooked grains and vegetables don't freeze as well as others and will become a bit mushy. These include potatoes, high-water-content vegetables, creamy foods, and cream sauces.
- Never go straight from the freezer to the microwave with glass containers. The rapid change in temperature can cause them to break! It's important to let food thaw in the refrigerator first.

---

question

Glass or Plastic?

Both can be great options, and there are stackable containers made from both materials. If you're concerned about BPA, look for plastic containers made without it or opt for glass.

You'll find storage information (refrigerator, freezer, room temperature) in each recipe in this book. To reheat a meal, use the microwave, stovetop, or oven, being careful to choose a method suitable for the type of food. Food that's been roasted or baked doesn't do as well if it's reheated in the microwave. In this case, reheat in the oven or toaster oven or on the stovetop. If you use the broiler, be sure to watch it carefully, as food can burn quickly under it. Most other foods, such as soups, stews, casseroles, pasta, and grain dishes (except breads) do well in the microwave or on the stovetop. Generally, leftovers should be reheated to 165°F.

CHAPTER 3
Staple Meal Prep Components

Whole Roasted Chicken 26

Homemade Chicken Stock 28

Basic Low-Sodium Broth 29

Rice-Quinoa Blend 30

Brown Rice 31

Quinoa 32

Homemade Cauliflower Rice 33

Overnight Oats 34

Sautéed Asparagus and Mushrooms 34

Roasted Sweet Potatoes 35

Roasted Red Potatoes, Carrots, and Brussels Sprouts 37

Roasted Broccoli and Cauliflower 38

Curry-Roasted Butternut Squash 39

Spicy and Tangy Barbecue Sauce 39

Spicy Lime, Cilantro, and Garlic Marinade 40

Basil Pesto 40

Salt-Free Mayonnaise 41

Asian-Inspired Low-Sodium Marinade 42

Salt-Free Chili Seasoning 42

Whole Roasted Chicken

Roasting a whole chicken at home is often a more budget-friendly way to enjoy poultry, especially compared to precut pieces at the store. With just a few ingredients and a little time, you can roast a beautiful chicken that can be used in multiple recipes through-out the week. This chicken is prepared by a technique called "spatchcock."

SERVES 4

Per Serving

Calories	263
Fat	8g
Sodium	103mg
Carbohydrates	0g
Fiber	0g
Sugar	0g
Protein	43g

SPATCHCOCK TECHNIQUE

Spatchcocking is a way to butterfly a chicken or a turkey by removing the backbone of the bird. One of the main advantages of this preparation technique is a shorter cooking time.

1 (6-pound) whole chicken

1 tablespoon olive oil

1 teaspoon salt-free garlic and herb seasoning

½ teaspoon garlic powder

¼ teaspoon ground black pepper

1 Preheat oven to 425°F. Remove giblets from inside chicken.

2 Place chicken in a roasting pan, breast side down. Find spine and cut alongside it with a knife or kitchen shears until back side of chicken is split in half. Flip chicken over so breast side is up.

3 Pour oil over chicken and use your hands or a paper towel to rub oil over chicken skin. Season chicken with garlic and herb seasoning, garlic powder, and pepper. Roast 8–10 minutes per pound for spatchcocked chicken or 15–20 minutes per pound if cooking whole. Internal temperature of chicken should be at least 165°F. Remove pan from oven.

4 Allow chicken to cool 30 minutes before breaking it down into quarters or shredding it into smaller pieces. Reserve bones and skin to make Homemade Chicken Stock (see recipe in this chapter). Store chicken in refrigerator up to 4 days. To reheat, place in a microwave-safe dish and microwave 60–75 seconds at a time.

Homemade Chicken Stock

MAKES 3¼ CUPS

Per Serving (¼ cup)

Calories	10
Fat	1g
Sodium	48mg
Carbohydrates	0g
Fiber	0g
Sugar	0g
Protein	1g

BROTH OR STOCK?

If you're wondering what the difference is, broth is usually made with meat and vegetables simmered in liquid, while a stock always includes bones. By cooking the bones, you end up with a thicker liquid with more collagen in the final product. That said, the terms "broth" and "stock" are often used interchangeably in conversation.

To reduce food waste, save money, and stick to the DASH diet, make homemade stock with leftover chicken bones, vegetable peelings, and scraps. Keep a bag in the freezer for vegetable stems, ends, and peelings. Once you roast a whole chicken, you will have everything needed for this homemade stock!

½ tablespoon olive oil

4 small carrots, chopped

3 medium stalks celery, chopped

½ medium yellow onion, peeled and quartered

2 cloves garlic, peeled and root end removed

¼ teaspoon salt

Leftover bones and skin from Whole Roasted Chicken (see recipe in this chapter)

2 bay leaves

½ sprig fresh rosemary

4 cups water

1 Heat oil in a large stockpot over medium heat. Add carrots, celery, onion, garlic, and salt. Cook about 6 minutes, stirring occasionally.

2 Add bones and skin, bay leaves, rosemary, and water. Increase heat to medium-high and bring to a boil. Reduce heat to low, cover, and simmer 2½ hours. Remove pot from heat. Use metal tongs to remove bones and any large pieces from stock, then pour stock through a fine-mesh strainer into a large glass bowl and let cool about 1 hour before dividing among glass storage containers.

3 Store in refrigerator up to 7 days. To reheat, place stock in a microwave-safe dish and microwave 45–60 seconds at a time, stirring in between, or place in a saucepan on the stovetop over medium heat until heated to 165°F.

Basic Low-Sodium Broth

This fat-free vegan broth is perfect for flavoring your favorite soup or sipping straight from a mug.

1 medium yellow onion, peeled and quartered

3 cloves garlic, peeled and halved

8 ounces white button mushrooms, roughly chopped

3 medium carrots, peeled and cut into chunks

2 medium stalks celery, cut into chunks

2 medium tomatoes, roughly chopped

1 (1") piece fresh ginger, peeled

6 whole peppercorns

2 bay leaves

10 cups water

1 Place all ingredients in a large stockpot.

2 Cover pot and bring to a boil over high heat. Reduce heat to medium-low and simmer 30 minutes.

3 Turn off the heat and let contents steep another 30 minutes.

4 Pour broth through a fine-mesh strainer, discarding solids. Store broth in refrigerator up to a week or in freezer up to 6 months. Thaw in refrigerator until defrosted. To reheat, place in a microwave-safe dish and microwave 2 minutes or in a saucepan over medium-high heat until heated through.

MAKES 8 CUPS

Per Serving (1 cup)

Calories	4
Fat	0g
Sodium	2mg
Carbohydrates	1g
Fiber	0g
Sugar	0g
Protein	0g

HOMEMADE VERSUS COMMERCIAL BROTH

Homemade broth is often tastier than store-bought. It's also additive- and preservative-free. Homemade broth can be made in batches and frozen for later use. However, when you're pressed for time, commercial low-sodium, low-fat broths can be a good alternative. Check nutrition facts carefully; some manufacturers sell "reduced-sodium" broths that contain hundreds of milligrams of sodium per serving.

Rice-Quinoa Blend

MAKES 8 CUPS

Per Serving (1 cup)

Calories	162
Fat	1g
Sodium	220mg
Carbohydrates	32g
Fiber	2g
Sugar	0g
Protein	5g

This wonderful blend is a good staple for weekly meal prep! It's light and fluffy, great for building protein bowls, and very easy to prepare for a busy week ahead. You will love that the quinoa and rice can be cooked together in one pot!

1 cup tri-color quinoa

1 cup white rice

4 cups water

¾ teaspoon salt

1 Rinse quinoa in a fine-mesh strainer, then transfer to a large saucepan. Add rice.

2 Add water and salt to pan. Bring to a boil over high heat. Once boiling, reduce heat to low and cover pan. Cook 20 minutes or until rice is tender.

3 To store, allow Rice-Quinoa Blend to cool before placing in an airtight container or resealable bag. Keep in refrigerator up to 4 days or in freezer up to 2 months. To reheat, place Rice-Quinoa Blend in a microwave-safe dish covered with a lid or moistened paper towel and microwave 30–45 seconds at a time, stirring in between.

Brown Rice

Brown rice takes longer to cook than white rice because of the fiber content, so it's great to cook this whole grain ahead of time. You can keep hearty brown rice in the refrigerator up to 4 days, so it will be ready to use in a quick stir-fry dish or power bowl during the week.

1 cup brown rice

2 cups water

¼ teaspoon salt

1 Rinse rice in a fine-mesh strainer, then transfer to a large saucepan. Add water and salt.

2 Bring to a boil over high heat. Once boiling, reduce heat to low and cover pan. Cook 40 minutes or until rice is tender.

3 To store, allow rice to cool before placing in an airtight container or resealable bag. Keep in refrigerator up to 4 days or in freezer up to 2 months. To reheat, place rice in a microwave-safe dish covered with a lid or moistened paper towel and microwave 30–45 seconds at a time, stirring in between.

SERVES 4

Per Serving

Calories	163
Fat	1g
Sodium	146mg
Carbohydrates	34g
Fiber	3g
Sugar	0g
Protein	3g

Quinoa

SERVES 4

Per Serving

Calories	223
Fat	3g
Sodium	12mg
Carbohydrates	40g
Fiber	5g
Sugar	0g
Protein	8g

QUINOA'S NUTRITION BENEFITS

This tiny whole grain is packed with nutritional benefits. In addition to providing high-quality carbohydrates, it's a good source of plant-based protein. One cup of cooked quinoa contains about 8 grams of protein. Quinoa also provides iron, manganese, magnesium, and 5 grams of fiber per cup.

Quinoa is available in different colors. Try any of them: white, red, or black! It's easy to cook and is a great base for a healthy meal. For breakfast, try the Breakfast Quinoa Salad (see recipe in Chapter 4). For lunch, use quinoa to create a power bowl with vegetables, a protein, and any additional toppings like avocado, cheese, or a homemade dressing.

1 cup tri-color quinoa
2 cups water
½ teaspoon garlic powder

1 Rinse quinoa in a fine-mesh strainer, then transfer to a large saucepan. Add remaining ingredients and bring to a boil over high heat. Once boiling, reduce heat to low and cover pan. Cook 18–20 minutes, until water is absorbed. Fluff with a fork.

2 To store, allow quinoa to cool before placing in an airtight container or resealable bag. Keep in refrigerator up to 4 days or in freezer up to 2 months. To reheat, place quinoa in a microwave-safe dish covered with a lid or moistened paper towel and microwave 30–45 seconds at a time, stirring in between.

Homemade Cauliflower Rice

It's super simple to make cauliflower rice at home if you have a food processor or box grater. You can use cauliflower rice as a lower-carb option to make power bowls or mix it into cooked rice or quinoa for a unique blend. Try the Greek Chicken and Cauliflower Rice Bowl (see recipe in Chapter 7) for a fast weeknight meal!

3 cups cauliflower florets
½ tablespoon olive oil
½ teaspoon dried oregano

1 To make rice, pulse cauliflower in a food processor or grate using the medium-sized holes on a box grater.

2 To cook cauliflower rice, heat oil in a large skillet over medium-high heat. Add cauliflower rice and oregano. Cook 4 minutes.

3 To store, place cooled cauliflower rice in an airtight container or resealable bag. Keep in refrigerator up to 4 days or in freezer up to 2 months. To reheat, place in a microwave-safe dish and micro-wave 45–60 seconds at a time, stirring in between.

SERVES 4	
Per Serving	
Calories	35
Fat	2g
Sodium	24mg
Carbohydrates	4g
Fiber	2g
Sugar	2g
Protein	2g

Overnight Oats

SERVES 1	
Per Serving	
Calories	272
Fat	7g
Sodium	88mg
Carbohydrates	38g
Fiber	5g
Sugar	4g
Protein	17g

Bookmark this super-simple recipe to make a basic overnight oatmeal that you can add any toppings to—such as fruit, chopped nuts, and seeds—when you're ready to enjoy! Top yours with blueberries and coconut, raspberries and almonds, or bananas and chopped pecans. The flavor combinations are endless, and this makes for a nourishing breakfast to start the day.

½ cup old-fashioned oats

½ cup low-fat milk

⅓ cup low-fat vanilla Greek yogurt

¼ teaspoon ground cinnamon

1 Combine all ingredients in a small bowl or 12-ounce Mason jar and stir until well combined.

2 Cover and refrigerate at least 6 hours or overnight. Use within 24 hours.

Sautéed Asparagus and Mushrooms

SERVES 4	
Per Serving	
Calories	29
Fat	2g
Sodium	2mg
Carbohydrates	3g
Fiber	1g
Sugar	1g
Protein	2g

Asparagus and mushrooms are a true match made in heaven! This easy vegetable combo works as a side dish, in a quick stir-fry or power bowl, or combined with scrambled eggs for breakfast.

½ tablespoon olive oil

8 ounces asparagus (about ½ bundle), ends removed

4 ounces white button mushrooms, sliced

2 cloves garlic, peeled and minced

⅛ teaspoon ground black pepper

1 Heat oil in a 12" skillet over medium-high heat. Carefully add asparagus and cook 1 minute.

2 Add mushrooms, garlic, and pepper. Cook 4–5 minutes, until asparagus is fork-tender. Remove from heat.

3 Allow vegetables to cool before storing in an airtight container in refrigerator up to 3 days. To reheat, place in a microwave-safe dish and microwave 45–60 seconds at a time, stirring in between.

Roasted Sweet Potatoes

Any sweet potato fan will adore this simple, delicious recipe. If you don't love the taste of chili powder, you can skip it. Try experimenting with other spices and herbs, such as rosemary, cumin, or thyme.

2 medium sweet potatoes, cut into 1" cubes (about 5 cups)

1 tablespoon olive oil

¼ teaspoon garlic powder

¼ teaspoon chili powder

¼ teaspoon salt

1 Preheat oven to 400°F.

2 Place sweet potatoes in a large mixing bowl. Add oil, garlic powder, chili powder, and salt. Toss to coat sweet potatoes. Spread on a baking sheet in a single layer. Roast 20–22 minutes, stirring halfway through.

3 Allow to cool before storing in an airtight container in refrigerator up to 4 days. To reheat, place in a microwave-safe dish and microwave 45–60 seconds at a time until heated through.

SERVES 4

Per Serving

Calories	86
Fat	3g
Sodium	185mg
Carbohydrates	13g
Fiber	2g
Sugar	3g
Protein	1g

Roasted Red Potatoes, Carrots, and Brussels Sprouts

This bright and cheery blend of roasted vegetables pairs well with meats like pork or beef tenderloin or with the Whole Roasted Chicken recipe in this chapter!

12 baby red potatoes, quartered

2 cups (¼"-thick) carrot slices

3 cups Brussels sprouts, stems removed and cut in half

2 tablespoons olive oil

2 teaspoons fresh thyme leaves

1 clove garlic, peeled and minced

¼ teaspoon salt

1 Preheat oven to 425°F. Line an 11" × 17" baking sheet with aluminum foil.

2 Place potatoes, carrots, and Brussels sprouts in a large bowl and toss with oil, thyme, garlic, and salt. Mix until evenly coated. Pour vegetables onto the prepared sheet and spread into a single layer. Place sheet in oven and roast 25–30 minutes, stirring vegetables halfway through. Vegetables are done when they can easily be pierced with a fork.

3 Allow vegetables to cool before storing in an airtight container in refrigerator up to 4 days. To reheat, place in a microwave-safe dish and microwave 45–60 seconds at a time, stirring in between.

SERVES 4

Per Serving

Calories	293
Fat	7g
Sodium	251mg
Carbohydrates	53g
Fiber	9g
Sugar	8g
Protein	8g

STAYING SEASONAL

Produce that is in season is usually more budget friendly and often better tasting. In the colder months, choose root vegetables like carrots, potatoes, and Brussels sprouts, which are great for roasting. In the summer months, you may opt for squash, tomatoes, and fresh lettuces.

Roasted Broccoli and Cauliflower

SERVES 4

Per Serving

Calories	59
Fat	3g
Sodium	31mg
Carbohydrates	6g
Fiber	2g
Sugar	2g
Protein	2g

Roasting vegetables can completely change the flavor thanks to the caramelization that occurs. If you haven't tasted roasted broccoli or cauliflower before, you should consider trying them. Having these roasted vegetables on hand will be super helpful for building healthy, balanced meals during the week.

2 cups broccoli florets

2 cups cauliflower florets

1 tablespoon olive oil

½ teaspoon garlic powder

¼ teaspoon ground black pepper

1 Preheat oven to 350°F.
2 Place broccoli and cauliflower in a large mixing bowl. Add oil, garlic powder, and pepper. Toss to coat broccoli and cauliflower.
3 Spread on a baking sheet into a single layer. Roast 25–30 minutes, stirring halfway through.
4 Allow to cool before storing in an airtight container in refrigerator up to 4 days. To reheat, place in a microwave-safe dish and microwave 45–60 seconds at a time, stirring in between.

Curry-Roasted Butternut Squash

When you roast a butternut squash, you bring out the sweetness of the squash. Save time by purchasing precut squash. Enjoy this squash in a grain bowl with a protein or serve it as a side dish.

1 medium butternut squash, peeled, seeded, and cut into 1" cubes

2 tablespoons olive oil

1 teaspoon curry powder

SERVES 6	
Per Serving	
Calories	66
Fat	4g
Sodium	2mg
Carbohydrates	7g
Fiber	1g
Sugar	1g
Protein	1g

1 Preheat oven to 450°F and adjust oven rack to middle position.

2 Place all ingredients in a large mixing bowl and toss to coat.

3 Spread squash into a single layer on a baking sheet. Place on middle oven rack and roast 20–25 minutes, until squash is tender and very lightly browned. Remove from oven.

4 Allow to cool before storing in an airtight container in refrigerator up to 4 days. To reheat, place in a microwave-safe dish and microwave 45–60 seconds at a time, stirring in between.

Spicy and Tangy Barbecue Sauce

Looking for a salt-free, fat-free, and absolutely delicious sauce? This authentic-tasting barbecue sauce is perfect for all your grilling, basting, and dipping needs.

2 (8-ounce) cans no-salt-added tomato sauce

2 tablespoons apple cider vinegar

2 tablespoons molasses

2 tablespoons chopped chipotle peppers in adobo sauce

1 tablespoon honey

1½ teaspoons onion powder

1 teaspoon ground smoked paprika

½ teaspoon garlic powder

½ teaspoon ground cumin

½ teaspoon ground black pepper

⅛ teaspoon ground cayenne pepper

MAKES 2 CUPS	
Per Serving (2 tablespoons)	
Calories	28
Fat	0g
Sodium	55mg
Carbohydrates	6g
Fiber	1g
Sugar	5g
Protein	0g

1 Combine all ingredients in a small saucepan and simmer over medium-low heat 10 minutes.

2 Remove from heat and pour into a clean lidded jar. Refrigerate up to 10 days.

Spicy Lime, Cilantro, and Garlic Marinade

MAKES ½ CUP

Per Serving (¼ cup)

Calories	56
Fat	4g
Sodium	3mg
Carbohydrates	5g
Fiber	0g
Sugar	1g
Protein	1g

This marinade provides the most amazing citrus-forward, garlicky, spicy Southwestern taste imaginable. Toss meat or tofu in the marinade and refrigerate it at least 1 hour.

2 teaspoons olive oil
½ cup finely chopped fresh cilantro
4 cloves garlic, peeled and minced
1 teaspoon dried red pepper flakes
¼ cup lime juice

Place all ingredients in a small bowl and whisk to combine. Cover and refrigerate up to 1 week.

Basil Pesto

MAKES ½ CUP

Per Serving (2 tablespoons)

Calories	164
Fat	15g
Sodium	45mg
Carbohydrates	3g
Fiber	1g
Sugar	0g
Protein	2g

Stir a little bit of this fragrant pesto into pasta or rice for a sensational taste, use it as a spread for sandwiches, or swirl some on top of a pizza. If you don't have pine nuts, you can use walnuts instead.

2 cups fresh basil leaves
4 cloves garlic, peeled
3 tablespoons olive oil
¼ cup pine nuts
2 tablespoons grated Parmesan cheese
¼ teaspoon ground black pepper

1 Place all ingredients in a food processor and pulse until smooth.
2 Store in an airtight container and refrigerate up to 7 days.

Salt-Free Mayonnaise

Want to know exactly how your mayonnaise is made? This mayonnaise is light and creamy and uses liquid egg substitute, eliminating cholesterol and the risk of salmonella. This recipe is adapted from Southern Living *magazine.*

¼ cup liquid egg substitute

2½ tablespoons distilled white vinegar

½ teaspoon ground white pepper

⅛ teaspoon garlic powder

⅛ teaspoon ground mustard

⅛ teaspoon ground cayenne pepper

⅔ cup canola oil

1 Place egg substitute, vinegar, white pepper, garlic powder, mustard, and cayenne in a food processor and pulse until smooth. Scrape down sides.

2 With food processor running, add oil in a slow and steady stream until mixture is thickened.

3 Store in an airtight container in refrigerator until ready to use. Use within 2 weeks.

MAKES 1 CUP

Per Serving (1 tablespoon)

Calories	82
Fat	9g
Sodium	7mg
Carbohydrates	0g
Fiber	0g
Sugar	0g
Protein	0g

LIQUID EGG SUBSTITUTES

Sold in cartons in the egg section, liquid egg substitutes are a great way of enjoying the flavor of whole eggs without the fat and cholesterol. You can use ¼ cup of liquid egg substitute in place of each egg in most recipes without a discernable difference in taste or texture. Liquid egg substitutes can be frozen as well, making them both healthy and convenient.

Asian-Inspired Low-Sodium Marinade

MAKES ½ CUP	
Per Serving (1 tablespoon)	
Calories	33
Fat	2g
Sodium	162mg
Carbohydrates	4g
Fiber	0g
Sugar	4g
Protein	1g

This low-sodium marinade has subtle nuances of garlic and ginger, five-spice powder, and the sweet tang of rice vinegar. Marinate your choice of meat, tofu, or tempeh for 2–4 hours, turning occasionally, before grilling or broiling.

3 tablespoons low-sodium soy sauce

1½ tablespoons honey

1 tablespoon unflavored rice vinegar

1 tablespoon sesame oil

2 cloves garlic, peeled and minced

1 tablespoon grated fresh ginger

¼ teaspoon five-spice powder

1 Combine all ingredients in a small bowl.
2 Store in an airtight container in refrigerator until ready to use, up to 1 week.

Salt-Free Chili Seasoning

MAKES ⅓ CUP	
Per Serving (¼ teaspoon)	
Calories	0
Fat	0g
Sodium	3mg
Carbohydrates	0g
Fiber	0g
Sugar	0g
Protein	0g

If you have difficulty finding commercial salt-free chili seasoning at the grocery store, make your own! It's quick and affordable, and you can adjust the ingredients to suit your taste.

2 tablespoons ground cumin

1 tablespoon chili powder

2 teaspoons dried oregano

1½ teaspoons ground paprika

½ teaspoon garlic powder

½ teaspoon onion powder

¼ teaspoon dried red pepper flakes

1 Place all ingredients in a small bowl and whisk to combine.
2 Store seasoning in a small lidded jar at room temperature. Use within 1 year.

CHAPTER 4

Breakfast

Blueberry Banana Oat Muffins 44

Vegetable Egg Muffins. 45

Honey-Sweetened Fruit and Ricotta Toast 46

Pistachio Cranberry Granola 48

Breakfast Quinoa Salad 49

Butternut Squash and Fajita Vegetable Frittata 51

Pumpkin Seed and Chia Granola 53

Raspberry Almond Overnight Oats 54

Grapefruit and Orange Yogurt Parfait 54

Swiss Cheese and Chive Mini Quiches 55

Asparagus, Swiss, and Ricotta Frittata 56

Maple Turkey Sausage 57

Scrambled Tofu with Mushrooms and Zucchini 58

Oven-Baked Apple Pancake 59

Whole-Wheat Cinnamon Pancakes with Banana 61

Orange Cornmeal Pancakes 62

Sweet Potato Breakfast Pie 63

Sunday Morning Waffles 64

Whole-Grain Spiced Pear Waffles 65

ABC Muffins. 66

Whole-Wheat Strawberry Corn Muffins. 67

Maple, Oatmeal, and Applesauce Muffins 68

Blueberry Banana Oat Muffins

SERVES 12

Per Serving

Calories	162
Fat	6g
Sodium	213mg
Carbohydrates	25g
Fiber	2g
Sugar	11g
Protein	4g

BANANAS AND POTASSIUM

Bananas are a good source of potassium, which is an important nutrient in the DASH diet. Buy more bananas than you plan to eat in a week so you can let them ripen to use in recipes like these Blueberry Banana Oat Muffins!

This recipe makes use of overripe bananas that are sitting on the counter. It offers a different twist to the usual banana muffin recipe with the addition of blueberries. What a delicious combination! You will bump up the fiber in these muffins by adding oats and using white whole-wheat flour.

1 cup quick oats

1 cup white whole-wheat flour

1½ teaspoons sodium-free baking powder

1 teaspoon baking soda

½ teaspoon salt

½ cup granulated sugar

1 large egg

1 medium overripe banana, peeled and mashed

⅓ cup low-fat plain Greek yogurt

⅓ cup low-fat milk

¼ cup canola oil

1 teaspoon vanilla extract

1 cup fresh blueberries

1 Preheat oven to 375°F. Line a twelve-cup muffin tin with paper liners or spray with nonstick cooking spray.

2 In a medium bowl, combine oats, flour, baking powder, baking soda, and salt. Whisk to combine.

3 In a second medium bowl, combine sugar, egg, banana, yogurt, milk, oil, and vanilla. Stir until combined.

4 Make a well in the center of the dry ingredients. Add liquid mixture to dry ingredients and stir until just combined, being careful not to overmix. Gently fold in blueberries and mix slightly.

5 Pour batter into prepared muffin tin, filling each cup three-quarters full. Place muffin tin in oven and bake 20 minutes or until a toothpick inserted into the center of a muffin comes out clean. Allow muffins to cool 10 minutes before removing from muffin tin and placing on a wire rack to cool completely. Store in an airtight container on the counter or in the refrigerator up to 3 days.

6 If freezing, store muffins in a freezer-safe resealable bag. Use within 3 months of freezing. To thaw, simply microwave a muffin 20–30 seconds or until warm.

Vegetable Egg Muffins

For a protein-rich breakfast on the go, try these Vegetable Egg Muffins! These cute mini frittatas are made in a muffin tin and reheat easily whenever you're ready to enjoy.

1 teaspoon olive oil

1 cup sliced zucchini (quartered lengthwise and sliced ¼" thick)

1 cup roughly chopped white button mushrooms

⅓ cup sliced green onion

¼ cup pitted Kalamata olives, chopped

¾ teaspoon dried oregano

8 large eggs

½ cup low-fat milk

⅛ teaspoon ground black pepper

¼ cup crumbled feta cheese

SERVES 6	
Per Serving	
Calories	159
Fat	11g
Sodium	318mg
Carbohydrates	3g
Fiber	1g
Sugar	1g
Protein	11g

1 Preheat oven to 350°F and adjust oven rack to middle position. Line a twelve-cup muffin tin with paper liners or spray with non-stick cooking spray.

2 Heat oil in a large skillet over medium heat. Add zucchini, mushrooms, and green onion. Sauté 2 minutes, stirring frequently. Reduce heat to medium-low and add olives and oregano. Stir to combine and cook 1 minute. Remove skillet from heat and allow vegetables to cool slightly.

3 In a large bowl, whisk eggs, milk, and pepper. Add cooked vegetables and cheese to egg mixture. Whisk until combined.

4 Measure out ¼ cup egg mixture into each of muffin tin's cups. Divide any remaining mixture among cups. Place muffin tin on middle oven rack and bake 20 minutes. Eggs should reach an internal temperature of 160°F and be set with no runny liquid on top. Allow to cool 5 minutes before removing egg muffins, using a table knife to loosen the edges.

5 Store in an airtight container in refrigerator up to 4 days. When ready to serve, microwave 30 seconds to reheat.

Honey-Sweetened Fruit and Ricotta Toast

SERVES 2

Per Serving

Calories	265
Fat	5g
Sodium	202mg
Carbohydrates	44g
Fiber	6g
Sugar	24g
Protein	12g

FRUIT SWAP

If you don't like peaches or want to change up this recipe a bit, you could substitute fresh figs or sliced strawberries. To take this recipe a step further, try adding chopped pistachios or pecans, or sprinkle on chia seeds to add some omega-3 fatty acids.

If you're looking to switch up your typical breakfast, look no further than this Honey-Sweetened Fruit and Ricotta Toast! It's the perfect balance of luxurious and light, sure to satisfy you and keep you full throughout the morning.

¼ cup plus 2 tablespoons part-skim ricotta cheese
1 teaspoon ground cinnamon
2 (1") slices hearty whole-grain bread
2 medium peaches, pitted and sliced ¼" thick
1 tablespoon honey

1   Mix together ricotta and cinnamon in a small bowl. Store mixture in an airtight container in refrigerator until ready to use, up to 2 days.
2   When ready to serve, toast bread in toaster. Spread ricotta mixture on toasted bread. Place peaches on top of ricotta mixture, then drizzle honey over fruit.

Pistachio Cranberry Granola

Per Serving

Calories	254
Fat	14g
Sodium	2mg
Carbohydrates	29g
Fiber	4g
Sugar	12g
Protein	6g

PISTACHIOS

Pistachios are grown all over Italy, Greece, and Turkey. These Mediterranean favorites are high in fiber, rich in B vitamins, and are a good source of heart-healthy monounsaturated and polyunsaturated fats. Shelled pistachios make an excellent snack, not only for the nutritional value, but also because removing shells as you eat slows you down.

Your house will smell so good while this is baking in the oven! Serve this crunchy and flavorful granola on top of yogurt, cottage cheese, or applesauce. It can also be enjoyed as is or like cereal with your milk of choice.

2 cups rolled oats

1 cup unsalted shelled pistachios, roughly chopped

¾ cup dried cranberries

¼ cup raw, unsalted shelled pumpkin seeds

2 tablespoons chia seeds

½ teaspoon ground cinnamon

½ teaspoon ground cardamom

¼ cup melted coconut oil

¼ cup 100 percent grade A maple syrup

1 Preheat oven to 350°F. Line an 11" × 17" baking sheet with parchment paper.

2 In a large bowl, combine oats, pistachios, cranberries, pumpkin seeds, chia seeds, cinnamon, and cardamom.

3 In a small bowl, whisk together oil and maple syrup until combined. Pour liquid mixture over dry mixture, then use a plastic spatula to mix well, making sure all dry ingredients become coated.

4 Pour granola mixture onto the prepared sheet and spread into a thin layer. Bake 20–22 minutes, stirring halfway through. Remove granola from oven and allow to cool on sheet. Granola will become crunchy as it dries out. Store in an airtight container at room temperature up to 2 weeks.

Breakfast Quinoa Salad

This Breakfast Quinoa Salad is perfect for those slow, cozy mornings when you're craving some comfort food. The possibilities for toppings are endless, so feel free to get creative! Make it creamy by adding a tablespoon of part-skim ricotta cheese or Greek yogurt at the end.

1 cup quinoa

2 cups water

1 cinnamon stick

1" piece fresh ginger, peeled

⅛ teaspoon salt

1 medium Bartlett pear, cored and diced into ½" pieces

½ cup chopped pecans

½ cup chopped dried cranberries

1 tablespoon fresh orange juice

2 teaspoons grated orange zest

2 teaspoons chia seeds

1 teaspoon honey

1 Rinse quinoa thoroughly in a fine-mesh strainer.

2 In a small saucepan, combine quinoa, water, cinnamon stick, ginger, and salt. Cover and bring to a boil over medium-high heat, then reduce heat to medium and cook 20 minutes or until water is absorbed. Remove from heat and fluff quinoa with a fork. Remove cinnamon stick and ginger. Allow to cool completely.

3 Mix in pear, pecans, cranberries, orange juice, orange zest, chia seeds, and honey. Salad will keep in refrigerator up to 2 days.

SERVES 4

Per Serving

Calories	407
Fat	13g
Sodium	13mg
Carbohydrates	63g
Fiber	10g
Sugar	18g
Protein	10g

QUINOA

Quinoa is a complete protein, meaning it contains all nine essential amino acids that your body cannot make on its own. For this reason, quinoa is a great option for vegetarians looking to up their complete protein intake!

Butternut Squash and Fajita Vegetable Frittata

Add some color and well-balanced spice to your breakfast with a simple frittata. This dish can come together quickly if the Chili-Roasted Butternut Squash is prepped in advance.

Chili-Roasted Butternut Squash

1½ cups diced butternut squash

1 tablespoon olive oil

1 teaspoon chili powder

¼ teaspoon ground black pepper

⅛ teaspoon salt

Frittata

4 large eggs

3 tablespoons low-fat milk

⅛ teaspoon ground black pepper

½ tablespoon olive oil

¼ cup diced yellow onion

¼ cup diced green bell pepper

¼ cup diced mushrooms

⅓ cup canned black beans, drained and rinsed

¾ cup Chili-Roasted Butternut Squash (half the amount from the recipe yield)

1 ounce shredded sharp Cheddar cheese

1 Preheat oven to 350°F.

2 For the squash: In a small bowl, combine squash, oil, chili powder, pepper, and salt. Stir to coat. Spread squash on a baking sheet in a single layer. Roast 25–30 minutes or until squash can easily be pierced with a fork. Cooked squash can be stored in an airtight container in refrigerator up to 1 week.

SERVES 4	
Per Serving	
Calories	172
Fat	10g
Sodium	215mg
Carbohydrates	9g
Fiber	2g
Sugar	2g
Protein	10g

continued on next page

3 For the frittata: Whisk together eggs, milk, and black pepper in a medium bowl. Set aside. Add oil to a medium oven-safe skillet and heat over medium heat. Add onion and bell pepper and cook 2 minutes. Add mushrooms, beans, and squash and cook 3 minutes. Before adding egg mixture, spread vegetables evenly around the skillet. Pour in egg mixture and cook about 3 minutes, slightly lifting cooked portions around the edges and tilting the pan to allow uncooked egg to reach the pan surface. Turn off heat and add Cheddar.

4 Turn oven broiler to high. Place skillet on top oven rack, about 8" from the broiler. Cook 2–3 minutes or until eggs are set and cheese starts to turn slightly golden brown.

5 Store frittata in an airtight container in refrigerator up to 3 days. To reheat, place frittata on a microwave-safe plate and microwave 30–45 seconds at a time.

Pumpkin Seed and Chia Granola

Both pumpkin seeds and chia seeds are high in fiber, potassium, iron, and magnesium, making this granola a nutritious and delicious breakfast or midday snack!

4 cups rolled oats

1 cup sweetened shredded coconut

1 cup pecan pieces

1 cup raw, unsalted shelled pumpkin seeds

3 tablespoons chia seeds

1 teaspoon ground cinnamon

½ teaspoon ground cardamom

¼ teaspoon salt

⅔ cup pumpkin purée

½ cup coconut oil

½ cup 100 percent grade A maple syrup

1 teaspoon vanilla extract

1 Preheat oven to 350°F.
2 In a large mixing bowl, combine oats, coconut, pecans, pumpkin seeds, chia seeds, cinnamon, cardamom, and salt. Mix well.
3 In a small saucepan over medium heat, combine pumpkin purée, oil, maple syrup, and vanilla. Whisk mixture to keep oil from separating, then pour over dry ingredients. Use a plastic spatula to mix well, making sure all dry ingredients become coated.
4 Pour granola mixture onto two large baking sheets and spread it out into a thin layer. Bake 22–24 minutes, stirring halfway through.
5 Remove granola from oven and allow to cool on sheets. The granola will become crunchy as it dries out. Store in an airtight container at room temperature up to 2 weeks.

SERVES 14

Per Serving

Calories	330
Fat	21g
Sodium	62mg
Carbohydrates	31g
Fiber	5g
Sugar	11g
Protein	7g

SERVING TIP

For a delightful and easy breakfast, place ½ cup Pumpkin Seed and Chia Granola, ½ cup low-fat plain Greek yogurt, and ½ cup diced apple on top. You'll be ready to take on the day after this balanced breakfast!

Raspberry Almond Overnight Oats

SERVES 1	
Per Serving	
Calories	418
Fat	17g
Sodium	88mg
Carbohydrates	49g
Fiber	12g
Sugar	8g
Protein	22g

When it comes to overnight oats, keep your toppings simple by adding fresh fruit, some nuts, and any other fun toppings you have on hand. You will love the bursting berries in your oats! You can portion chopped almonds and ground flaxseed as you prep the oats to save even more time in the morning.

1 serving Overnight Oats (see recipe in Chapter 3)
⅓ cup fresh raspberries
2 tablespoons chopped almonds
1 teaspoon ground flaxseed

Prepare oats at least 6 hours before serving. When ready to serve, add raspberries, almonds, and flaxseed.

Grapefruit and Orange Yogurt Parfait

SERVES 2	
Per Serving	
Calories	187
Fat	3g
Sodium	50mg
Carbohydrates	30g
Fiber	2g
Sugar	23g
Protein	11g

Start the day with a bright, citrusy yogurt parfait! For a crunchy element, this recipe calls for pumpkin seeds. These delicious seeds also are rich in magnesium.

1 cup low-fat vanilla Greek yogurt
½ medium orange, peeled, segmented, and diced
½ medium grapefruit, peeled, segmented, and diced
1 tablespoon unsalted shelled pumpkin seeds

1 Place ½ cup yogurt in each of two small bowls. Top each bowl with half of orange pieces and half of grapefruit pieces. Repeat in a second bowl with remaining yogurt, orange slices, and grapefruit slices.
2 Store in refrigerator up to 24 hours. To serve, top each bowl with ½ tablespoon pumpkin seeds.

Swiss Cheese and Chive Mini Quiches

These tasty quiches look impressive but require very little preparation and equipment. You just need a rolling pin, a biscuit cutter, and a muffin tin, in addition to a couple bowls, measuring cups, and measuring spoons.

¾ cup plus 2 tablespoons unbleached all-purpose flour, divided

½ teaspoon salt-free all-purpose seasoning

¼ teaspoon dried dill

2 tablespoons unsalted butter

Cold water

2 large eggs

⅔ cup low-fat milk

⅓ cup low-fat sour cream

6 tablespoons shredded Swiss cheese

¼ cup chopped fresh chives

¼ teaspoon ground black pepper

SERVES 12	
Per Serving	
Calories	93
Fat	5g
Sodium	25mg
Carbohydrates	8g
Fiber	0g
Sugar	0g
Protein	4g

1 Preheat oven to 350°F. Put oven rack in middle position. Line a twelve-cup muffin tin with liners or spray with nonstick spray.

2 Place ¾ cup flour, all-purpose seasoning, and dill in a large bowl. Whisk to combine. Add butter and use your fingers to cut butter into flour mixture until mixture resembles fine crumbs.

3 Add cold water ½ tablespoon at a time until dough just comes together. Roll dough out thinly and cut into 12 (2") circles using a biscuit cutter or a drinking glass.

4 Line cups of prepared muffin tin with 1 dough round. Set aside.

5 Beat eggs, milk, sour cream, and remaining 2 tablespoons flour in a medium bowl until combined.

6 Divide mixture evenly among muffin cups. Top each with ½ tablespoon Swiss cheese and 1 teaspoon chives. Sprinkle with pepper.

7 Place muffin tin on middle oven rack and bake 25 minutes. Remove from oven and let rest for a few minutes. Remove mini quiches by sliding a knife around edges and gently lifting.

8 Store in an airtight container in refrigerator up to 4 days. To reheat, microwave 30–45 seconds.

Asparagus, Swiss, and Ricotta Frittata

SERVES 4

Per Serving	
Calories	83
Fat	2g
Sodium	232mg
Carbohydrates	6g
Fiber	1g
Sugar	4g
Protein	11g

Frittatas are impressive yet ridiculously easy to make and easy to reheat for a quick breakfast choice. This frittata has a complex and delicious flavor profile with asparagus and two different cheeses. Liquid egg replacement is stocked beside the eggs in most supermarkets.

8 stalks fresh asparagus, trimmed and cut into thirds

1 small shallot, peeled and minced

1¼ cups liquid egg replacement

¼ cup sliced jarred roasted red peppers

¼ cup shredded Swiss cheese

1 tablespoon part-skim ricotta cheese

¼ teaspoon ground black pepper

1 Preheat oven to 450°F and adjust oven rack to top position.

2 Steam asparagus in a small saucepan over high heat for 5 minutes.

3 Spray a medium oven-safe skillet with nonstick cooking spray. Place over medium heat, add shallot, and sauté 2 minutes.

4 Add egg replacement to skillet and remove from heat. Top with asparagus, red peppers, and Swiss cheese. Dollop ricotta over the top and season with black pepper.

5 Place skillet on the top oven rack and bake 10 minutes. Remove from oven. Slide a spatula around and under frittata to loosen. Remove and cut into wedges.

6 Store in an airtight container in refrigerator up to 4 days. To reheat, place in a microwave-safe dish and microwave 45–60 seconds.

Maple Turkey Sausage

Perfect for those avoiding pork or simply looking for another lean breakfast meat, these homemade patties are subtly sweet and delicious. Because these store well in the freezer, reheating them and elevating your breakfast is very easy.

2 pounds lean ground turkey

1 large egg white

1 tablespoon 100 percent grade A maple syrup

1 tablespoon ground sage

½ teaspoon dried red pepper flakes

½ teaspoon fennel seed

½ teaspoon ground black pepper

½ teaspoon ground rosemary

¼ teaspoon garlic powder

1 Combine all ingredients in a large bowl and mix using a fork or your hands. The mixture will be sticky. Form into 16 (2") patties.

2 Heat a griddle or large skillet over medium heat and brown patties on both sides, about 4 minutes per side. Reduce heat to medium-low or low if patties seem to be burning. Drain patties on paper towels.

3 Store in an airtight container in refrigerator up to 4 days or in a freezer-safe resealable bag in freezer up to 3 months. To reheat, place in a microwave-safe dish and microwave 45–60 seconds.

SERVES 8

Per Serving

Calories	184
Fat	9g
Sodium	80mg
Carbohydrates	2g
Fiber	0g
Sugar	2g
Protein	23g

Scrambled Tofu with Mushrooms and Zucchini

SERVES 4

Per Serving	
Calories	130
Fat	6g
Sodium	6mg
Carbohydrates	7g
Fiber	3g
Sugar	3g
Protein	12g

WHAT IS TURMERIC?

Turmeric is a spice made from the ground root of the turmeric plant. Its bright yellow color and distinct flavor are used in many types of food, from Indian cuisine to prepared mustard. Turmeric has a slightly bitter taste that works well in combination with other seasonings. It's high in manganese and iron and may help reduce the risk of some cancers.

This is a great salt-free dish, especially good for vegans or those watching their cholesterol. The turmeric adds a great color to the tofu, making it look like eggs. You can add other vegetables that you have on hand.

1 small onion, peeled and diced

1 clove garlic, peeled and minced

½ cup sliced mushrooms

½ cup diced zucchini

1 small red bell pepper, seeded and diced

1 pound extra-firm tofu, drained

½ teaspoon salt-free garlic and herb seasoning

½ teaspoon ground black pepper

½ teaspoon ground turmeric

1 Place a large nonstick skillet over medium heat. Add onion, garlic, mushrooms, zucchini, and bell pepper and cook 5 minutes, stirring regularly.

2 Crumble tofu over vegetable mixture, keeping it in rather large chunks. Add garlic and herb seasoning, black pepper, and turmeric. Stir gently to combine. Cook another 5 minutes, stirring gently. Remove from heat.

3 Allow to cool before storing in an airtight container in refrigerator up to 4 days. To reheat, place in a microwave-safe dish and microwave 45–60 seconds.

Oven-Baked Apple Pancake

Moist, airy, and delicious, this low-cholesterol pancake will impress with its taste and simplicity. Just whisk together the ingredients, pour, and bake. The oven does all the rest of the work. Use Pink Lady apples instead of Honeycrisp if you'd like.

2 cups diced Honeycrisp apple

1 tablespoon vanilla extract

1 tablespoon sodium-free baking powder

1 cup unbleached all-purpose flour

⅓ cup unsweetened applesauce

⅓ cup 100 percent grade A maple syrup

¾ cup low-fat milk

1 tablespoon granulated sugar

½ teaspoon ground cinnamon

1 Preheat oven to 400°F and adjust oven rack to middle position. Lightly spray a large oven-safe skillet with nonstick cooking spray.

2 Place apple, vanilla, baking powder, flour, applesauce, maple syrup, and milk in a large bowl and stir to combine. Pour batter into the prepared skillet and smooth the top with a spatula.

3 Combine sugar and cinnamon in a small bowl and sprinkle evenly over batter.

4 Place skillet on middle oven rack and bake 25 minutes. Remove from oven. Carefully loosen pancake from skillet using a spatula. Slice into 8 wedges.

5 Store in an airtight container in refrigerator up to 4 days. To reheat, place on a microwave-safe plate and microwave 45–60 seconds.

SERVES 8	
Per Serving	
Calories	133
Fat	1g
Sodium	14mg
Carbohydrates	29g
Fiber	1g
Sugar	14g
Protein	3g

Whole-Wheat Cinnamon Pancakes with Banana

These delicious pancakes—flavored with ripe banana, cinnamon, and vanilla—make a fabulous low-fat breakfast.

1⅓ cups white whole-wheat flour

¼ cup granulated sugar

1 tablespoon sodium-free baking powder

1⅓ cups low-fat milk

1 large egg white

1 teaspoon ground cinnamon

1 tablespoon vanilla extract

1 medium banana, peeled and sliced

SERVES 4

Per Serving	
Calories	277
Fat	3g
Sodium	56mg
Carbohydrates	54g
Fiber	5g
Sugar	17g
Protein	9g

1 Place flour, sugar, and baking powder in a large bowl and whisk to combine.

2 Add milk, egg white, cinnamon, and vanilla. Mix and let sit 1–2 minutes to thicken.

3 Heat a nonstick griddle or medium skillet over medium heat. Pour ¼ of batter onto the heated griddle. Arrange ¼ of banana slices over top of batter. When pancake has bubbled on top and is nicely browned on bottom, 2–4 minutes, flip over and cook another 2–3 minutes. Transfer cooked pancake to a plate.

4 Repeat with remaining batter and banana slices.

5 Allow pancakes to cool before freezing in a freezer-safe resealable bag, separating each pancake using parchment paper. Use within 1 month. To thaw pancakes, place on a microwave-safe plate and microwave 30 seconds.

Orange Cornmeal Pancakes

SERVES 4

Per Serving

Calories	235
Fat	2g
Sodium	52mg
Carbohydrates	47g
Fiber	4g
Sugar	14g
Protein	7g

These light, fluffy pancakes are so good you may even pass on the syrup. You'll want to make plenty of these to keep stashed in the freezer.

⅔ cup white whole-wheat flour

⅔ cup cornmeal

1 tablespoon sodium-free baking powder

¼ cup granulated sugar

3 tablespoons orange juice

1½ teaspoons grated orange zest

1 cup low-fat milk

1 large egg white

1 Stir together all ingredients in a medium bowl.
2 Heat a nonstick griddle or medium skillet over medium-low heat. Pour about ¼ cup batter onto the heated griddle. When pancake has bubbled on top and is nicely browned on bottom, about 2 minutes, flip over and cook another 2 minutes. Transfer cooked pancake to a plate.
3 Repeat with remaining batter.
4 Allow pancakes to cool before freezing in a freezer-safe resealable bag, separating each pancake using parchment paper. Use within 1 month. To thaw pancakes, place on a microwave-safe dish and microwave 30 seconds.

Sweet Potato Breakfast Pie

A cross between hash browns and a pancake, this super-healthy, oven-baked breakfast will garner rave reviews. Serve plain or drizzled lightly with maple syrup.

2 cups shredded sweet potato

1 cup shredded carrot

¼ cup white whole-wheat flour

2 large egg whites

1 tablespoon 100 percent grade A maple syrup

1 tablespoon orange juice

½ teaspoon grated orange zest

¼ teaspoon ground cinnamon

1 Preheat oven to 425°F and adjust oven rack to middle position. Spray a pie pan lightly with nonstick cooking spray and set aside.

2 Place all ingredients in a large bowl and stir to combine. Spread mixture in the prepared pan and smooth the top.

3 Place pan on the middle oven rack and bake 20 minutes. Remove from oven and cut into wedges.

4 Store in an airtight container in refrigerator up to 4 days. To reheat, place on a microwave-safe plate and microwave 45–60 seconds.

SERVES 8

Per Serving

Calories	59
Fat	0g
Sodium	41mg
Carbohydrates	13g
Fiber	2g
Sugar	4g
Protein	2g

Sunday Morning Waffles

Homemade waffles make a simple but tasty breakfast. As a bonus, they freeze beautifully. You can make them in bulk, store them in the freezer, and then toast them for quick weekday breakfasts.

SERVES 6

Per Serving

Calories	236
Fat	7g
Sodium	50mg
Carbohydrates	36g
Fiber	3g
Sugar	9g
Protein	8g

WAFFLE TIP

After removing waffles from the waffle iron, place them directly on the middle rack of a pre-heated 200°F oven until all the waffles are done. When serving, do not stack the waffles. The moisture from the waffles will condense and cause them to become limp. Always serve waffles in a single layer to keep them fresh and crisp.

1⅔ cups white whole-wheat flour

¼ cup granulated sugar

1 tablespoon sodium-free baking powder

2 large egg whites

1½ cups low-fat milk

2 teaspoons vanilla extract

2 tablespoons canola oil

1 Place flour, sugar, and baking powder in a large bowl and whisk to combine.

2 Place egg whites in a medium bowl and beat until they form stiff peaks.

3 Stir milk, vanilla, and oil into flour mixture. Set aside for 1–2 minutes to thicken, then gently fold in beaten egg whites.

4 Heat a waffle iron. Spray lightly with nonstick cooking spray, then ladle batter onto the hot surface, being careful to avoid the edges. Close waffle iron and bake until waffle is golden brown, 4–5 minutes.

5 Remove baked waffle from the iron and repeat with remaining batter.

6 Allow waffles to cool before freezing in a freezer-safe resealable bag, separating each waffle using parchment paper. Use within 1 month. To thaw waffles, place on a microwave-safe dish and microwave 30 seconds, and then place in toaster oven or toaster to make crisp again.

Whole-Grain Spiced Pear Waffles

Crisp and hearty, these healthy waffles are also great with chopped apple and pecans. Prep a batch of these to enjoy on a lazy week-end morning or as a quick breakfast option during the week.

2 medium pears, peeled, cored, and diced, divided

1⅔ cups white whole-wheat flour

⅓ cup granulated sugar

1½ tablespoons sodium-free baking powder

2 cups low-fat milk

1 large egg white

2 tablespoons canola oil

2 teaspoons vanilla extract

1 teaspoon ground cinnamon

½ teaspoon ground ginger

¼ teaspoon ground nutmeg

1 cup chopped walnuts, divided

SERVES 8	
Per Serving	
Calories	315
Fat	15g
Sodium	39mg
Carbohydrates	39g
Fiber	5g
Sugar	13g
Protein	8g

1 Measure ½ cup diced pears and set aside. Place remaining pears in a large bowl.

2 Add flour, sugar, baking powder, milk, egg white, oil, vanilla, cinnamon, ginger, nutmeg, and ½ cup walnuts to the bowl and beat until smooth.

3 Heat a waffle iron. Spray lightly with nonstick cooking spray, then ladle batter onto the hot surface, being careful to avoid the edges. Close waffle iron and bake until waffle is golden brown, 4–5 minutes.

4 Remove baked waffle from the iron and repeat with remaining batter. Top waffles with reserved ½ cup pears and remaining ½ cup walnuts.

5 Allow waffles to cool before freezing in a freezer-safe resealable bag, separating each waffle using parchment paper. Use within 1 month. To thaw waffles, place on a microwave-safe dish and microwave 30 seconds, and then place in toaster oven or toaster to make crisp again.

ABC Muffins

SERVES 12

Per Serving

Calories	131
Fat	4g
Sodium	18mg
Carbohydrates	22g
Fiber	2g
Sugar	10g
Protein	2g

SODIUM-FREE BAKING POWDER

Standard baking powder, the kind typically sold in supermarkets, contains hundreds of milligrams of sodium per serving and is not recommended on the DASH diet. Two brands of sodium-free baking powder are available and provide the same great rise in baked goods. Ener-G sodium-free baking powder can be purchased online. Hain Pure Foods sodium-free baking powder is sold online and at select stores.

The alphabet never tasted so delicious! Apple, banana, and carrot give these muffins superb moistness and flavor. Packed with vitamins and nutrients, they make a great cholesterol-free breakfast or quick snack. Use Jonagold apples instead of Braeburn if you like.

2 medium Braeburn apples, cored and chopped

2 medium carrots, peeled and shredded

1 medium banana, peeled and mashed

3 tablespoons canola oil

¼ cup unsweetened almond milk

¼ cup packed light brown sugar

1 tablespoon vanilla extract

1 cup unbleached all-purpose flour

¼ cup white whole-wheat flour

1½ teaspoons sodium-free baking powder

1 Preheat oven to 350°F and adjust oven rack to middle position. Line a twelve-cup muffin tin with paper liners or spray with non-stick cooking spray. Set aside.

2 Place all ingredients in a large bowl and mix.

3 Divide batter evenly among the prepared muffin cups. Place muffin tin on middle oven rack and bake 20–25 minutes or until an inserted toothpick comes out clean.

4 Remove muffin tin from oven and place on a wire rack to cool. Let cool completely before removing muffins from tin. Store in an airtight container at room temperature up to 5 days.

Whole-Wheat Strawberry Corn Muffins

The combination of plump, moist berries and the subtle crunch of cornmeal is irresistible in these fabulous muffins.

1 cup white whole-wheat flour

½ cup cornmeal

½ cup granulated sugar

1 tablespoon sodium-free baking powder

1 cup chopped strawberries

1 cup low-fat milk

3 tablespoons canola oil

2 teaspoons vanilla extract

1 Preheat oven to 375°F and adjust oven rack to middle position. Line a twelve-cup muffin tin with paper liners or spray with non-stick cooking spray.

2 Place flour, cornmeal, sugar, and baking powder in a large bowl and whisk to combine.

3 Add strawberries, milk, oil, and vanilla and stir until incorporated.

4 Fill each muffin cup two-thirds full with batter. Place muffin tin on middle oven rack and bake 20 minutes or until an inserted toothpick comes out clean.

5 Remove muffin tin from oven and place on a wire rack to cool. Let muffins cool at least 10 minutes before removing from muffin tin and allowing muffins to cool completely. Store in an airtight container at room temperature up to 3 days.

SERVES 12

Per Serving

Calories	134
Fat	4g
Sodium	12mg
Carbohydrates	22g
Fiber	2g
Sugar	9g
Protein	3g

Maple, Oatmeal, and Applesauce Muffins

SERVES 12

Per Serving

Calories	166
Fat	5g
Sodium	17mg
Carbohydrates	26g
Fiber	1g
Sugar	11g
Protein	3g

MAPLE SYRUP GRADING

According to the United States Department of Agriculture, all 100 percent maple syrup sold in grocery stores in consumer-sized containers—less than 5 gallons—qualify as US Grade A maple syrup. The color may vary but the syrup should always be free from cloudiness and sediment.

With all the comforting flavor of a bowl of oatmeal in a convenient package, these yummy muffins make any busy morning better. Bake a batch ahead of time, freeze, and then pop one out the night before to thaw.

1 cup low-fat milk

1 tablespoon distilled white vinegar

1 cup old-fashioned rolled oats

1 large egg white

1/4 cup canola oil

1/4 cup unsweetened applesauce

1/3 cup packed light brown sugar

1/4 cup 100 percent grade A maple syrup

1 teaspoon ground cinnamon

2 teaspoons sodium-free baking powder

1 teaspoon sodium-free baking soda

1 cup unbleached all-purpose flour

1/4 cup whole-wheat flour

1 Preheat oven to 425°F and adjust oven rack to middle position. Line a twelve-cup muffin tin with paper liners or spray with non-stick cooking spray. Set aside.

2 Pour milk into a measuring cup and add vinegar. Set aside for 5 minutes. Pour mixture into a large bowl and stir in oats. Set aside for 10 minutes.

3 Add egg white, oil, and applesauce to oat mixture and stir. Stir in sugar, maple syrup, cinnamon, baking powder, and baking soda. Gradually add both flours and stir to combine.

4 Divide batter evenly among the prepared muffin cups. Place muffin tin on middle oven rack and bake 20–25 minutes or until an inserted toothpick comes out clean.

5 Remove muffin tin from oven, then carefully remove muffins from cups and place on a wire rack to cool. Store in an airtight container at room temperature up to 3 days or in a freezer-safe resealable bag in the freezer up to 2 months. Thaw at room temperature before serving.

CHAPTER 5

Salads and Sides

Kale and Roasted Beet Salad 70

Fresh Corn, Pepper, and Avocado Salad 72

Spring Pea Salad 74

Tuscan Kale Salad 75

Grapefruit Salmon Salad 77

Green Beans with Pecans, Cranberries, and Parmesan 79

Sautéed Cabbage, Kale, and Bacon 80

Garlic Rosemary Potato Salad 81

Southwestern Beet Slaw 82

Salade Niçoise 83

Tart Apple Salad with Fennel and Honey Yogurt Dressing 84

Italian Vinaigrette 84

Thai-Inspired Pasta Salad 85

Whole-Wheat Couscous Salad with Citrus and Cilantro 86

Simple Autumn Salad 87

Tabbouleh Salad 88

Arugula with Pears and Red Wine Vinaigrette 90

Zucchini Cakes 91

Lemon Parmesan Rice with Fresh Parsley 92

Israeli Couscous with Sautéed Spinach, Bell Pepper, and Onion . . 93

Wheat Berry Pilaf with Roasted Vegetables 95

Sautéed Spinach with Shallots and Garlic 96

Whole-Wheat Couscous with Plums, Ginger, and Allspice 97

Garlic Rosemary Mashed Potatoes 98

Sun-Dried Tomato Couscous with Pine Nuts, Garlic, and Basil 99

Perfect Corn Bread 100

Kale and Roasted Beet Salad

This is a colorful, confetti-like bowl of salad featuring a delicious medley of dried cranberries, roasted golden beets, tomatoes, and chickpeas. Bookmark the Honey Mustard Vinaigrette recipe included with this salad to use on other salads at home!

SERVES 4

Per Serving

Calories	298
Fat	19g
Sodium	464mg
Carbohydrates	30g
Fiber	5g
Sugar	19g
Protein	5g

TO PEEL OR NOT TO PEEL?

Wondering if you need to peel beets before roasting? No need to take the extra step! Be sure to scrub beets well before using them, but the skin is perfectly edible and softens with baking.

Roasted Beets

2 medium golden beets, cut into ¼" cubes

1 tablespoon olive oil

¼ teaspoon finely chopped dried rosemary

¼ teaspoon salt

⅛ teaspoon garlic powder

Kale Salad

1 bunch curly kale, finely chopped

½ cup canned chickpeas, rinsed

6 cherry tomatoes, quartered

½ cup sliced green onions

½ cup chopped dried cranberries

¼ cup chopped walnuts

1 tablespoon fresh lemon zest

Honey Mustard Vinaigrette

3 tablespoons extra-virgin olive oil

1 tablespoon Dijon mustard

1 tablespoon honey

1 tablespoon lemon juice

1 clove garlic, peeled and finely minced

¼ teaspoon salt

⅛ teaspoon ground black pepper

1 For the roasted beets: Preheat oven to 400°F. Spray a small baking sheet with nonstick cooking spray.

2 In a medium bowl, toss together beets, oil, rosemary, salt, and garlic powder. Spread on the prepared sheet and roast 30–40 minutes or until beets can be easily pierced with a fork. Let cool before adding to salad.

3 For the kale salad: Combine kale, chickpeas, tomatoes, green onions, cranberries, walnuts, lemon zest, and cooled roasted beets in a large bowl. Store in an airtight container in refrigerator up to 3 days.

4 For the vinaigrette: In a small bowl, whisk together oil, mustard, honey, lemon juice, garlic, salt, and pepper. Store in an airtight container in refrigerator up to 3 days.

5 Toss salad with dressing when ready to serve.

Fresh Corn, Pepper, and Avocado Salad

SERVES 6

Per Serving

Calories	130
Fat	8g
Sodium	10mg
Carbohydrates	14g
Fiber	3g
Sugar	4g
Protein	2g

CORN FACTS

The fiber and antioxidants in corn provide many of its cardiovascular benefits. Sweet corn, however, is the only variety that contains vitamin C. It can be eaten hot or cold, on the cob or in single kernels, and even popped. Corn grows easily in the home garden. Its sweet taste and vibrant color add flavor, interest, and nutrition to any meal.

The next time you make corn on the cob, set aside a few ears for this fabulous summer salad. You can also serve this on top of tacos or burrito bowls made with Spicy Lime Chicken (see recipe in Chapter 10).

3 large ears fresh corn, cooked

1 medium red bell pepper, seeded and diced

1 medium avocado, peeled, pitted, and diced

1 small jalapeño pepper, seeded and minced

1 green onion, thinly sliced

1 clove garlic, peeled and minced

2 tablespoons lime juice

2 tablespoons extra-virgin olive oil

¼ teaspoon ground black pepper

1 Cut kernels from corncobs carefully, using a very sharp knife. Place kernels in a large bowl. Add bell pepper, avocado, jalapeño, green onion, and garlic.

2 In a small bowl, whisk together lime juice and oil. Drizzle over salad and toss to coat. Season with black pepper.

3 Store in an airtight container in refrigerator up to 3 days.

Spring Pea Salad

SERVES 6

Per Serving

Calories	105
Fat	5g
Sodium	181mg
Carbohydrates	12g
Fiber	4g
Sugar	4g
Protein	4g

RADISHES

Radishes are an excellent source of vitamin C, providing about 30 percent of the recommended Daily Value in a 1-cup serving. Vitamin C is essential for a healthy immune system, vision, and skin health.

This healthy Spring Pea Salad is the perfect easy side dish and can be prepared ahead of time. A win-win!

16 ounces frozen peas

⅓ cup diced red radishes

¼ cup finely torn fresh mint leaves

2 tablespoons finely diced shallot

2 tablespoons lemon zest

2 tablespoons extra-virgin olive oil

1 tablespoon lemon juice

1 tablespoon finely minced garlic

¼ teaspoon kosher salt

¼ teaspoon ground black pepper

⅛ teaspoon ground cayenne pepper

1 Allow peas to thaw at room temperature or rinse them in a colander under cool water. Place peas in a medium bowl and add radishes.

2 Combine remaining ingredients in a small bowl and stir. Pour dressing over peas and radishes. For best flavor, allow salad to sit 2 hours in refrigerator before serving. Store in an airtight container in refrigerator up to 4 days.

Tuscan Kale Salad

Get dinner on the table fast with this easy salad topped with roasted chicken. If you don't have time to make the Whole Roasted Chicken recipe in this book, pick up a rotisserie chicken at the store instead.

3 tablespoons extra-virgin olive oil

2 tablespoons balsamic vinegar

1 clove garlic, peeled and minced

¼ teaspoon salt

8 cups finely chopped curly kale

4 cups baby kale leaves

½ cup thinly sliced green onions

½ cup chopped sun-dried tomatoes (not packed in oil)

½ cup chopped marinated artichoke hearts

16 ounces Whole Roasted Chicken (see recipe in Chapter 3), shredded

1 ounce shredded Asiago cheese

1 medium avocado, peeled, pitted, and diced

1 In a small bowl, whisk together oil, vinegar, garlic, and salt. Set aside.

2 Toss together both types of kale, green onions, sun-dried tomatoes, and artichoke hearts in a large mixing bowl. Top with chicken and Asiago.

3 Store salad and dressing in separate airtight containers in refrigerator, up to 2 days for the salad and 7 days for the dressing. To serve, place prepared salad in a bowl and top with avocado and dressing.

SERVES 4

Per Serving

Calories	422
Fat	23g
Sodium	561mg
Carbohydrates	16g
Fiber	6g
Sugar	5g
Protein	36g

KALE YEAH!

When using kale in salads, it's best to chop it very fine to help decrease the bitterness and to make it easier to chew. You can use a food processor to make this task super easy! Leafy greens like kale are a good source of vitamins K, A, and C, and fiber.

Grapefruit Salmon Salad

Brighten up your salad routine with this refreshing, nutrient-rich salad. The grapefruit, salmon, and creamy avocado go so well together, and it's all topped off with a homemade citrus vinaigrette. The salmon and citrus vinaigrette can be prepared in advance of the salad.

Citrus Vinaigrette

¼ cup fresh orange juice

2 tablespoons fresh grapefruit juice

2 tablespoons extra-virgin olive oil

1 tablespoon minced cilantro leaves

2 teaspoons white wine vinegar

1 teaspoon lime juice

1 clove garlic, peeled and minced

⅛ teaspoon salt

Salmon Salad

2 (6-ounce) salmon fillets

⅛ teaspoon salt

⅛ teaspoon ground black pepper

1 teaspoon olive oil

1 (5-ounce) package baby kale and spinach mix

1 medium grapefruit, peeled and segmented

½ medium avocado, peeled, pitted, and sliced thin

½ cup frozen shelled edamame, thawed

¼ cup thinly sliced red onion

2 tablespoons unsalted shelled pumpkin seeds

1 For the citrus vinaigrette: Combine all ingredients in a small bowl or liquid measuring cup. Whisk together and set aside.

2 For the salmon salad: Place salmon skin side down on a plate. Pat with a paper towel to dry. Season with salt and pepper.

continued on next page

SERVES 2

Per Serving

Calories	636
Fat	35g
Sodium	416mg
Carbohydrates	33g
Fiber	10g
Sugar	14g
Protein	46g

SALMON

Salmon is one of the best sources of omega-3 fatty acids, which may help lower the risk of heart disease and lower inflammation levels in the body. Your body cannot make these acids, so it's important to regularly include foods like salmon in your diet!

3 Heat a 10" skillet over medium-high heat, then add oil. Carefully place salmon fillets skin side up in the skillet and reduce heat to medium. Cook 4–5 minutes on one side, until golden brown and salmon easily releases from the pan, before turning fillets over with tongs. Continue to cook for 3–5 minutes. Once cooked through, place fillets on a clean plate.

4 Prepare salads in two large bowls, starting with baby kale and spinach mix. Top with grapefruit, avocado, edamame, onion, and pumpkin seeds.

5 Store salmon, dressing, and salad in separate airtight containers in refrigerator up to 3 days, 5 days for the dressing. Salmon does not have to be reheated to eat with salad. If you choose to reheat it, place it in a microwave-safe dish covered with a lid and micro-wave 2–3 minutes or until internal temperature reaches 165°F.

Green Beans with Pecans, Cranberries, and Parmesan

Salty, sweet, crunchy, and oh so satisfying! These Green Beans with Pecans, Cranberries, and Parmesan are so delicious they'll convert any vegetable hater into a vegetable lover. Swap the pecans for almonds if you want an added crunch.

1 pound fresh green beans, ends snapped off

2 cloves garlic, peeled and minced

1½ tablespoons balsamic vinegar

1½ tablespoons olive oil

¼ teaspoon ground black pepper

¼ teaspoon salt

¼ cup pecan pieces

¼ cup dried cranberries, roughly chopped

¼ cup freshly grated Parmesan cheese

SERVES 6	
Per Serving	
Calories	119
Fat	8g
Sodium	176mg
Carbohydrates	11g
Fiber	3g
Sugar	6g
Protein	3g

1 Preheat oven to 325°F. Lay out green beans on a large baking sheet.

2 In a small bowl, use a fork to stir together garlic, vinegar, oil, and pepper. Drizzle vinaigrette over green beans and toss to coat them well. Season green beans with salt. Roast green beans 20–22 minutes, tossing them halfway through. Green beans should be slightly browned and easily pierced with a fork when cooked through.

3 While green beans are cooking, lightly toast pecan pieces in a small skillet over low heat 5 minutes, shaking the skillet occasionally.

4 Remove sheet from oven and place green beans in a large bowl. Top with cranberries, pecan pieces, and Parmesan. Store in an airtight container in refrigerator up to 3 days. To reheat, place in a microwave-safe dish and microwave 30–60 seconds until heated through.

Sautéed Cabbage, Kale, and Bacon

SERVES 4

Per Serving

Calories	77
Fat	3g
Sodium	119mg
Carbohydrates	8g
Fiber	3g
Sugar	4g
Protein	5g

Load up on your green vegetables with this hearty side dish! The low-sodium bacon adds just the right amount of salt and flavor to the leafy green vegetables, and the dish pairs well with pork tenderloin or Whole Roasted Chicken (see recipe in Chapter 3).

4 slices low-sodium bacon

¼ cup diced yellow onion

5 cups chopped green cabbage

4 ounces reduced-sodium vegetable broth, divided

3 cups chopped kale

1 Cook bacon in a large skillet over medium heat until crisp. Remove from skillet and place on a paper towel–lined plate to remove grease. Once cool, chop into small pieces.

2 In a clean large skillet, cook onion over medium heat 2 minutes. Add cabbage and 2 ounces vegetable broth, cover, and cook 5 minutes. Add kale and remaining 2 ounces broth. Cover and cook 5 minutes.

3 Store cooked bacon and cooked vegetables in separate airtight containers in refrigerator up to 3 days. To reheat, place vegetables in a microwave-safe dish and microwave 45–60 seconds at a time, stirring in between. Top with chopped bacon before serving.

Garlic Rosemary Potato Salad

This savory concoction of potatoes, green onions, and garlic is hefty enough to fill you up yet light enough to be refreshing. Pair this potato salad with Mediterranean Turkey Burgers (see recipe in Chapter 10) or Salmon Cakes (see recipe in Chapter 8).

6 medium potatoes

3 cloves garlic, peeled and minced

1 cup sliced green onions

¼ cup extra-virgin olive oil

2 tablespoons unflavored rice vinegar

2 teaspoons chopped fresh rosemary

¼ teaspoon ground black pepper

¼ teaspoon salt

SERVES 6	
Per Serving	
Calories	235
Fat	9g
Sodium	134mg
Carbohydrates	35g
Fiber	6g
Sugar	3g
Protein	4g

1 Put potatoes in a large saucepan and add enough water to cover by 1". Bring to a boil over high heat. Boil until fork-tender but still solid, 20–25 minutes.

2 Remove from heat and place under cold running water. Drain potatoes and set aside to cool 15 minutes. Cut into cubes and place in a large bowl.

3 Add garlic and green onions and toss to combine.

4 In a small bowl, whisk together oil, vinegar, rosemary, pepper, and salt. Pour dressing over salad and stir gently to coat. Cover and refrigerate at least 3 hours before serving. Store in refrigerator up to 2 days.

Southwestern Beet Slaw

SERVES 6

Per Serving

Calories	38
Fat	1g
Sodium	48mg
Carbohydrates	7g
Fiber	2g
Sugar	4g
Protein	1g

Shredded beets are combined with carrots, green onions, garlic, cilantro, and a lime vinaigrette. The resulting salad is subtly sweet, spicy, and spectacular.

3 medium beets, trimmed, peeled, and shredded

3 green onions, sliced

2 medium carrots, peeled and shredded

¼ cup chopped fresh cilantro

2 cloves garlic, peeled and minced

3 tablespoons lime juice

1 teaspoon extra-virgin olive oil

½ teaspoon Salt-Free Chili Seasoning (see recipe in Chapter 3)

¼ teaspoon ground black pepper

1 Place beets in a large bowl. Add green onions, carrots, cilantro, and garlic and stir to combine.

2 In a small bowl, whisk together lime juice, oil, chili seasoning, and pepper. Pour dressing over beet mixture and toss to coat.

3 Cover and refrigerate at least 2 hours before serving. Store in refrigerator up to 3 days.

Salade Niçoise

The famous French salad is re-created in a low-sodium style. Delightful and impressive, it's a plate full of color, flavor, and protein with a dreamy dressing that pulls it all together. Prep the vegetables ahead of time for quick salad assembly when you're ready to eat!

2 medium red potatoes

1 tablespoon distilled white vinegar

2 large eggs

1 pound green beans, trimmed

2 tablespoons extra-virgin olive oil

2 tablespoons red wine vinegar

1 teaspoon no-salt-added prepared mustard

1 clove garlic, peeled and minced

½ teaspoon ground black pepper

1 small head butter lettuce, torn into bite-sized pieces

1 small cucumber, peeled, seeded, and sliced

2 small tomatoes, quartered

1 (5-ounce) can no-salt-added light tuna in water, drained

SERVES 2	
Per Serving	
Calories	570
Fat	23g
Sodium	259mg
Carbohydrates	60g
Fiber	12g
Sugar	15g
Protein	33g

1 Place potatoes in a medium saucepan and add enough water to cover. Bring to a boil over high heat. Reduce heat to medium-low and simmer until tender, about 20 minutes. Drain potatoes and transfer to a cutting board. Dice potatoes and place in a large bowl. Add white vinegar and toss to coat. Set aside.

2 Place eggs in a small saucepan, add enough water to cover, and bring to a boil over high heat. Boil 12 minutes. Drain and cool in a bowl of cold water 5 minutes. Carefully crack, peel, and quarter eggs. Set aside.

3 Bring a small saucepan of water to a boil over high heat. Add green beans and cook 2 minutes. Remove beans from the pan and immediately place in a bowl of ice water. Set aside.

4 In a small bowl, whisk together oil, red wine vinegar, mustard, garlic, and pepper.

5 Assemble salad on a platter, placing lettuce on the bottom and then grouping cucumber, potatoes, eggs, green beans, tomatoes, and tuna on top. Drizzle dressing evenly over salad. Store in an airtight container in refrigerator up to 2 days.

Tart Apple Salad with Fennel and Honey Yogurt Dressing

SERVES 6	
Per Serving	
Calories	81
Fat	0g
Sodium	24mg
Carbohydrates	19g
Fiber	3g
Sugar	14g
Protein	2g

The fennel really makes this salad, and the plant can be used in its entirety—bulb, stalks, and fronds. Leave the peel on the apples for added nutrients and fiber.

2 medium Granny Smith apples, cored and diced

1 small bulb fennel, trimmed and chopped

1½ cups halved seedless red grapes

2 tablespoons lemon juice

¼ cup low-fat vanilla Greek yogurt

1 teaspoon honey

1 Combine all ingredients in a medium bowl and stir.
2 Cover and refrigerate up to 2 days.

Italian Vinaigrette

MAKES ¼ CUP	
Per Serving **(2 tablespoons)**	
Calories	38
Fat	3g
Sodium	1mg
Carbohydrates	1g
Fiber	0g
Sugar	0g
Protein	0g

This simple all-purpose salad dressing also works well as a marinade.

3 tablespoons distilled white vinegar

1½ teaspoons extra-virgin olive oil

2 cloves garlic, peeled and minced

½ teaspoon salt-free Italian seasoning

½ teaspoon salt-free all-purpose seasoning

Place all ingredients in a small bowl and whisk to combine. Store in an airtight container in refrigerator up to 10 days.

Thai-Inspired Pasta Salad

Colorful fresh vegetables and the flavors of sesame and ginger make this hearty pasta salad a treat. Serve it warm or cold.

1 pound spaghetti

2 tablespoons plus ⅓ cup peanut oil, divided

1 medium yellow squash, trimmed and julienned

1 medium zucchini, trimmed and julienned

1 medium green bell pepper, seeded and julienned

1 medium red bell pepper, seeded and julienned

1 medium orange bell pepper, seeded and julienned

6 green onions, sliced

3 cloves garlic, peeled and minced

1 small jalapeño pepper, seeded and minced

¾ cup chopped walnuts

1 tablespoon sesame oil

¼ cup unflavored rice vinegar

2 tablespoons salt-free peanut butter

1 tablespoon no-salt-added tomato paste

¼ cup chopped fresh cilantro

1 tablespoon minced fresh ginger

1 teaspoon granulated sugar

¼ teaspoon Salt-Free Chili Seasoning (see recipe in Chapter 3)

SERVES 8	
Per Serving	
Calories	470
Fat	23g
Sodium	24mg
Carbohydrates	51g
Fiber	5g
Sugar	5g
Protein	12g

1 Bring a large pot of water to a boil over high heat. Break spaghetti in half and add to the pot. Cook 10 minutes, stirring occasionally. Remove from heat, drain, and set aside.

2 Heat 2 tablespoons peanut oil in a large skillet over medium heat. Add julienned vegetables, green onions, garlic, jalapeño, and walnuts and cook, stirring occasionally, 3–4 minutes.

3 Remove skillet from heat and transfer vegetable mixture to a very large bowl. Add cooked spaghetti.

4 Whisk together remaining ⅓ cup peanut oil, sesame oil, vinegar, peanut butter, tomato paste, cilantro, ginger, sugar, and chili seasoning in a small bowl. Pour over pasta salad and toss to coat. Cover and refrigerate up to 3 days.

5 To reheat, place in a microwave-safe bowl covered with a lid and microwave 60 seconds.

Whole-Wheat Couscous Salad with Citrus and Cilantro

SERVES 6

Per Serving

Calories	148
Fat	1g
Sodium	8mg
Carbohydrates	30g
Fiber	5g
Sugar	6g
Protein	5g

WHAT IS COUSCOUS?

Couscous is a tiny grain-like pasta made from semolina (wheat) flour. It comes in white and whole-wheat varieties. Couscous is low in fat and sodium and is a good source of protein and fiber. It's sold in most supermarkets and natural food stores, both in packages and dry bulk bins, and is often stocked alongside rice and other grains.

This whole-grain salad strikes the perfect balance between light and filling. Its refreshing taste can be enjoyed year-round, but it is best in summer with freshly picked produce from the garden. You may substitute cherry tomatoes as desired.

1½ cups water

1 cup whole-wheat couscous

1 medium cucumber, peeled, seeded, and sliced

1 pint grape tomatoes, halved

1 small jalapeño pepper, seeded and minced

2 small shallots, peeled and minced

2 green onions, sliced

2 cloves garlic, peeled and minced

2 tablespoons lemon juice

2 tablespoons lime juice

1 teaspoon extra-virgin olive oil

¼ cup chopped fresh cilantro

¼ teaspoon ground black pepper

1 Bring water to a boil in a medium saucepan over high heat. Stir in couscous, reduce heat to medium-low, cover, and simmer 2 minutes. Remove pan from heat, uncover, and fluff couscous with a fork. Set aside to cool 5 minutes.

2 Transfer couscous to a large bowl and add all remaining ingredients. Stir to combine.

3 Cover and refrigerate up to 3 days.

Simple Autumn Salad

This healthy salad is a tasty combination of red leaf lettuce, red onion, fruit, and walnuts in a light and tangy vinaigrette.

1 large head red leaf lettuce, torn into bite-sized pieces

½ small red onion, peeled and thinly sliced

½ cup chopped dried figs

⅓ cup chopped walnuts

2 tablespoons white balsamic vinegar

2 tablespoons extra-virgin olive oil

1 clove garlic, peeled and minced

¼ teaspoon ground black pepper

1 medium pear, cored and thinly sliced

1   Prepare salad in advance by placing lettuce, red onion, dried figs, and walnuts in a storage container. These can be prepped into individual salads if preferred by distributing ingredients evenly among four containers. Keep in refrigerator up to 4 days.

2   In a small bowl, whisk together vinegar, oil, garlic, and pepper. Store dressing in an airtight container in the refrigerator up to 7 days.

3   When ready to serve, add pear to salad and pour dressing over salad. Toss to coat.

SERVES 4

Per Serving

Calories	192
Fat	13g
Sodium	22mg
Carbohydrates	17g
Fiber	4g
Sugar	10g
Protein	3g

STOCK UP AND SAVE

There's nothing more irritating than running out of a crucial ingredient when you're ready to cook. This goes double for when you're following a specialized diet and don't have the luxury of ordering out. By buying items in bulk, you'll not only be saving money due to lesser unit costs, but you'll also be hedging against future inconvenience.

Tabbouleh Salad

SERVES 4

Per Serving

Calories	123
Fat	3g
Sodium	8mg
Carbohydrates	20g
Fiber	2g
Sugar	2g
Protein	3g

PARSLEY FACTS

Parsley is an easily grown herb that comes in two varieties: flat-leaf and curly. Use it to add refreshing taste and color to salads, dressings, and pastas. Parsley contains high levels of vitamins A, C, and K as well as antioxidants and may help prevent cardio-vascular disease.

This refreshing low-sodium salad is a wonderful way to start any meal. Throwing a party? Set out this salad with other sliced fresh vegetables and a bowl of homemade hummus.

⅔ cup couscous

1 cup boiling water

1 small tomato, diced

1 small green bell pepper, seeded and diced

1 small shallot, peeled and finely diced

⅓ cup chopped fresh parsley

1 clove garlic, peeled and minced

3 tablespoons lemon juice

1 tablespoon extra-virgin olive oil

½ teaspoon ground black pepper

1 Place couscous in a small bowl. Stir in boiling water, cover, and set aside for 5 minutes.

2 Place tomato, bell pepper, shallot, and parsley in a salad bowl. Add couscous and stir to combine.

3 In a small bowl, whisk together garlic, lemon juice, oil, and black pepper. Pour garlic mixture over couscous mixture and toss to coat.

4 Cover and refrigerate up to 3 days.

Arugula with Pears and Red Wine Vinaigrette

SERVES 4

Per Serving

Calories	171
Fat	12g
Sodium	12mg
Carbohydrates	16g
Fiber	4g
Sugar	10g
Protein	2g

The peppery taste of arugula is paired with crisp, sweet pears and a tangy red wine vinaigrette. Add grilled chicken, dried figs, and/or shredded cheese for a main-course salad.

8 cups fresh baby arugula

¼ cup chopped pecans

4 tablespoons red wine vinegar

2 tablespoons extra-virgin olive oil

1 clove garlic, peeled and minced

½ teaspoon dried marjoram

¼ teaspoon ground mustard

¼ teaspoon ground black pepper

2 medium pears, cored and thinly sliced

1 Place arugula and pecans in a large bowl.

2 In a small bowl, whisk together vinegar, oil, garlic, marjoram, mustard, and pepper.

3 Store salad and dressing in separate airtight containers in the refrigerator until ready to use, up to 4 days for the salad and 7 days for the dressing. Add pears to arugula bowl when ready to serve. Pour dressing over salad and toss to coat.

Zucchini Cakes

These scrumptious oven-baked patties are a perfect way to use some of your garden surplus. Garnish them with homemade horseradish sauce or no-salt-added ketchup.

1 medium zucchini, trimmed and shredded

1 small red onion, peeled and minced

1 large egg white

¾ cup salt-free bread crumbs

2 teaspoons salt-free all-purpose seasoning

¼ teaspoon ground black pepper

1. Preheat oven to 400°F and adjust oven rack to middle position. Spray a baking sheet lightly with nonstick cooking spray and set aside.
2. Press zucchini gently between paper towels to release excess liquid.
3. In a large bowl, combine zucchini, onion, egg white, bread crumbs, seasoning, and pepper.
4. Shape mixture into 4 patties and place on the prepared sheet.
5. Place sheet on middle oven rack and bake 10 minutes. Remove from oven and gently flip patties, then return to oven and bake another 10 minutes.
6. Remove from oven. Allow to cool, then store in an airtight container in refrigerator up to 3 days. Reheat in a preheated toaster oven at 400°F for about 5 minutes.

SERVES 4

Per Serving

Calories	94
Fat	1g
Sodium	17mg
Carbohydrates	19g
Fiber	3g
Sugar	2g
Protein	4g

HOMEMADE HORSERADISH SAUCE

Combine 2 tablespoons store-bought horse-radish with ¼ cup low-fat sour cream. Add 2 tablespoons chopped fresh herbs, such as dill or chives; 1 minced garlic clove; and freshly ground black pepper. Cover and refrigerate. Use within 5 days.

Lemon Parmesan Rice with Fresh Parsley

SERVES 4

Per Serving

Calories	160
Fat	1g
Sodium	99mg
Carbohydrates	33g
Fiber	1g
Sugar	1g
Protein	4g

This healthy, quick, and easy side has lots of flavor. Vary the fresh herbs to suit your mood; swap the parsley for cilantro, oregano, or basil. Use low-sodium chicken broth for a richer flavor.

1 cup basmati rice

1½ cups low-sodium vegetable broth

2 tablespoons grated Parmesan cheese

2 tablespoons chopped fresh parsley

1 tablespoon lemon juice

½ teaspoon grated lemon zest

½ teaspoon ground black pepper

1 Rinse rice in a fine-mesh strainer, then place in a medium saucepan. Add broth and bring to a boil over medium-high heat.

2 Reduce heat to low, cover, and simmer 15 minutes.

3 Remove pan from heat. Stir in Parmesan, parsley, lemon juice, lemon zest, and pepper. Store in an airtight container in refrigerator up to 3 days. If serving warm, place in a microwave-safe dish and microwave 60 seconds.

Israeli Couscous with Sautéed Spinach, Bell Pepper, and Onion

Featuring earthy flavors accented with a splash of citrus, this yummy side can be served either warm or cold. You can use low-sodium chicken broth instead of vegetable broth for a richer flavor.

1⅓ cups Israeli couscous

1¾ cups boiling water

1 teaspoon olive oil

3 cloves garlic, peeled and minced

1 medium red onion, peeled and diced

1 medium red bell pepper, seeded and diced

6 cups baby spinach

¼ cup low-sodium vegetable broth

2 tablespoons lemon juice

¼ teaspoon ground black pepper

1. Place couscous in a small saucepan and add boiling water. Bring to a boil over high heat. Reduce heat to medium-low, cover, and simmer 12 minutes. Drain excess water.

2. Heat oil in a large skillet over medium heat. Add garlic and onion and sauté 2 minutes. Add bell pepper and sauté 4 minutes. Add spinach and sauté until wilted, 3–5 minutes. Remove skillet from heat.

3. Add broth and stir to release the browned bits from the bottom of the skillet. Stir in couscous, lemon juice, and black pepper. Store in an airtight container in refrigerator up to 3 days. If serving warm, place in a microwave-safe dish and microwave 60 seconds.

SERVES 6

Per Serving

Calories	161
Fat	1g
Sodium	36mg
Carbohydrates	32g
Fiber	3g
Sugar	2g
Protein	6g

WHAT IS ISRAELI COUSCOUS?

Israeli couscous, also known as ptitim, is a type of small round pasta made from wheat flour. It's like standard couscous but larger in diameter. Israeli couscous cooks quickly and is very versatile, making it a great alternative to rice and other grains. It's sold in supermarkets and specialty food stores in both white and whole-wheat varieties.

Wheat Berry Pilaf with Roasted Vegetables

This pilaf is chewy, bright, and incredibly flavorful thanks to the quartet of roasted vegetables. It makes a great potluck dish and can be served either hot or cold.

¾ cup parboiled wheat berries

2 cups water

1 small bulb fennel, trimmed

3 medium carrots, peeled and sliced

1 medium red onion, peeled and diced

8 cloves garlic, peeled and roughly chopped

1 teaspoon olive oil

¼ teaspoon ground cinnamon

¼ teaspoon ground black pepper

1 Preheat oven to 425°F and adjust oven rack to middle position. Lightly spray a baking sheet with nonstick cooking spray and set aside.

2 Place wheat berries and water in a small saucepan and bring to a boil over high heat. Reduce heat to low, cover, and simmer 15 minutes. Drain excess water and set aside.

3 Dice white bulb and stalks of fennel and place in a medium bowl. Coarsely chop green fronds and set aside.

4 Add carrots, onion, and garlic to the bowl with diced fennel. Add oil and toss to coat.

5 Arrange vegetable mixture in a single layer on the prepared sheet. Place on middle oven rack and roast 15 minutes. Remove from oven.

6 Transfer roasted vegetables to a medium bowl and add wheat berries, fennel fronds, cinnamon, and pepper. Stir to combine.

7 Cover and refrigerate up to 3 days. If serving warm, place in a microwave-safe dish and microwave 60 seconds.

SERVES 6

Per Serving

Calories	129
Fat	1g
Sodium	42mg
Carbohydrates	26g
Fiber	7g
Sugar	4g
Protein	5g

WHAT ARE WHEAT BERRIES?

Wheat berries, a whole grain, are individual kernels of wheat with the outer husk removed. They come in red and white varieties and can be eaten whole or ground into flour. They're high in fiber and protein, low in fat, and sodium-free. Standard wheat berries take about an hour to cook. Look for parboiled (partly cooked) wheat berries to speed preparation.

Sautéed Spinach with Shallots and Garlic

SERVES 2

Per Serving

Calories	54
Fat	2g
Sodium	73mg
Carbohydrates	7g
Fiber	3g
Sugar	2g
Protein	3g

Baby spinach requires nothing more than a good rinsing. When using larger spinach leaves, remove stems, then chop coarsely. Add this dish to scrambled eggs to get vegetables at breakfast!

1 teaspoon olive oil

1 large shallot, peeled and minced

2 cloves garlic, peeled and minced

6 cups trimmed fresh spinach

¼ teaspoon ground black pepper

1 Heat oil in a large skillet over medium heat. Add shallot and garlic and sauté 2 minutes.

2 Add spinach and sauté just until wilted, 3–5 minutes. Remove from heat.

3 Season with pepper. Store in an airtight container in refrigerator up to 3 days. Reheat in a microwave-safe dish for 60 seconds.

Whole-Wheat Couscous with Plums, Ginger, and Allspice

An appealing medley of flavors in a simple package, this side dish is terrific served warm or cold. It pairs well with the Sheet Pan Pork Roast and Vegetables from Chapter 6.

1½ cups water

1 cup whole-wheat couscous

2 medium plums, peeled, pitted, and diced

3 green onions, sliced

2 teaspoons minced fresh ginger

¼ cup chopped walnuts

¼ teaspoon ground black pepper

¼ teaspoon ground allspice

1 Place water in a small saucepan and bring to a boil over high heat. Stir in couscous, reduce heat to medium-low, cover, and simmer 2 minutes.

2 Remove pan from heat, uncover, and fluff couscous with a fork. Let stand for 5 minutes.

3 Place remaining ingredients in a medium bowl. Add couscous and toss to combine.

4 Cover and refrigerate up to 3 days. If serving warm, place in a microwave-safe dish and microwave 60 seconds.

SERVES 6

Per Serving

Calories	155
Fat	4g
Sodium	3mg
Carbohydrates	26g
Fiber	4g
Sugar	5g
Protein	5g

Garlic Rosemary Mashed Potatoes

SERVES 6

Per Serving

Calories	151
Fat	5g
Sodium	33mg
Carbohydrates	25g
Fiber	3g
Sugar	2g
Protein	3g

ROSEMARY FACTS

Rosemary is a perennial herb with a strong taste and fragrance. It grows in sturdy sprigs with leaves like soft pine needles. Rosemary can be used either fresh or dried and is often ground into a fragrant powder. It contains iron and several antioxidants believed to ward off neurological disorders such as Alzheimer's disease and Parkinson's disease.

Potatoes often fall flat without the boost of salt, but these salt-free mashed potatoes, made without butter and milk, too, may be the best you've ever had. Make a batch to serve alongside Beef Tenderloin and Roasted Vegetables (see recipe in Chapter 6) or Whole Roasted Chicken (see recipe in Chapter 3).

6 cloves garlic, peeled
2 tablespoons extra-virgin olive oil
¼ cup low-sodium vegetable broth
1 teaspoon unflavored rice vinegar
1 teaspoon ground rosemary
½ teaspoon ground white pepper
¼ teaspoon ground mustard
6 cups cubed red potatoes

1 Place garlic, oil, broth, vinegar, rosemary, pepper, and mustard in a food processor and purée until smooth. Set aside.

2 Place potatoes in a large saucepan and add enough water to cover. Bring to a boil over high heat. Reduce heat to medium-high, cover, and simmer 15 minutes.

3 Remove from heat and drain. Mash potatoes. Stir in garlic mixture.

4 Cover and refrigerate up to 4 days. To reheat, place in a microwave-safe dish and microwave 60–75 seconds until heated through.

Sun-Dried Tomato Couscous with Pine Nuts, Garlic, and Basil

Sun-dried tomatoes provide an astronomical amount of flavor to this whole-grain couscous dish with absolutely no salt. Select sun-dried tomatoes packed without oil.

1 cup chopped sun-dried tomatoes (not packed in oil)

2 cups boiling water

1 cup whole-grain couscous

2 teaspoons olive oil

4 cloves garlic, peeled and minced

⅓ cup pine nuts

¼ teaspoon ground black pepper

2 tablespoons chopped fresh basil

SERVES 4	
Per Serving	
Calories	299
Fat	10g
Sodium	37mg
Carbohydrates	43g
Fiber	7g
Sugar	9g
Protein	10g

1 Place sun-dried tomatoes in a small bowl and cover with boiling water. Set aside for 15 minutes.

2 Remove tomatoes and set aside, then pour soaking liquid into a measuring cup and add enough additional water to make 2 cups.

3 Pour tomato-water liquid into a small saucepan and bring to a boil over high heat. Stir in couscous, reduce heat to medium-low, cover, and simmer 2 minutes. Remove pan from heat, uncover, and fluff couscous with a fork. Set aside to cool 5 minutes.

4 Heat oil in a medium skillet over medium heat. Add tomatoes, garlic, and pine nuts and sauté 3 minutes. Remove from heat. Add couscous, pepper, and basil and toss to combine.

5 Cover and refrigerate up to 4 days. Reheat in a microwave-safe dish for 60–75 seconds.

Perfect Corn Bread

SERVES 16

Per Serving

Calories	104
Fat	4g
Sodium	14mg
Carbohydrates	15g
Fiber	1g
Sugar	4g
Protein	2g

FABULOUS FAT-FREE CORN BREAD!

Make an equally delicious fat-free version of this corn bread by substituting ¼ cup unsweetened applesauce for the canola oil, and skim milk for the low-fat milk. Add ½ cup frozen corn to the batter for an added treat.

This foolproof corn bread strikes the ideal balance between sweet and savory. Plus, it pairs well with just about any soup! Substitute white whole-wheat flour for all-purpose flour if you prefer. You can also substitute 100 percent grade A maple syrup for the granulated sugar.

1 cup cornmeal

¾ cup unbleached all-purpose flour

1 tablespoon sodium-free baking powder

⅓ cup granulated sugar

1 cup low-fat milk

1 large egg white

¼ cup canola oil

1 teaspoon vanilla extract

1 Preheat oven to 425°F and adjust oven rack to middle position. Grease an 8" × 8" baking dish and set aside.

2 Place all ingredients in a large bowl and stir to combine. Pour batter into the prepared dish. Place dish on middle oven rack and bake 20 minutes.

3 Remove dish from oven and place on a wire rack to cool briefly before cutting corn bread into squares. Store in an airtight container at room temperature up to 4 days.

CHAPTER 6

Beef and Pork Entrées

Sheet Pan Pork Roast and Vegetables........................ 102

Easy Deconstructed Wonton Soup 103

Beef Tenderloin and Roasted Vegetables 104

Red Lentil Soup with Bacon 106

30-Minute Ground Beef Pizza........................... 107

Whole-Grain Pasta with Meat Sauce 108

Beef with Pea Pods 109

Pressure Cooker Beef Bourguignon........................ 110

Pressure Cooker Harvest Stew 111

Asian-Inspired Mini Meatloaves with Salt-Free Hoisin Glaze...... 113

Seared Sirloin Steaks with Garlicky Greens.................. 114

Whole-Grain Rotini with Pork, Pumpkin, and Sage 115

Ginger and Garlic Pork Stir-Fry 116

Pork Chops with Sautéed Apples and Shallots 117

Sheet Pan Pork Roast and Vegetables

SERVES 4

Per Serving

Calories	453
Fat	24g
Sodium	417mg
Carbohydrates	17g
Fiber	4g
Sugar	4g
Protein	41g

SWEET POTATOES

Swapping out the sweet potatoes for red potatoes in this dish would be delicious! However, the sweet potatoes' sweetness pairs well with the pork roast in this recipe, and they provide a great pop of color!

This Sheet Pan Pork Roast and Vegetables is a delicious one pan meal your whole family will love. It can be served for dinner, or easily portioned out and packed for lunches!

4½ tablespoons olive oil, divided

1 tablespoon minced fresh rosemary

2 cloves garlic, peeled and minced

½ teaspoon paprika

½ teaspoon salt, divided

1½ pounds boneless pork loin roast

9 ounces halved Brussels sprouts

2 small sweet potatoes, cut into ½" cubes

¾ teaspoon garlic powder

¼ teaspoon ground black pepper

1 In a small bowl, mix 1½ tablespoons oil, rosemary, garlic, paprika, and ¼ teaspoon salt. Rub mixture over all sides of pork and marinate for 30 minutes.

2 Meanwhile, preheat oven to 400°F. Prepare a baking sheet for pork by cutting a piece of aluminum foil about 12" long. Starting from the long side, roll the aluminum foil into a coil. Once you have a coil, bring the two ends together to form a circle. Place the foil ring on the sheet and place pork on top so it does not touch the sheet. Roast pork in oven 20 minutes.

3 While pork is roasting, prepare vegetables by mixing them in a large bowl with remaining 3 tablespoons olive oil, remaining ¼ teaspoon salt, garlic powder, and pepper, tossing to coat well.

4 Before adding vegetables to the sheet with pork, spray the sheet with nonstick cooking spray. Spread vegetables out in a single layer on the sheet. Return sheet to oven and cook 25–30 minutes or until pork reaches an internal temperature of 145°F and vegetables are fork-tender. Allow pork to rest 5–10 minutes before slicing.

5 Store in an airtight container in refrigerator up to 3 days. To reheat, place in a microwave-safe dish covered with a lid and microwave 45–60 seconds at a time until heated to 165°F.

Easy Deconstructed Wonton Soup

This low-sodium soup is so similar to classic wonton soup, you'll be hard-pressed to tell the difference. Add your choice of fresh mushrooms: basic white button, baby bella, oyster, or shiitake.

½ pound lean ground pork

1 tablespoon minced fresh ginger

4 cloves garlic, peeled and minced

8 cups low-sodium chicken broth

2 cups sliced fresh baby bella mushrooms

6 ounces whole-grain yolk-free egg noodles

¼ teaspoon ground white pepper

4 green onions, sliced

1 Place a large stockpot over medium heat. Add pork, ginger, and garlic and sauté 5 minutes. Drain any excess fat, then return to stovetop over medium heat.

2 Add broth and bring to a boil. Stir in mushrooms, noodles, and pepper. Cover and simmer 10 minutes.

3 Remove pot from heat. Stir in green onions.

4 Allow soup to cool before storing in airtight containers in refrigerator up to 2 days. To reheat, place in a microwave-safe dish and microwave 60–90 seconds until heated through.

SERVES 8	
Per Serving	
Calories	151
Fat	4g
Sodium	173mg
Carbohydrates	17g
Fiber	2g
Sugar	1g
Protein	10g

CHOOSING LOW-SODIUM BROTHS

It's important to become familiar with reading the nutrition label to assess what is in the products you purchase. First, look at the serving size noted for a specific product. When it comes to managing blood pressure, look at the milligrams of sodium in a serving and for broths, aim to stay under 150 milligrams of sodium per 1 cup serving.

Beef Tenderloin and Roasted Vegetables

SERVES 3

Per Serving

Calories	679
Fat	23g
Sodium	404mg
Carbohydrates	71g
Fiber	12g
Sugar	10g
Protein	47g

This Beef Tenderloin and Roasted Vegetables is impressively easy. The dish pairs well with the Roasted Red Potatoes, Carrots, and Brussels Sprouts from Chapter 3. If you would like a nice fresh bite to the dish, garnish with fresh thyme.

2 teaspoons olive oil

1 teaspoon salt-free garlic and herb seasoning

1 teaspoon fresh thyme, stems removed

1 pound beef tenderloin (about 4" thick)

Roasted Red Potatoes, Carrots, and Brussels Sprouts (see recipe in Chapter 3)

1 Preheat oven to 475°F. Line a small rimmed baking sheet with aluminum foil. Tear off another piece of aluminum foil, about 12" long, and roll it lengthwise into a long coil, then bring the ends together to form a circle. Beef tenderloin will be placed on top of this while it roasts in the oven.

2 In a small bowl, combine oil, garlic and herb seasoning, and thyme. Press mixture onto tenderloin, coating all sides. Place tenderloin on top of aluminum ring so that it does not touch the sheet.

3 Roast tenderloin 35–40 minutes for medium-rare doneness or 45–50 minutes for medium doneness. Use a meat thermometer to test the internal temperature: 135°F for medium-rare and 145°F for medium.

4 Once beef has reached desired internal temperature, remove from the oven, loosely place a piece of aluminum foil over beef, and let rest 10 minutes.

5 Store in an airtight container in refrigerator up to 3 days. When ready to serve, slice beef 1" thick. To reheat, place in a microwave-safe dish covered with a lid and microwave 45–60 seconds at a time until heated to 165°F. Serve with Roasted Red Potatoes, Carrots, and Brussels Sprouts.

Red Lentil Soup with Bacon

SERVES 8

Per Serving	
Calories	184
Fat	1g
Sodium	117mg
Carbohydrates	29g
Fiber	11g
Sugar	4g
Protein	14g

Filled with vegetables, this low-fat lentil soup has a light, delicious broth enhanced by the smoky flavor of low-sodium bacon. Red lentils are used here because of their smaller size and shorter cooking time. If you want to substitute brown lentils, increase the simmering time to 40 minutes.

2 slices low-sodium bacon, diced

1 medium onion, peeled and diced

3 cloves garlic, peeled and minced

2 medium carrots, peeled and diced

2 medium stalks celery, diced

2 cups dried red lentils, rinsed

8 cups low-sodium beef broth

2 bay leaves

½ teaspoon dried savory

½ teaspoon dried thyme

¼ teaspoon dried basil

¼ teaspoon dried oregano

⅛ teaspoon dried red pepper flakes

¼ teaspoon ground black pepper

1 Place a large stockpot over medium heat. Add bacon, onion, and garlic and sauté 5 minutes. Add carrots and celery and sauté 2 minutes.

2 Add lentils, broth, bay leaves, savory, thyme, basil, oregano, red pepper flakes, and black pepper and stir to combine. Increase heat to high and bring to a boil.

3 Reduce heat to low, cover, and simmer, stirring occasionally, until lentils are tender, 20–30 minutes.

4 Remove from heat and remove bay leaves.

5 Allow soup to cool before storing in airtight containers in refrigerator up to 2 days. To reheat, place in a microwave-safe dish and microwave 60–90 seconds until heated through.

30-Minute Ground Beef Pizza

This supremely delicious pizza is flavored with lean ground beef and fresh vegetables. If you thought "real" pizza was gone from your life, think again!

1 cup white whole-wheat flour

1 teaspoon salt-free all-purpose seasoning

1 teaspoon salt-free Italian seasoning

½ teaspoon garlic powder

2 large egg whites

⅔ cup low-fat milk

½ pound lean ground beef

1 medium onion, peeled and chopped

½ cup no-salt-added pasta sauce

2 plum tomatoes, sliced

1 cup sliced mushrooms

1 small green bell pepper, seeded and diced

3 cloves garlic, peeled and minced

¼ cup chopped fresh basil

¼ cup shredded Swiss cheese

¼ cup part-skim ricotta cheese

SERVES 4	
Per Serving	
Calories	330
Fat	10g
Sodium	115mg
Carbohydrates	35g
Fiber	6g
Sugar	5g
Protein	24g

1 Preheat oven to 425°F and adjust oven rack to middle position. Grease and flour a 12" nonstick pizza pan and set aside.

2 Place flour, all-purpose seasoning, Italian seasoning, and garlic powder in a medium bowl and whisk to combine. Stir in egg whites and milk. Pour batter onto the prepared pan and set aside.

3 Heat a large skillet over medium heat. Add beef and onion and cook, stirring frequently, 5 minutes. Remove from heat and carefully drain any excess fat.

4 Spoon beef mixture evenly over batter on pan. Place pan on middle oven rack and bake 20 minutes.

5 Remove pan from oven. Spread pasta sauce evenly over pizza. Top with tomatoes, mushrooms, bell pepper, garlic, and basil. Sprinkle Swiss cheese over pizza, then dollop with ricotta.

6 Return pan to oven and bake 5 minutes, until cheese has melted.

7 Remove pizza from oven. Gently remove from pan and cut into 8 slices. Allow to cool before storing in an airtight container in refrigerator up to 3 days.

8 To reheat, preheat toaster oven or oven to 375°F. Place pizza on a toaster oven tray or a baking sheet and heat for 8 minutes.

Whole-Grain Pasta with Meat Sauce

Per Serving

Calories	357
Fat	3g
Sodium	60mg
Carbohydrates	59g
Fiber	11g
Sugar	6g
Protein	25g

Top your favorite whole-grain pasta with this thick, rich, and hearty salt-free sauce. If you prefer more spice, increase the amount of red pepper flakes. If not, omit the red pepper flakes. Serve the pasta with a green salad for a complete meal.

1 pound whole-grain pasta

1 pound extra-lean ground beef

1 medium onion, peeled and diced

3 cloves garlic, peeled and minced

2 (8-ounce) cans no-salt-added tomato sauce

⅓ cup red wine

1 tablespoon balsamic vinegar

1 teaspoon dried basil

½ teaspoon dried marjoram

½ teaspoon dried oregano

½ teaspoon dried red pepper flakes

½ teaspoon dried thyme

½ teaspoon ground black pepper

1 Cook pasta according to package directions, omitting salt. Drain and set aside.

2 Combine beef, onion, and garlic in a medium skillet over medium heat. Cook, stirring frequently, until beef has browned, about 5 minutes.

3 Add all remaining ingredients and stir to combine. Simmer 10 minutes, stirring occasionally.

4 Remove pan from heat and spoon sauce over pasta. Allow to cool before storing in an airtight container in refrigerator up to 3 days.

5 To reheat, place in a microwave-safe dish covered with a lid and microwave 60–90 seconds until heated through.

Beef with Pea Pods

This beautifully delicious and salt-free take on a Chinese classic, with tasty beef and crunchy pea pods, is great served with cooked brown rice. The sauce used in the recipe can be made in advance and stored in the refrigerator.

1 tablespoon sesame oil

3 green onions, sliced

2 cloves garlic, peeled and minced

2 teaspoons minced fresh ginger

¾ pound thin beef steak, sliced into ½" × 3" strips

4 cups fresh pea pods, trimmed

3 tablespoons Asian-Inspired Low-Sodium Marinade (see recipe in Chapter 3)

4 cups cooked brown rice

SERVES 4	
Per Serving	
Calories	536
Fat	13g
Sodium	172mg
Carbohydrates	72g
Fiber	11g
Sugar	11g
Protein	32g

1 Heat oil in a wok over medium heat. Add green onions, garlic, and ginger and stir-fry 30 seconds. Add beef and stir-fry 5 minutes, until beef has browned.

2 Add pea pods and marinade and stir-fry 3 minutes.

3 Remove from heat. Allow to cool before storing in an airtight container in refrigerator up to 3 days.

4 To reheat, place in a microwave-safe dish and microwave 60–90 seconds until heated through. Serve over rice.

Pressure Cooker Beef Bourguignon

SERVES 6

Per Serving

Calories	300
Fat	11g
Sodium	127mg
Carbohydrates	11g
Fiber	2g
Sugar	5g
Protein	36g

**INSTANT POT®
INSTRUCTIONS**

Press the Sauté button and melt butter in the Instant Pot®. Sauté onions 5 minutes. Move onions to the side of the pan, add beef, and brown on all sides, about 5 minutes. Press the Cancel button. Add remaining ingredients, close lid, press the Manual button, and set for 20 minutes. Let pressure release naturally for 10 minutes, then quick-release any remaining pressure until the float valve drops.

A pressure cooker cuts the cooking time of this traditional French dish by two-thirds, so it's ready in just 30 minutes! The heavenly smell of simmering beef and onions will have you (and any fortunate guests) salivating.

2 tablespoons unsalted butter

3 large onions, peeled and sliced

2 pounds lean beef stew meat, cubed

2 cups water

1½ cups red wine

2 teaspoons sodium-free beef bouillon granules

½ teaspoon dried marjoram

½ teaspoon dried thyme

½ teaspoon ground black pepper

1 pound white button mushrooms, sliced

1 Melt butter in a pressure cooker over medium-high heat. Add onions and cook, stirring occasionally, 5 minutes.

2 Move onions to the side of the pan, add beef, and brown on all sides, about 5 minutes.

3 Add remaining ingredients and stir to combine. Secure the lid on the pressure cooker and set to high. Bring the contents to a boil. Once you hear sizzling, reduce heat to medium and cook 20 minutes.

4 Allow pressure cooker to depressurize naturally. Allow to cool before storing in an airtight container in refrigerator up to 3 days.

5 To reheat, place in a microwave-safe dish and microwave 90 seconds or until heated to 165°F.

Pressure Cooker Harvest Stew

This hearty low-sodium dish is savory and filling, with an appealing subtle sweetness. Although it looks and tastes impressive, it couldn't be easier. Just pop everything into the pressure cooker and it's done in 30 minutes!

1 tablespoon olive oil

2 pounds lean beef stew meat, cubed

3 medium carrots, peeled and sliced into thick rounds

2 medium Granny Smith apples, peeled, cored, and cut into chunks

1 large onion, peeled and diced

1 cup fresh cranberries

4 cloves garlic, peeled and minced

2 cups water

2 teaspoons sodium-free beef bouillon granules

⅓ cup unsweetened apple juice

1 teaspoon dried marjoram

½ teaspoon dried savory

½ teaspoon dried thyme

½ teaspoon ground cinnamon

½ teaspoon ground rosemary

¼ teaspoon ground allspice

¼ teaspoon ground black pepper

1 Heat oil in a pressure cooker over medium-high heat. Add beef and brown on all sides, 3–5 minutes.

2 Add remaining ingredients and stir to combine. Secure the lid on the pressure cooker. Once pressurized, reduce heat to medium and cook 20 minutes.

3 Remove pressure cooker from heat and place in a sink under cold running water. Once cooker is depressurized, remove from sink. Allow stew to cool before storing in an airtight container in refrigerator up to 3 days.

4 To reheat, place in a microwave-safe dish and microwave 90 seconds or until heated to 165°F.

SERVES 6

Per Serving

Calories	382
Fat	13g
Sodium	121mg
Carbohydrates	17g
Fiber	3g
Sugar	10g
Protein	50g

**INSTANT POT®
INSTRUCTIONS**

Press the Sauté button and heat oil in the Instant Pot®. Brown beef on all sides, 3–5 minutes. Press the Cancel button. Add remaining ingredients, close lid, press the Manual button, and set for 20 minutes. Let pressure release naturally for 10 minutes, then quick-release any remaining pressure until the float valve drops.

Asian-Inspired Mini Meatloaves with Salt-Free Hoisin Glaze

Deliciously meaty, these tender little loaves are loaded with vegetables and the flavors of ginger, garlic, and five-spice powder. They are also easily pre-portioned into single servings!

SERVES 4	
Per Serving	
Calories	238
Fat	10g
Sodium	182mg
Carbohydrates	18g
Fiber	5g
Sugar	5g
Protein	18g

½ pound lean ground pork

1 medium red bell pepper, seeded and diced

¾ cup shelled edamame

3 green onions, sliced

3 cloves garlic, peeled and minced

1 tablespoon minced fresh ginger

1 large egg white

⅓ cup salt-free bread crumbs

½ teaspoon five-spice powder

¼ teaspoon ground white pepper

3 tablespoons Asian-Inspired Low-Sodium Marinade (see recipe in Chapter 3), divided

1 tablespoon no-salt-added tomato paste

1 Preheat oven to 375°F and adjust oven rack to middle position. Line a four cups of a jumbo muffin tin with paper liners or spray with nonstick cooking spray.

2 Place pork, bell pepper, edamame, green onions, garlic, ginger, egg white, bread crumbs, five-spice powder, and white pepper in a large bowl. Add 1 tablespoon marinade and mix using a wooden spoon or your hands.

3 Divide mixture into 4 equal portions and press into the prepared muffin cups.

4 Combine remaining 2 tablespoons marinade and tomato paste in a small bowl and stir until smooth. Brush onto tops of meatloaves, dividing evenly.

5 Place muffin tin on middle oven rack and bake 30 minutes.

6 Remove from oven, gently run a knife around the sides of each loaf, and remove from muffin tin. Allow to cool before storing in an airtight container in refrigerator up to 3 days. To reheat, place in a microwave-safe dish covered with a lid and microwave 60 seconds at a time until heated to 165°F.

Seared Sirloin Steaks with Garlicky Greens

SERVES 6

Per Serving

Calories	311
Fat	15g
Sodium	82mg
Carbohydrates	9g
Fiber	3g
Sugar	3g
Protein	28g

Serve this juicy, medium-rare beef accented with tart and tangy kale to hungry guests. Serve with roasted potatoes and fresh corn for a balanced, filling meal. This recipe is adapted from Fine Cooking.

1½ pounds sirloin steak (1" thick)

1 tablespoon chopped fresh rosemary

¾ teaspoon ground black pepper, divided

1 tablespoon olive oil

¾ cup dry white wine

4 cloves garlic, peeled and minced

2 tablespoons white balsamic vinegar

1 teaspoon no-salt-added prepared mustard

1½ pounds fresh kale, stems removed and chopped

1 Preheat oven to 400°F and adjust oven rack to middle position.

2 Trim and cut steak into 6 portions. Season both sides with rosemary and ½ teaspoon pepper.

3 Heat oil in a heavy oven-safe skillet over medium-high heat. Carefully place steaks in skillet and cook until browned, about 3 minutes per side. Transfer skillet to middle oven rack and roast 5 minutes. Remove from oven and set steaks aside, allowing them to rest 10 minutes before slicing.

4 Meanwhile, return the skillet to medium heat on the burner, being careful to not touch handle, which will be hot from the oven. Add wine and cook 3 minutes, scraping up any browned bits from the bottom of the pan. Add garlic, vinegar, mustard, and remaining ¼ teaspoon pepper and stir to combine.

5 Add kale and toss to coat. Cover the skillet and cook, stirring once or twice, until kale is tender, about 5 minutes. Place equal amounts kale on top of each steak.

6 Allow to cool before storing in an airtight container in refrigerator up to 3 days.

7 To reheat, place in a microwave-safe dish covered with a lid and microwave 45–60 seconds at a time until heated to 165°F.

Whole-Grain Rotini with Pork, Pumpkin, and Sage

Pumpkin adds color, nutrients, and subtle flavor to this deliciously filling dish. Rotini, corkscrew-shaped pasta with a lot of surface area, allows the sauce to really cling. Feel free to substitute a different variety of pasta if you prefer.

1 (13-ounce) package whole-grain rotini

1 pound lean ground pork

1 medium red onion, peeled and diced

3 cloves garlic, peeled and minced

1 medium yellow bell pepper, seeded and diced

1 cup pumpkin purée

2 teaspoons ground sage

1 teaspoon ground rosemary

½ teaspoon ground black pepper

SERVES 6	
Per Serving	
Calories	412
Fat	12g
Sodium	61mg
Carbohydrates	51g
Fiber	9g
Sugar	4g
Protein	26g

1 Cook pasta according to package directions, omitting salt. Drain and set aside.

2 Heat a medium skillet over medium heat. Add pork, onion, and garlic and sauté 2 minutes. Add bell pepper and sauté 5 minutes.

3 Remove from heat. Add pasta, pumpkin, sage, rosemary, and black pepper to the skillet and stir to combine. Allow to cool before storing in an airtight container in refrigerator up to 3 days.

4 To reheat, place in a microwave-safe dish covered with a lid and microwave 60 seconds at a time until heated to 165°F.

Ginger and Garlic Pork Stir-Fry

SERVES 4

Per Serving

Calories	220
Fat	5g
Sodium	370mg
Carbohydrates	25g
Fiber	7g
Sugar	12g
Protein	17g

Intensely flavorful and speedy to prepare, this low-sodium stir-fry features tender pork loin and crisp vegetables in a delectable sauce. Serve it over the Brown Rice from Chapter 3. Replace pea pods with sugar snap peas if desired.

8 ounces pork tenderloin, thinly sliced

1½ tablespoons minced fresh ginger

3 cloves garlic, peeled and minced

2 tablespoons Asian-Inspired Low-Sodium Marinade (see recipe in Chapter 3)

¾ cup low-sodium vegetable broth

2 teaspoons cornstarch

2 teaspoons sesame oil

1 head bok choy, sliced

½ pound pea pods, trimmed

2 medium carrots, peeled and sliced

1 medium red bell pepper, seeded and diced

1 small red onion, peeled and diced

4 green onions, sliced

¼ teaspoon ground black pepper

1 Place pork in a large bowl. Add ginger, garlic, and marinade and stir to coat. Set aside.

2 In a small bowl, whisk together broth and cornstarch. Set aside.

3 Heat oil in a wok over medium heat. Add bok choy, pea pods, carrots, bell pepper, and red onion and cook, stirring occasionally, 5 minutes.

4 Add pork mixture and cook, stirring occasionally, 5 minutes. Add broth mixture and cook, stirring frequently, until sauce thickens, 30 seconds to 1 minute.

5 Remove from heat. Stir in green onions and season with black pepper. Allow to cool before storing in an airtight container in refrigerator up to 3 days.

6 To reheat, place in a microwave-safe dish covered with a lid and microwave 60 seconds at a time until heated to 165°F.

Pork Chops with Sautéed Apples and Shallots

Fill your house with the heavenly smell of apples and cinnamon. This delicious dish of boneless medallions in a white wine sauce is low in sodium. The sautéed apples can be made in advance and kept in the refrigerator if you prefer.

1 pound pork loin chops

1 teaspoon ground black pepper, divided

1 teaspoon olive oil

3 small shallots, peeled and minced, divided

¾ cup white wine

2 tablespoons unsalted butter

4 medium apples, cored and thinly sliced

½ cup apple juice

¼ cup packed light brown sugar

½ teaspoon ground cinnamon

SERVES 4	
Per Serving	
Calories	441
Fat	16g
Sodium	85mg
Carbohydrates	45g
Fiber	5g
Sugar	36g
Protein	25g

1 Preheat oven to 350°F and adjust oven rack to middle position.

2 Season chops with ½ teaspoon pepper. Heat oil in a large skillet over medium-high heat. Place chops in skillet and brown quickly on both sides, 2–3 minutes each side. Remove from skillet and transfer to a medium baking dish.

3 Reduce heat to medium. Add 2 shallots to skillet and cook, stirring frequently, 2–3 minutes, scraping pan to remove drippings.

4 Add wine and remaining ½ teaspoon pepper. Cook, stirring occasionally, 1 minute, then pour over chops.

5 Cover baking dish with foil, place on middle oven rack, and bake 30 minutes, until internal temperature reaches 145°F.

6 Meanwhile, melt butter in a medium skillet over medium heat. Add remaining shallot and sauté 2 minutes. Add apples, apple juice, sugar, and cinnamon. Cook, stirring occasionally, 10–15 minutes, until apples are tender.

7 Remove skillet from heat. Remove pork chops from oven. Allow apples and pork chops to cool before storing in an airtight container in refrigerator up to 3 days.

8 To reheat, place in a microwave-safe dish covered with a lid and microwave 60 seconds at a time until heated to 165°F.

PORK FACTS

Lean pork is considered a healthy meat, containing roughly the same cholesterol per serving as chicken and turkey. It is an excellent source of protein, vitamins B_6 and B_{12}, and minerals. Its mild flavor pairs well with fruit, both fresh and dried. As a lean meat, pork can dry out quickly, so it's important not to overcook it.

CHAPTER 7
Chicken and Turkey Entrées

Italian Chicken Kebabs. 120

Greek Chicken and Cauliflower Rice Bowl. 122

Asian Turkey Lettuce Wraps 123

Cheesy Potato Chowder 124

Classic Chicken Noodle Soup 125

Chicken, Black Bean, and Vegetable Soft Tacos. 127

Chicken, Corn, and Black Bean Chili. 128

Grilled Tequila Chicken with Sautéed Peppers and Onion 129

Saucy Barbecued Chicken with Rice 130

Spicy Yogurt-Marinated Chicken Tenders 131

Chicken Curry with Creamy Tomato Sauce. 132

Oven-Baked Chicken Tenders. 134

Chicken with Rice, Lemon, and Kale 135

Honey Mustard Chicken Breasts. 136

Tropical Chicken Salad Wraps. 137

Broccoli, Ground Turkey, and Pesto Pizza 139

Ground Turkey Meatloaf Minis. 140

Turkey and Brown Rice–Stuffed Peppers 141

Seasoned Turkey Burgers with Sautéed Mushrooms and Swiss. . . 142

Italian Chicken Kebabs

SERVES 3

Per Serving

Calories	300
Fat	14g
Sodium	93mg
Carbohydrates	7g
Fiber	2g
Sugar	4g
Protein	36g

These easy kebabs can be served with a side of seasoned rice, quinoa, or farro or a leafy green side salad for a balanced meal. If you don't own an outdoor grill, cook these kebabs on a grill pan on the stovetop or use an indoor grill. You can use store-bought pesto if you do not have the ingredients for Basil Pesto (see recipe in Chapter 3). If you don't want to remove the skewer during reheating, use wooden skewers instead of metal.

1 pound boneless, skinless chicken breast, cut into 1" cubes

½ cup Basil Pesto (see recipe in Chapter 3)

1 medium zucchini, trimmed and cut into ½"-thick half-moon pieces

1 medium orange bell pepper, seeded and cut into 1" pieces

¼ medium red onion, peeled and cut into 1" pieces

6 metal skewers

1 Place chicken in a medium bowl and pour pesto over top, stirring to coat chicken. Allow to marinate at least 20 minutes but no longer than 60 minutes in the refrigerator.

2 Preheat grill and, if using bamboo skewers, soak them in water for 20 minutes. Assemble Italian Chicken Kebabs by alternating pieces of marinated chicken, zucchini, bell pepper, and red onion until each skewer is filled.

3 Place kebabs over medium heat on a gas grill or over medium ash-covered coals. Cook 4 minutes, then turn kebabs over and cook another 3–5 minutes, until chicken reaches an internal temperature of 165°F.

4 Store in an airtight container in refrigerator up to 3 days. To reheat, remove chicken and vegetables from skewers, place in a microwave-safe dish covered with a lid, and microwave 45–60 seconds at a time until heated to 165°F.

Greek Chicken and Cauliflower Rice Bowl

SERVES 4

Per Serving

Calories	268
Fat	10g
Sodium	440mg
Carbohydrates	14g
Fiber	5g
Sugar	7g
Protein	33g

Enjoy flavors of the Mediterranean for dinner in under 30 minutes with this simple and filling Greek Chicken and Cauliflower Rice Bowl! Make the cauliflower rice ahead of time using the Homemade Cauliflower Rice recipe in Chapter 3. If you cannot find the dressing mentioned in this recipe, pick another low-sodium Greek yogurt dressing of your choice.

1 pound boneless, skinless chicken breasts

1 teaspoon dried oregano

1 teaspoon dried thyme

1 teaspoon garlic powder

½ teaspoon ground black pepper

1 (24-ounce) package cauliflower rice, cooked

¼ cup diced red bell pepper

¼ cup diced yellow bell pepper

⅓ cup sliced cucumbers

¼ cup sliced green onion

¼ cup shredded carrots

½ cup crumbled feta cheese

½ cup Greek dressing with feta

1 Season both sides of each chicken breast with oregano, thyme, garlic powder, and black pepper. Lightly coat a grill pan or medium skillet with nonstick cooking spray and place over medium heat. Add chicken and cook 8–10 minutes or until internal temperature reaches 165°F. Let cool before storing in an airtight container in refrigerator up to 4 days.

2 When ready to serve, add cauliflower rice to a bowl and top with chicken, vegetables, feta, and dressing.

3 To reheat chicken, place in a microwave-safe dish covered with a lid and microwave 45–60 seconds at a time until heated to 165°F. To reheat cauliflower rice, place in a microwave-safe dish and microwave 60 seconds before adding toppings.

Asian Turkey Lettuce Wraps

Make the Asian-Inspired Low-Sodium Marinade ahead of time so you can have dinner ready in 10 minutes or less! This dish stores well, and you can easily double the recipe to make a larger batch.

4 tablespoons Asian-Inspired Low-Sodium Marinade (see recipe in Chapter 3)

½ teaspoon cornstarch

1 pound 90 percent lean ground turkey

12 romaine lettuce leaves

¼ cup shredded carrots

¼ cup diced radishes

SERVES 4	
Per Serving	
Calories	245
Fat	11g
Sodium	257mg
Carbohydrates	8g
Fiber	2g
Sugar	5g
Protein	26g

1 Whisk together marinade and cornstarch in a small bowl. Set aside.

2 Cook turkey in a large skillet over medium-high heat until no longer pink, about 5–6 minutes, using a spatula to break turkey into small pieces. Turn off heat and use a paper towel to blot liquid from cooked turkey.

3 Add marinade to turkey and mix well.

4 Store cooked turkey in an airtight container in refrigerator up to 3 days. To reheat, place in a microwave-safe dish covered with a lid and microwave 45–60 seconds at a time until heated to 165°F. To serve, add about 3 tablespoons turkey to each lettuce leaf and top with carrots and radishes.

Cheesy Potato Chowder

SERVES 6

Per Serving

Calories	231
Fat	7g
Sodium	432mg
Carbohydrates	31g
Fiber	5g
Sugar	5g
Protein	10g

This creamy, dreamy concoction of potatoes, chicken broth, and cheese will make a low-sodium soup fan of anyone.

1 tablespoon olive oil

2 cups diced onion

1 cup diced celery

2 cloves garlic, peeled and minced

6 cups diced potatoes

4 cups low-sodium chicken broth

⅓ cup dry white wine

½ teaspoon dried thyme

¼ teaspoon ground rosemary

¼ teaspoon dried basil

¼ teaspoon ground black pepper

1 cup shredded Swiss cheese

1 Heat oil in a large stockpot over medium heat. Add onion, celery, and garlic and sauté 5 minutes. Add potatoes and cook, stirring, 1 minute. Add broth, wine, thyme, rosemary, basil, and pepper. Bring to a boil.

2 Reduce heat to low, cover, and simmer 20 minutes.

3 Remove pot from heat. Using a blender or food processor, purée half the soup. Return puréed soup to pot and stir to combine. Add cheese and stir until melted.

4 Allow soup to cool before storing in airtight containers in refrigerator up to 3 days. To reheat, place in a microwave-safe dish and microwave 60–90 seconds until heated through.

Classic Chicken Noodle Soup

No cookbook would be complete without this perennial favorite. This low-fat, low-sodium version makes the most of meaty chicken and tender vegetables.

SERVES 4

Per Serving

Calories	215
Fat	3g
Sodium	651mg
Carbohydrates	18g
Fiber	2g
Sugar	3g
Protein	27g

2 cups shredded cooked chicken

2 medium carrots, peeled and sliced

1 medium stalk celery, sliced

1 small onion, peeled and diced

3 cloves garlic, peeled and minced

4 cups low-sodium chicken broth

1 teaspoon salt-free all-purpose seasoning

½ teaspoon ground sage

¼ teaspoon ground rosemary

¼ teaspoon ground black pepper

1½ cups yolk-free egg noodles

1 Combine chicken, carrots, celery, onion, garlic, broth, seasoning, sage, rosemary, and pepper in a medium stockpot. Bring to a boil over high heat.

2 Add noodles, reduce heat to medium-low, and simmer 10 minutes. Remove from heat.

3 Allow soup to cool before storing in airtight containers in refrigerator up to 3 days. To reheat, place in a microwave-safe dish and microwave 60–90 seconds until heated through.

Chicken, Black Bean, and Vegetable Soft Tacos

In this dish, soft corn tortillas are filled with a saucy and spicy combination of chicken, vegetables, and beans. If you're using a commercial chili seasoning, start with 1 teaspoon and work up from there.

½ cup low-sodium chicken broth

1 medium carrot, peeled and diced

1 medium sweet potato, peeled and diced

3 boneless, skinless chicken thighs, cut into bite-sized pieces

1 medium onion, peeled and diced

1 medium red bell pepper, seeded and diced

1 medium jalapeño pepper, seeded and minced

3 cloves garlic, peeled and minced

1 (15-ounce) can no-salt-added black beans, not drained

½ cup corn kernels

2 tablespoons no-salt-added tomato paste

2 tablespoons Salt-Free Chili Seasoning (see recipe in Chapter 3)

12 (5") corn tortillas, warmed

½ cup low-fat sour cream

¼ cup chopped fresh cilantro

1 Heat a medium skillet over medium heat. Add broth, carrot, and sweet potato. Cover and cook 5 minutes. Add chicken, onion, peppers, and garlic. Cover and cook another 5 minutes, stirring halfway through.

2 Add beans with liquid, corn, tomato paste, and chili seasoning. Cook, stirring occasionally, 5 minutes. Remove from heat.

3 Store filling in an airtight container in refrigerator up to 3 days until ready to serve. To reheat, place in a microwave-safe dish and microwave 60–90 seconds until heated to 165°F. Spoon filling into tortillas and top with sour cream and cilantro.

SERVES 6	
Per Serving	
Calories	357
Fat	8g
Sodium	167mg
Carbohydrates	47g
Fiber	9g
Sugar	5g
Protein	23g

SALT-FREE CHILI SEASONING

Not all salt-free seasoning blends are the same, and nowhere is this more apparent than when it comes to chili seasonings. Some brands are fiery, while others are bland. Taste seasonings before adding them to food. Carefully assess how much or how little needs to be added to your food and you'll never risk over-seasoning.

Chicken, Corn, and Black Bean Chili

SERVES 8

Per Serving

Calories	245
Fat	3g
Sodium	197mg
Carbohydrates	34g
Fiber	8g
Sugar	5g
Protein	21g

SLOW COOKER MAGIC

Slow cookers take the work out of many meals and have an almost magical ability to transform the toughest, most inexpensive cuts of meat into tender, succulent feasts. To make this chicken chili in a slow cooker, simply measure ingredients into the appliance, stir to combine, and cover. Set the slow cooker to low and simmer 6–8 hours.

This yummy low-sodium chili is a little different from the standard variety, thanks to the addition of corn and meaty chunks of chicken and the absence of diced tomatoes. Serve it with Perfect Corn Bread (see recipe in Chapter 5) for a truly heavenly meal. This recipe is adapted from Kitchen Basics Healthy Cooking with Stock.

2 teaspoons olive oil

1 pound boneless, skinless chicken breasts, cut into ½" cubes

1 medium red onion, peeled and diced

3 cloves garlic, peeled and minced

1 medium green bell pepper, seeded and diced

1 medium red bell pepper, seeded and diced

1 (6-ounce) can no-salt-added tomato paste

2 tablespoons Salt-Free Chili Seasoning (see recipe in Chapter 3)

1 teaspoon ground cumin

2 cups low-sodium chicken broth

2 (15-ounce) cans no-salt-added black beans, drained and rinsed

2 cups frozen corn kernels

¼ cup chopped fresh cilantro

¼ teaspoon ground black pepper

1   Heat oil in a large stockpot over medium heat. Add chicken and sauté until the outside is no longer pink, 3–5 minutes.

2   Add onion and garlic and sauté 2 minutes. Add bell peppers and sauté 2 minutes. Stir in tomato paste, chili seasoning, cumin, broth, and beans. Increase heat to high and bring to a boil.

3   Reduce heat to medium-low, cover, and simmer 20 minutes.

4   Stir in corn, cover, and cook another 5 minutes. Remove from heat and stir in cilantro and black pepper.

5   Allow soup to cool before storing in airtight containers in refrigerator up to 3 days. To reheat, place in a microwave-safe dish and microwave 60–90 seconds until heated through.

Grilled Tequila Chicken with Sautéed Peppers and Onion

This fabulous chicken is succulently moist and unbelievably flavorful thanks to the tequila marinade. The longer the chicken marinates, the greater the flavor. Serve the chicken with fresh corn on the cob and chopped fresh cilantro.

1 cup lime juice

⅓ cup tequila

3 cloves garlic, peeled and chopped

¼ cup chopped fresh cilantro

1 tablespoon agave nectar

½ teaspoon ground black pepper

1 teaspoon ground cumin

½ teaspoon ground coriander

4 (4-ounce) boneless, skinless chicken breasts

2 teaspoons canola oil

1 large green bell pepper, seeded and diced

1 large red bell pepper, seeded and diced

1 large onion, peeled and diced

½ cup low-fat sour cream

SERVES 4	
Per Serving	
Calories	279
Fat	13g
Sodium	66mg
Carbohydrates	11g
Fiber	2g
Sugar	5g
Protein	28g

1 Place lime juice, tequila, garlic, cilantro, agave nectar, black pepper, cumin, and coriander in a large bowl and whisk to combine.

2 Add chicken and turn several times to coat. Cover and place in refrigerator to marinate at least 6 hours, preferably overnight.

3 Heat a gas or charcoal grill. Grill chicken until no longer pink but still juicy and tender, 10–15 minutes per side.

4 Meanwhile, heat oil in a medium skillet over medium heat. Add bell peppers and onion and sauté 5 minutes. Remove from heat.

5 Remove chicken from grill. Store in an airtight container with the peppers and onion in refrigerator up to 3 days.

6 To reheat, place in a microwave-safe dish and microwave 60–90 seconds until heated to 165°F. Serve with sautéed vegetables and a dollop of sour cream.

Saucy Barbecued Chicken with Rice

SERVES 4

Per Serving

Calories	494
Fat	8g
Sodium	283mg
Carbohydrates	76g
Fiber	10g
Sugar	21g
Protein	25g

This simple and satisfying low-sodium chicken recipe is full of bar-becue flavor and amazingly tender meat. Try it spooned over baked potatoes instead of rice.

1 teaspoon canola oil

1 small onion, peeled and finely diced

2 cloves garlic, peeled and minced

1 pound boneless, skinless chicken thighs, cut into bite-sized pieces

1 large green bell pepper, seeded and diced

2 cups Spicy and Tangy Barbecue Sauce (see recipe in Chapter 3)

¼ cup chopped fresh cilantro

4 cups cooked brown rice

1 Heat oil in a medium skillet over medium heat. Add onion and garlic and sauté 2 minutes. Add chicken and bell pepper and sauté another 2 minutes.

2 Add barbecue sauce and stir to combine. Bring to a boil.

3 Reduce heat to medium-low, cover, and simmer until chicken is cooked through, 10–15 minutes.

4 Remove from heat. Stir in cilantro.

5 Store chicken and rice in an airtight container in refrigerator up to 3 days. To reheat, place in a microwave-safe dish and micro-wave 60–90 seconds until heated to 165°F.

Spicy Yogurt-Marinated Chicken Tenders

Although this recipe uses chicken tenders, the marinade works equally well with any cut of chicken, from bone-in breasts to a whole roaster. For maximum impact, allow the chicken to marinate as long as possible.

¾ cup low-fat plain Greek yogurt

1 medium onion, peeled and minced

3 cloves garlic, peeled and minced

2 tablespoons lime juice

1 tablespoon honey

1 teaspoon ground smoked paprika

1 teaspoon ground cumin

¼ teaspoon ground cayenne pepper

1 pound boneless, skinless chicken tenders

1 Combine yogurt, onion, garlic, lime juice, honey, paprika, cumin, and cayenne in a large bowl and stir to combine. Add chicken and toss to coat. Cover and refrigerate 30 minutes up to 12 hours.

2 Preheat oven to 375°F and adjust oven rack to middle position. Line a baking sheet with parchment paper or foil and arrange chicken in a single layer.

3 Place sheet on middle oven rack and bake until chicken is golden brown, 10–15 minutes.

4 Allow to cool before storing in an airtight container in refrigerator up to 3 days. To reheat, place in a microwave-safe dish and microwave 60–90 seconds until heated to 165°F.

SERVES 4

Per Serving

Calories	131
Fat	1g
Sodium	113mg
Carbohydrates	5g
Fiber	0g
Sugar	4g
Protein	24g

DIFFERENT TYPES OF MARINADES

Marinades can be divided into three types. Acidic marinades are those made with fruit juice, wine, or vinegar. Enzymatic marinades rely on fruit enzymes, like those found in papaya, pineapple, or kiwi. Dairy-based marinades use either buttermilk or yogurt as their base. Only dairy marinades reliably tenderize without the risk of toughening or disintegrating meat.

Chicken Curry with Creamy Tomato Sauce

SERVES 4

Per Serving

Calories	219
Fat	4g
Sodium	187mg
Carbohydrates	14g
Fiber	3g
Sugar	7g
Protein	31g

CHICKEN FACTS

Chicken's mild flavor and affordable nature make it one of the most popular proteins. When preparing chicken, remove the skin to cut down on fat. White meat contains less fat, but dark meat contains a higher concentration of some nutrients. Skinless chicken is an excellent source of protein, vitamin B$_6$, and minerals.

This quick and easy chicken curry tastes terrific. As a bonus, it will leave your house smelling amazing. Serve it over cooked basmati rice or quinoa. You can substitute low-sodium vegetable broth for the chicken broth if you prefer.

1 teaspoon canola oil

1 pound boneless, skinless chicken breasts, cut into bite-sized pieces

1 large onion, peeled and diced

3 cloves garlic, peeled and minced

1 tablespoon minced fresh ginger

1 small jalapeño pepper, seeded and minced

1 (15-ounce) can no-salt-added diced tomatoes, not drained

2 tablespoons no-salt-added tomato paste

¾ cup low-sodium chicken broth

½ cup low-fat plain Greek yogurt

2 teaspoons salt-free curry powder

½ teaspoon ground paprika

¼ teaspoon ground black pepper

¼ cup chopped fresh cilantro

1 Heat oil in a large skillet over medium heat. Add chicken, onion, garlic, and ginger and cook, stirring frequently, 5 minutes. Add jalapeño, tomatoes with juice, tomato paste, broth, yogurt, curry powder, paprika, and black pepper and stir to combine. Bring to a boil.

2 Reduce heat to medium-low, cover, and simmer, stirring frequently, until chicken is fully cooked, about 20 minutes. Remove from heat. Stir in cilantro.

3 Store in an airtight container in refrigerator up to 3 days. To reheat, place in a microwave-safe dish covered with a lid and microwave 45–60 seconds until heated to 165°F.

Oven-Baked Chicken Tenders

SERVES 8

Per Serving

Calories	189
Fat	1g
Sodium	163mg
Carbohydrates	9g
Fiber	1g
Sugar	0g
Protein	33g

Baked rather than fried, these flavorful, crispy tenders are much lower in fat than the frozen kind. Serve them with salt-free ketchup, barbecue sauce, and honey for dipping.

½ cup unbleached all-purpose flour

½ cup white whole-wheat flour

½ cup salt-free bread crumbs

2 teaspoons garlic powder

2 teaspoons onion powder

1 teaspoon ground paprika

1 teaspoon ground black pepper

½ cup low-fat milk

1 large egg white

3 pounds boneless, skinless chicken breast tenderloins

1 Preheat oven to 375°F and adjust oven rack to middle position. Line a large baking sheet with foil, spray lightly with nonstick cooking spray, and set aside.

2 Combine both flours, bread crumbs, garlic powder, onion powder, paprika, and pepper in a large resealable bag. Seal bag and shake to combine.

3 Whisk together milk and egg white in a shallow bowl.

4 One piece at a time, dip chicken into milk mixture, then place in the bag with flour mixture, seal, and shake vigorously to coat. Place breaded tenders on the prepared sheet.

5 Place on middle oven rack and bake 10–15 minutes, until golden brown.

6 Store chicken in an airtight container in refrigerator up to 3 days. To reheat, place in a microwave-safe dish covered with a lid and microwave 45–60 seconds until heated to 165°F.

Chicken with Rice, Lemon, and Kale

In this easy oven-baked meal, hearty kale, meaty chunks of chicken, and rice are bathed in a delicious lemony broth. This works well for meal preppers, as this can be a complete meal served as is. If you would prefer a refreshing taste, use 1 tablespoon of fresh thyme instead of dried.

8 boneless, skinless chicken thighs, cut into bite-sized pieces

1 cup basmati rice

4 cups chopped fresh kale

2 medium shallots, peeled and chopped

2 cups low-sodium chicken broth

½ cup white wine

3 tablespoons lemon juice

1 tablespoon grated lemon zest

4 cloves garlic, peeled and minced

1 teaspoon dried thyme

¼ teaspoon ground black pepper

1 Preheat oven to 425°F and adjust oven rack to middle position. Spray a 9" × 13" casserole pan lightly with nonstick cooking spray. Arrange chicken in a single layer in the prepared pan. Scatter rice, kale, and shallots over the top.

2 Place broth, wine, lemon juice, lemon zest, garlic, thyme, and pepper in a medium bowl and whisk to combine. Carefully pour mixture over the contents in the pan.

3 Cover pan tightly with foil, place on middle oven rack, and bake 30 minutes.

4 Store in an airtight container in refrigerator up to 3 days. To reheat, place in a microwave-safe dish covered with a lid and microwave 45–60 seconds until heated to 165°F.

SERVES 4

Per Serving

Calories	601
Fat	17g
Sodium	466mg
Carbohydrates	43g
Fiber	2g
Sugar	2g
Protein	60g

COOKING WITH WINE

Wine can add depth and interest to many foods. This is especially true when it comes to salt-free cooking. If you're wary of wine's intoxicating effects, add it only to foods that will be heated. The cooking process evaporates the alcohol, leaving only its flavor behind. When cooking with wine, opt for inexpensive bottles.

Honey Mustard Chicken Breasts

SERVES 4

Per Serving

Calories	158
Fat	4g
Sodium	42mg
Carbohydrates	5g
Fiber	0g
Sugar	5g
Protein	26g

This moist and flavorful dish will leave you wanting more. These breasts can be cooked on a grill instead of in the oven. Grill them over medium heat, turning once, until the chicken is slightly crisp outside and no longer pink inside, 10–15 minutes per side.

2 tablespoons mustard seeds

1 tablespoon ground mustard

1 tablespoon distilled white vinegar

2 tablespoons water

¼ cup white wine

2 tablespoons honey

1 pound boneless, skinless chicken breasts

1 Crush mustard seeds slightly using a mortar and pestle or small spice grinder. Place in a medium bowl or large resealable bag. Add ground mustard, vinegar, water, wine, and honey and mix to combine.

2 Add chicken to the marinade and coat completely. Cover bowl or seal bag tightly and refrigerate 4–12 hours.

3 Preheat oven to 375°F and adjust oven rack to middle position.

4 Remove chicken from marinade and place in a 9" × 13" baking dish. Cover dish tightly with foil.

5 Place dish on middle oven rack and bake until chicken reaches an internal temperature of 165°F, about 30 minutes. Remove from oven.

6 Store in an airtight container in refrigerator up to 3 days. To reheat, place in a microwave-safe dish covered with a lid and microwave 45–60 seconds until heated to 165°F.

Tropical Chicken Salad Wraps

Colorfully festive, with a fresh, spicy kick, these sandwiches make great party fare when sliced in half and arranged on a platter. Rather than a mayonnaise-based filling, this chicken salad is dressed in a light vinaigrette. Add sliced avocado to the wraps if you like.

SERVES 6

Per Serving

Calories	321
Fat	8g
Sodium	188mg
Carbohydrates	39g
Fiber	8g
Sugar	10g
Protein	25g

1 pound boneless, skinless chicken breasts

1 medium mango, peeled, pitted, and diced

1 small red onion, peeled and diced

1 small red bell pepper, seeded and diced

1 small jalapeño pepper, seeded and minced

2 cloves garlic, peeled and minced

1 cup canned no-salt-added black beans, drained and rinsed

2 tablespoons apple cider vinegar

2 tablespoons lime juice

2 tablespoons extra-virgin olive oil

¼ cup chopped fresh cilantro

½ teaspoon ground white pepper

4 cups mixed salad greens

6 (8") reduced-sodium whole-wheat wraps

1 Place chicken in a large saucepan and add enough water to cover. Bring to a boil over high heat. Reduce heat slightly and continue boiling about 20 minutes, until chicken reaches an internal temperature of 165°F.

2 Remove from heat, drain, and set aside to cool 20 minutes.

3 Cut chicken into bite-sized pieces. Place in a large bowl and add mango, onion, peppers, garlic, and beans.

4 Place vinegar, lime juice, oil, cilantro, and white pepper in a small bowl and whisk to combine. Pour over chicken mixture and stir to coat. Assemble chicken salad wraps or store chicken salad in refrigerator up to 3 days until ready to use.

5 To assemble wraps, divide greens and chicken salad evenly among wraps, then roll up. Slice each in half using a sharp knife. Cover and refrigerate up to 24 hours.

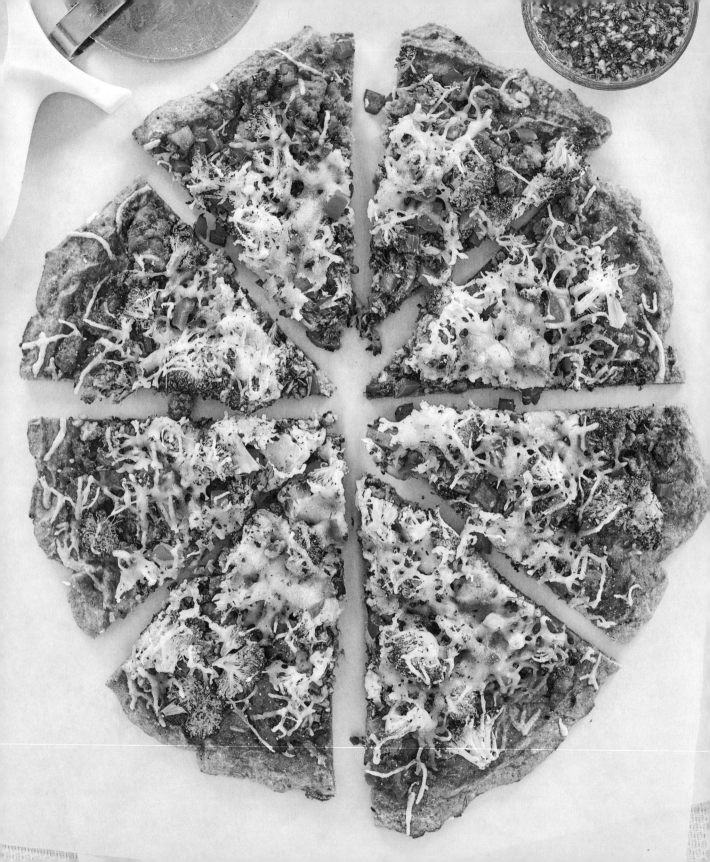

Broccoli, Ground Turkey, and Pesto Pizza

Lean ground turkey, savory red onion, and pesto make this a pizza you won't forget. And it's ready in about 30 minutes!

1 cup white whole-wheat flour

1 teaspoon salt-free all-purpose seasoning

1 teaspoon salt-free Italian seasoning

½ teaspoon garlic powder

2 large egg whites

⅔ cup low-fat milk

½ pound lean ground turkey

1 medium red onion, peeled and chopped

1 teaspoon olive oil

1 medium red bell pepper, seeded and diced

1 medium head broccoli, chopped

4 tablespoons Basil Pesto (see recipe in Chapter 3)

½ cup shredded Swiss cheese

¼ teaspoon ground black pepper

SERVES 4

Per Serving

Calories	427
Fat	19g
Sodium	149mg
Carbohydrates	36g
Fiber	7g
Sugar	4g
Protein	27g

1 Preheat oven to 425°F and adjust oven rack to middle position. Grease and flour a 12" nonstick pizza pan and set aside.

2 Place flour, all-purpose seasoning, Italian seasoning, and garlic powder in a medium bowl and whisk to combine. Stir in egg whites and milk. Pour batter onto the prepared pan and set aside.

3 Place a large skillet over medium heat. Add turkey and onion and cook, stirring occasionally, 5 minutes.

4 Remove from heat. Carefully drain any excess fat. Spoon mixture evenly over batter. Place pan on middle oven rack. Bake 20 minutes.

5 While pizza is baking, heat oil in a large skillet over medium heat. Add bell pepper and broccoli and sauté 5 minutes. Remove skillet from heat and set aside.

6 Once crust is baked, remove pan from oven. Top pizza with pesto, spreading evenly. Arrange broccoli and bell pepper evenly over the top, then sprinkle with cheese and black pepper. Return pan to oven and bake 3–5 minutes, until cheese has melted completely.

7 Remove pizza from oven. Gently remove pizza from pan and cut into 8 slices. Allow to cool before storing in an airtight container in refrigerator up to 3 days. To reheat, preheat toaster oven or conventional oven to 400°F. Place pizza on toaster oven tray or a baking sheet and cook until heated through.

Ground Turkey Meatloaf Minis

SERVES 6

Per Serving

Calories	303
Fat	10g
Sodium	116mg
Carbohydrates	23g
Fiber	4g
Sugar	8g
Protein	27g

HOMEMADE BREAD CRUMBS

To make your own salt-free bread crumbs, crisp several pieces of salt-free or low-sodium bread in the toaster. Tear or use a food processor to pulse the toasted bread into tiny pieces. Looking for an alternative? Wonderful low-sodium bread crumbs can also be made from finely chopped unsalted nuts, matzo, and salt-free potato chips.

A deliciously lighter version of the all-American meal, these mini meatloaves can also be made with lean ground chicken. Serve them with Garlic Rosemary Mashed Potatoes (see recipe in Chapter 5).

1½ pounds lean ground turkey

1 medium onion, peeled and finely diced

2 medium stalks celery, finely diced

1 small green bell pepper, seeded and finely diced

4 cloves garlic, peeled and minced

1 (8-ounce) can no-salt-added tomato sauce

1 large egg white

¾ cup salt-free bread crumbs

1 tablespoon molasses

¼ teaspoon liquid smoke

½ teaspoon dried basil

½ teaspoon dried oregano

½ teaspoon dried savory

½ teaspoon dried thyme

½ teaspoon ground black pepper

¼ cup salt-free ketchup

1 Preheat oven to 375°F and adjust oven rack to middle position. Line a six-cup muffin tin with paper liners or spray with nonstick cooking spray.

2 Place turkey, onion, celery, bell pepper, garlic, tomato sauce, egg white, bread crumbs, molasses, liquid smoke, basil, oregano, savory, thyme, and black pepper in a large bowl and mix using a wooden spoon or your hands.

3 Divide mixture evenly among the prepared muffin cups and press in firmly. Top meatloaves with ketchup and spread evenly.

4 Place muffin tin on middle oven rack and bake 30 minutes.

5 Remove from oven. Gently run a knife around the sides of each loaf and remove from muffin tin. Allow to cool before storing in an airtight container in refrigerator up to 4 days.

6 To reheat, place in a microwave-safe dish covered with a lid and microwave 45–60 seconds until heated to 165°F.

Turkey and Brown Rice–Stuffed Peppers

This healthier version of the comfort-food classic uses ground turkey and brown rice, with juicy tomatoes and raisins for a little added sweetness.

4 large red bell peppers

1 pound lean ground turkey

1 medium onion, peeled and diced

3 cloves garlic, peeled and minced

2 medium stalks celery, diced

2 cups cooked brown rice

1 (15-ounce) can no-salt-added diced tomatoes

2 tablespoons no-salt-added tomato paste

¼ cup raisins

2 teaspoons ground cumin

1 teaspoon dried oregano

½ teaspoon ground cinnamon

½ teaspoon ground black pepper

SERVES 4	
Per Serving	
Calories	443
Fat	11g
Sodium	136mg
Carbohydrates	53g
Fiber	9g
Sugar	18g
Protein	31g

1 Preheat oven to 425°F and adjust oven rack to middle position. Lightly spray a 9" × 13" baking dish with nonstick cooking spray and set aside.

2 Trim about ½" off the top of each bell pepper and set tops aside. Carefully core and seed, leaving peppers intact. Trim bottoms if necessary so that peppers sit flat. Set aside.

3 Heat a medium skillet over medium heat. Add turkey, onion, garlic, and celery and sauté 5 minutes. Remove from heat. Stir in the remaining ingredients.

4 Fill each bell pepper with one-quarter of turkey mixture, pressing firmly to pack. Stand peppers in the prepared dish, replace pepper tops, and then cover dish tightly with foil. Place dish on middle oven rack and bake until bell peppers are tender, 25–30 minutes.

5 Remove from oven and allow to cool before storing in an airtight container in refrigerator up to 3 days.

6 To reheat, place in a microwave-safe dish covered with a lid and microwave 90 seconds or until heated to 165°F.

Seasoned Turkey Burgers with Sautéed Mushrooms and Swiss

SERVES 4

Per Serving

Calories	418
Fat	16g
Sodium	446mg
Carbohydrates	31g
Fiber	5g
Sugar	4g
Protein	36g

CLEAN YOUR GRILL EASILY

The easiest way to clean your charcoal or propane grill is to do it right after use. After removing food from the grill, close the lid and allow the flames to burn off excess grease and debris. After 10 minutes, scrape the grates with a heavy wire brush. Turn off the gas (if applicable) and close the lid again.

These juicy, salt-free burgers will have you oohing and aahing your way to the last mushroom-topped bite. Make a batch of these burgers ahead of time so they're ready to pop on the grill for dinner after a workday!

1 pound lean ground turkey

2 cloves garlic, peeled and minced

1 tablespoon no-salt-added prepared mustard

2 teaspoons low-sodium Worcestershire sauce

1 teaspoon salt-free Italian seasoning

½ teaspoon ground black pepper

1 teaspoon olive oil

3 cups sliced mushrooms

4 whole-wheat burger buns

½ cup shredded Swiss cheese

1 Place turkey in a large bowl. Add garlic, mustard, Worcestershire sauce, Italian seasoning, and pepper and mix using your hands.

2 Divide mixture into four equal portions. Roll each portion into a ball, then flatten and form into a patty. Store prepped patties in an airtight container in refrigerator, with parchment paper between patties. Use within 3 days.

3 When ready to cook, grill or broil patties until they reach an internal temperature of 165°F. If grilling, they'll take 5–6 minutes per side; if broiling, they'll take 4–6 minutes per side. Remove burgers from heat, cover, and set aside.

4 Heat oil in a medium skillet over medium heat. Add mushrooms and sauté 5 minutes. Remove from heat.

5 Sandwich each burger in a bun, dividing sautéed mushrooms and cheese evenly among burgers.

CHAPTER 8

Seafood Entrées

Shrimp and Bok Choy Noodle Soup 144

Sheet Pan Salmon. 145

Zesty Tuna Lettuce Wraps. 146

Sesame Shrimp Stir-Fry. 148

Baked Tuna Cakes 149

Healthy Fish and Chips 150

Roasted Steelhead Trout with Grapefruit Sauce 152

Ahi Tuna with Grape Tomato Salsa. 155

Spicy Tilapia with Pineapple Relish 156

Salmon Cakes 157

Shrimp Creole 158

Open-Faced Tuna Melts. 159

Tuna Pasta Salad with Broccoli and Sun-Dried Tomatoes. 160

Shrimp and Bok Choy Noodle Soup

SERVES 4

Per Serving

Calories	189
Fat	4g
Sodium	691mg
Carbohydrates	26g
Fiber	3g
Sugar	6g
Protein	15g

LEFTOVER INGREDIENT TIP

You'll have leftover savoy cabbage after making this soup, but don't let it go to waste! Chop it up to use in a weeknight stir-fry dish or sauté it with minced garlic and a bit of salt for a quick side dish.

Dinner in 30 minutes or less? Yes, please! A delicious and comforting noodle soup can get you through those chilly days and nights. This is a flavorful and filling soup that has plenty of green vegetables.

1 tablespoon olive oil

2 cloves garlic, peeled and minced

2 green onions, white and green parts divided, sliced

6 ounces baby bella mushrooms, sliced

6 cups low-sodium vegetable broth

1 tablespoon low-sodium soy sauce

½ teaspoon dried red pepper flakes

¼ teaspoon ground ginger

2 cups chopped savoy cabbage

1 head baby bok choy, sliced

3 ounces uncooked soba noodles

½ pound (41–50) shrimp, peeled and deveined

¼ cup fresh cilantro leaves

1. Heat oil in a large stockpot over medium heat. Add garlic and white parts of onions and sauté 2 minutes, stirring frequently. Add mushrooms and cook 2 minutes.

2. Add broth, soy sauce, red pepper flakes, ginger, cabbage, and bok choy. Reduce heat to medium-low and cook 10 minutes.

3. Meanwhile, bring 3 cups water to a boil in a medium saucepan over high heat. Add noodles and cook 5–7 minutes or until cooked through. Drain noodles and add to stockpot.

4. Add shrimp to soup and cook 3–4 minutes over medium-low heat. Shrimp will turn pink when cooked through.

5. Allow soup to cool before storing in airtight containers in refrigerator up to 2 days. To reheat, place in a microwave-safe dish and microwave 90 seconds or until heated through. Garnish with cilantro and green parts of onions before serving.

Sheet Pan Salmon

When it comes to preparing the perfect salmon in the oven, be sure to rely on aluminum foil packets. Pair your salmon with vegetables you've cooked ahead of time, like the Roasted Broccoli and Cauliflower from Chapter 3.

4 (4-ounce) wild Alaskan salmon fillets

2 tablespoons olive oil

1 teaspoon garlic powder

½ teaspoon salt

SERVES 4

Per Serving

Calories	235
Fat	12g
Sodium	358mg
Carbohydrates	1g
Fiber	0g
Sugar	0g
Protein	25g

1 Preheat oven to 400°F. Tear off four sheets of aluminum foil large enough to wrap each salmon fillet.

2 Place each salmon fillet skin side down in the center of a piece of foil. Season fillets by dividing oil, garlic powder, and salt evenly among them. Fold up the edges of the foil over each fillet to create a packet, making sure there are no openings in the foil so steam does not escape from the packet.

3 Place foil packets on a large baking sheet and bake 10–12 minutes, depending on thickness of salmon. Salmon should reach an internal temperature of 145°F.

4 Once salmon is cooked through, use a spatula to carefully remove salmon from foil packets. It should easily release from the skin. Discard foil.

5 Store in an airtight container in refrigerator up to 3 days.

6 To reheat, place in a microwave-safe dish covered with a lid and microwave 60 seconds at a time until heated through.

Zesty Tuna Lettuce Wraps

SERVES 2

Per Serving

Calories	202
Fat	5g
Sodium	133mg
Carbohydrates	6g
Fiber	3g
Sugar	2g
Protein	32g

This tuna salad is made with avocado in place of the typical mayonnaise, which gives it the familiar creaminess without the added saturated fats! Make the tuna salad ahead of time to make lettuce wraps in as little as 5 minutes. If you like it spicy, add a drizzle of sriracha before you eat the wrap.

2 (5-ounce) cans no-salt-added light tuna in water, drained

½ small ripe avocado, peeled, pitted, and diced

2 tablespoons chopped cilantro leaves

¾ teaspoon sriracha

¼ teaspoon Dijon mustard

⅛ teaspoon ground black pepper

6 large Bibb lettuce leaves

¼ cup finely diced carrots

¼ cup diced cucumber

1 In a small bowl, combine tuna, avocado, cilantro, sriracha, mustard, and pepper and stir well until no chunks of avocado remain. Store tuna salad in refrigerator up to 3 days.

2 When ready to make lettuce wraps, divide tuna salad evenly among lettuce leaves and top with carrots and cucumber.

Sesame Shrimp Stir-Fry

SERVES 4

Per Serving

Calories	226
Fat	5g
Sodium	303mg
Carbohydrates	37g
Fiber	3g
Sugar	5g
Protein	8g

Stir-fry dishes are often some of the quickest meals to make, and this one is no exception! You can blanch vegetables ahead of time to save even more time when making this recipe during the week.

1 cup sugar snap peas

⅓ cup diced carrot

2 cups broccoli florets

1 tablespoon sesame oil

¼ cup diced white onion

2 cloves garlic, peeled and minced

16 (31–35) frozen peeled and deveined shrimp, thawed

3 tablespoons Asian-Inspired Low-Sodium Marinade (see recipe in Chapter 3)

2 cups cooked brown rice

1 Bring 4 cups water to a boil in a medium saucepan over high heat. Carefully add sugar snap peas and carrot. Cook 2 minutes. Add broccoli and cook 3 minutes. Use a strainer to drain vegetables and run under cold water 30 seconds.

2 Heat oil in a large skillet over medium heat. Add onion and garlic and sauté 2 minutes. Add shrimp and cook 2 minutes on each side.

3 Add cooked vegetables and marinade to shrimp, stirring to coat. Cook until shrimp are pink and reach an internal temperature of 145°F.

4 Store in an airtight container in refrigerator up to 3 days.

5 To reheat, place in a microwave-safe dish and microwave 60 seconds at a time until heated through. Serve over rice.

Baked Tuna Cakes

This moist and healthy twist on crab cakes is accented with vegetables and a crisp oven-fried crust. Prep the cakes as appetizers for an important dinner party or for a family holiday.

2 (5-ounce) cans no-salt-added light tuna in water, drained

1 small carrot, peeled and shredded

1 medium stalk celery, finely diced

1 small shallot, peeled and minced

2 cloves garlic, peeled and minced

1 large egg white

¼ cup salt-free bread crumbs

2 tablespoons Salt-Free Mayonnaise (see recipe in Chapter 3)

½ teaspoon dried dill

½ teaspoon dried thyme

¼ teaspoon ground rosemary

¼ teaspoon ground black pepper

1 Preheat oven to 400°F and adjust oven rack to middle position. Spray a baking sheet lightly with nonstick cooking spray and set aside.

2 Place all ingredients in a medium bowl and stir to combine. Shape mixture into 4 cakes and place on the prepared sheet.

3 Place sheet on middle oven rack and bake 10 minutes. Remove from oven and gently flip cakes, then return to oven and bake another 5 minutes. Allow to cool before storing in an airtight container in refrigerator up to 3 days.

4 To reheat, place in a microwave-safe dish covered with a lid and microwave 60 seconds at a time until heated through.

SERVES 4

Per Serving

Calories	148
Fat	5g
Sodium	67mg
Carbohydrates	9g
Fiber	2g
Sugar	1g
Protein	17g

COOKING SPRAY

Cooking spray is oil in an aerated form. When sprayed, it provides a nonstick surface and cuts down on the amount of oil used. You can make your own cooking spray too! Refillable oil spray bottles are sold at many kitchen stores and online. They are chemical-free and can be filled with your choice of oil.

Healthy Fish and Chips

SERVES 4

Per Serving

Calories	547
Fat	12g
Sodium	314mg
Carbohydrates	82g
Fiber	12g
Sugar	4g
Protein	29g

LOW-SODIUM TARTAR SAUCE

Make your own low-sodium tartar sauce by combining ½ cup Salt-Free Mayonnaise (see recipe in Chapter 3) with 1 tablespoon salt-free pickle relish. Cover and refrigerate until serving, up to 1 week. Salt-free pickle relish is sold at select stores and online.

This healthy version of the beloved coastal dinner is baked rather than fried. Choose your favorite white-fleshed fish, such as haddock, pollock, or cod. Serve this with lemon wedges, malt vinegar, and salt-free ketchup. Substitute panko for bread crumbs if you prefer. This recipe is adapted from Let's Cook!

2 tablespoons unbleached all-purpose flour

2 tablespoons white whole-wheat flour

1 teaspoon ground black pepper, divided

2 large egg whites

2 cups salt-free bread crumbs

1 teaspoon dried parsley

1 teaspoon dried dill

1 teaspoon dried thyme

1 pound haddock, cut into 8 pieces

4 large potatoes, cut into 8 wedges each

3 tablespoons olive oil

1 Preheat oven to 425°F and adjust oven racks to top and middle positions. Cover a large baking sheet with foil and set aside.

2 Place both flours and ½ teaspoon pepper in a wide, shallow bowl and whisk to combine.

3 Place egg whites in a second shallow bowl.

4 Place bread crumbs, parsley, dill, and thyme in a large resealable bag. Seal bag and shake well.

5 Dredge 1 haddock fillet completely in seasoned flour, then dip in egg whites, coating completely.

6 Place fillet in bag with bread crumb mixture, seal, and shake gently to coat. Carefully remove fillet from bag and place on the prepared sheet. Repeat with remaining fillets. Place sheet with fillets in refrigerator.

7 Line a second large baking sheet with parchment paper. Arrange potato wedges on the sheet and brush both sides of potato wedges with oil. Sprinkle with remaining ½ teaspoon pepper. Place on middle oven rack and bake 15 minutes. Remove from oven and flip potatoes over, then return to oven.

8 Remove baking sheet with fish from the refrigerator and place it on the top oven rack. Bake potatoes and fish 15 minutes, until both are crispy and brown. Allow fish and potatoes to cool before storing in separate airtight containers in refrigerator up to 3 days.

9 To reheat fish and potatoes, preheat toaster oven or conventional oven to 375°F. Place fish and potatoes on toaster oven tray or a baking sheet and cook until fish is heated throughout.

Roasted Steelhead Trout with Grapefruit Sauce

SERVES 4

Per Serving

Calories	319
Fat	10g
Sodium	59mg
Carbohydrates	31g
Fiber	4g
Sugar	20g
Protein	26g

The fish is roasted simply; just a brush of olive oil and dusting of black pepper is all it takes to make this fish melt in your mouth. The sweet, spicy citrusy sauce elevates the dish to stardom. This recipe is adapted from Fine Cooking.

Trout

1 pound steelhead trout

2 teaspoons olive oil

¼ teaspoon ground black pepper

Grapefruit Sauce

2 medium ruby red grapefruits

1 teaspoon extra-virgin olive oil

1 medium shallot, peeled and minced

1 clove garlic, peeled and minced

1 teaspoon minced fresh ginger

2 teaspoons agave nectar

⅛ teaspoon ground cayenne pepper

2 tablespoons thinly sliced fresh basil

1 Preheat oven to 350°F and adjust oven rack to middle position.

2 For the trout: Place trout in a large baking dish, brush with oil, and sprinkle with pepper. Place the dish on the middle oven rack and roast 15 minutes.

3 For the sauce: Cut the top and bottom off 1 grapefruit. Stand grapefruit on one end and cut down to remove the white pith and peel. Use a sharp knife to remove each grapefruit segment from its membrane. Cut the segments in half and set aside. Juice the remaining grapefruit and set aside.

4 Heat oil in a small saucepan over medium heat. Add shallot and garlic and sauté 2 minutes.

5 Add ginger, grapefruit juice, agave nectar, and cayenne and stir to combine. Bring to a simmer, then cook until reduced by half, about 10 minutes.

6 Remove saucepan from heat. Stir in grapefruit and basil.

7 Remove trout from oven. Slice into 4 portions.

8 Store trout and sauce in separate airtight containers in refrigerator. Use fish and sauce within 2 days.

9 To reheat trout, place in a microwave-safe dish covered with a lid and microwave 60 seconds at a time until heated through. To reheat, place sauce in a microwave-safe dish and microwave 20 seconds and spoon over trout to serve.

Ahi Tuna with Grape Tomato Salsa

Fish always makes a fresh, light, and easy main course, and it's naturally low in sodium. This recipe calls for broiling the tuna, but keep a close eye on it, as it can quickly become overcooked!

SERVES 4

Per Serving

Calories	176
Fat	4g
Sodium	55mg
Carbohydrates	5g
Fiber	1g
Sugar	3g
Protein	29g

Grape Tomato Salsa

2 cups halved grape tomatoes

¼ cup finely diced onion

¼ cup finely diced green bell pepper

1 clove garlic, peeled and minced

1 tablespoon apple cider vinegar

1 tablespoon chopped fresh cilantro

½ teaspoon ground cumin

¼ teaspoon ground coriander

⅛ teaspoon ground black pepper

⅛ teaspoon dried red pepper flakes

Tuna Steaks

1 pound ahi (yellowfin) tuna, cut into 4 steaks

1 tablespoon olive oil, divided

¼ teaspoon ground black pepper, divided

1 For the salsa: Place all ingredients in a medium bowl and stir to combine. Store in an airtight container in refrigerator up to 3 days.

2 For the tuna steaks: Preheat broiler to high. Adjust oven rack to top position. Place tuna steaks on a broiler pan or in a shallow baking dish that is safe for broiler use, brush with ½ tablespoon oil, and sprinkle with ⅛ teaspoon pepper. Place on top oven rack and broil 4 minutes.

3 Remove pan from oven and carefully flip steaks. Brush with remaining ½ tablespoon oil, sprinkle with remaining ⅛ teaspoon pepper, and return to oven. Broil another 4 minutes. Remove from oven.

4 Store tuna steaks in an airtight container in refrigerator. Tuna steaks should be used within 2 days.

5 To reheat tuna steaks, place in a microwave-safe dish covered with a lid and microwave 60 seconds at a time until heated through. Serve with cold grape tomato salsa.

YELLOWFIN TUNA

Yellowfin tuna, also known as ahi, live in the warm waters of the equator and can grow as large as 300–400 pounds. Yellowfin tuna is an excellent source of protein, vitamins B_6 and B_{12}, minerals, and omega-3 fatty acids. It's low in sodium, fat, and calories, making it a great choice on the DASH diet.

Spicy Tilapia with Pineapple Relish

SERVES 4

Per Serving

Calories	205
Fat	4g
Sodium	61mg
Carbohydrates	19g
Fiber	2g
Sugar	13g
Protein	24g

Tilapia is mild in flavor, meaty, and often inexpensive. This recipe calls for salt-free Cajun seasoning, which you can usually find in the seasonings section at your local grocery store. If you have an aversion to spicy food, omit the red pepper flakes and jalapeño. This recipe is adapted from Cooking Light.

Pineapple Relish

½ medium pineapple, peeled, cored, and diced

1 small red onion, peeled and diced

1 small tomato, diced

1 small jalapeño pepper, seeded and minced

2 cloves garlic, peeled and minced

2 tablespoons unflavored rice vinegar

2 tablespoons chopped fresh cilantro

Spicy Tilapia

2 teaspoons canola oil

1 teaspoon salt-free Cajun seasoning

¼ teaspoon dried red pepper flakes

1 pound boneless tilapia fillets

1 For the pineapple relish: Combine pineapple, onion, tomato, jalapeño, and garlic in a medium bowl. Add vinegar and cilantro and stir to combine.

2 For the spicy tilapia: Heat oil in a large skillet over medium-high heat.

3 Combine Cajun seasoning and red pepper flakes in a small bowl and sprinkle evenly over fish fillets. Place fish in skillet and cook 2 minutes per side or until fish flakes easily when tested with a fork. Remove from heat.

4 Store tilapia and pineapple relish separately in refrigerator. The tilapia and relish should be used within 2 days.

5 To reheat tilapia, place in a microwave-safe dish covered with a lid and microwave 60 seconds at a time until heated through. Serve with pineapple relish.

Salmon Cakes

Delicately crisp outside and flavorfully moist inside, these Salmon Cakes are a real treat, whether sandwiched in rolls or eaten plain.

1 (15-ounce) can no-salt-added boneless salmon, drained

4 tablespoons Salt-Free Mayonnaise (see recipe in Chapter 3)

½ cup salt-free bread crumbs

1 small onion, peeled and minced

1 small yellow bell pepper, seeded and minced

1 large egg white

1 teaspoon dried herbes de Provence

½ teaspoon ground paprika

¼ teaspoon ground mustard

⅛ teaspoon celery seed

¼ teaspoon ground black pepper

1 Preheat oven to 400°F and adjust oven rack to middle position. Spray a baking sheet lightly with nonstick cooking spray and set aside.

2 Place all ingredients in a large bowl. Mix using a spoon or your hands. Divide mixture into 6 equal portions and shape into patties.

3 Place patties on the prepared sheet. Place sheet on middle oven rack and bake 10 minutes. Remove from oven and gently flip patties, then return to oven and bake another 5 minutes.

4 Store salmon cakes in an airtight container in refrigerator up to 2 days.

5 To reheat, place in a microwave-safe dish covered with a lid and microwave 60 seconds at a time until heated through.

SERVES 6

Per Serving

Calories	180
Fat	8g
Sodium	84mg
Carbohydrates	10g
Fiber	2g
Sugar	1g
Protein	18g

MAYONNAISE SUBSTITUTE

Instead of adding salt-free mayonnaise to a recipe, try an equal amount of plain low-fat Greek yogurt. Its thick and creamy consistency works well in many types of salads and sandwiches, from tuna and salmon to chicken and egg. To thin the yogurt, add a little lemon juice or low-sodium broth. For extra flavor, add minced garlic and some chopped fresh herbs.

Shrimp Creole

SERVES 6

Per Serving

Calories	141
Fat	2g
Sodium	482mg
Carbohydrates	15g
Fiber	4g
Sugar	7g
Protein	12g

SHRIMP FACTS

Shrimp are naturally high in sodium, at roughly 160 milligrams per 3-ounce serving, so they should be consumed carefully. Shrimp come in a variety of sizes and are sold by weight and size. Most shrimp consumed in the United States are processed and may have added salt. Read package labels carefully and buy fresh, unprocessed shrimp whenever possible.

This spicy and beautiful shrimp dish is made for special occasions but also functions as a warm comfort food. Serve it over leftover cooked brown or white rice.

2 teaspoons canola oil

1 medium onion, peeled and thinly sliced

1 medium red bell pepper, seeded and thinly sliced

2 medium stalks celery, thinly sliced

3 cloves garlic, peeled and minced

2 (15-ounce) cans no-salt-added diced tomatoes

1 (8-ounce) can no-salt-added tomato sauce

⅓ cup white wine

½ teaspoon apple cider vinegar

2 bay leaves

2 teaspoons Salt-Free Chili Seasoning (see recipe in Chapter 3)

1 teaspoon ground paprika

½ teaspoon ground black pepper

⅛ teaspoon ground cayenne pepper

1 pound (31–35) shrimp, peeled and deveined

1 Heat oil in a medium skillet over medium heat. Add onion, bell pepper, celery, and garlic and cook, stirring occasionally, 5 minutes.

2 Add tomatoes, tomato sauce, wine, vinegar, bay leaves, chili seasoning, paprika, black pepper, and cayenne and stir to combine. Simmer 10 minutes, stirring frequently. If sauce begins to splatter, cover and reduce heat to medium-low.

3 Stir in shrimp and simmer 5 minutes.

4 Remove from heat and remove bay leaves from pan. Allow to cool before storing in an airtight container in refrigerator up to 3 days.

5 To reheat, place in a microwave-safe dish covered with a lid and microwave 60 seconds at a time until heated through.

Open-Faced Tuna Melts

This lightened version of the beloved diner sandwich uses home-made salt-free mayonnaise, which leaves the sandwiches lower in sodium, fat, and cholesterol. Make the tuna salad in advance so you can make a tuna melt in under 5 minutes!

1 (5-ounce) can no-salt-added light tuna in water, drained

1 small shallot, peeled and finely chopped

1 small stalk celery, finely diced

1 small carrot, peeled and finely diced

2 tablespoons Salt-Free Mayonnaise (see recipe in Chapter 3)

½ teaspoon dried herbes de Provence

¼ teaspoon ground black pepper

2 slices low-sodium bread

2 romaine lettuce leaves

1 small tomato, sliced

2 (1-ounce) slices Swiss cheese

1 Place tuna in a medium bowl. Add shallot, celery, carrot, mayonnaise, herbes de Provence, and pepper and stir to combine. Store in an airtight container in refrigerator up to 3 days.

2 When ready to serve, preheat broiler. Place bread slices on a baking sheet and top each with 1 lettuce leaf and half of tuna mixture. Smooth out tuna mixture and top with sliced tomato and cheese.

3 Broil sandwiches 1–2 minutes, until cheese melts.

SERVES 2

Per Serving

Calories	362
Fat	18g
Sodium	175mg
Carbohydrates	22g
Fiber	3g
Sugar	5g
Protein	28g

HERBES DE PROVENCE

Herbes de Provence is a classic blend of French herbs, typically composed of dried basil, thyme, savory, fennel, and lavender. This blend gives a distinct flavor to many dishes and is particularly well suited to grilled meats and seafood. Commercial blends are sold in supermarkets and online.

Tuna Pasta Salad with Broccoli and Sun-Dried Tomatoes

SERVES 8

Per Serving

Calories	221
Fat	2g
Sodium	44mg
Carbohydrates	36g
Fiber	7g
Sugar	4g
Protein	16g

HOW IS VINEGAR MADE?

Vinegar is produced when an alcoholic liquid is fermented and ethanol within it oxidizes. The remaining liquid, which becomes highly acidic, is the vinegar. Balsamic vinegar is made from the leftover pressings, or must, of white grapes that are first boiled down to form a syrup and then aged. Apple cider vinegar is made using apple must.

Bold flavors combine flawlessly in this healthy salad. With whole grains, low-fat protein, vitamins, and nutrients, it's a one dish meal that's wonderful served warm or cold.

½ cup chopped sun-dried tomatoes (not packed in oil)

1 cup boiling water

1 (13-ounce) package whole-grain penne

1 tablespoon olive oil

1 large head broccoli, cut into small florets

2 small shallots, peeled and finely diced

2 (5-ounce) cans no-salt-added light tuna in water, drained

2 tablespoons balsamic vinegar

½ teaspoon ground black pepper

1 Place sun-dried tomatoes in a medium bowl, add water, and let soak 10 minutes. Drain, reserving 2 tablespoons of soaking liquid.

2 Cook penne according to package directions, omitting salt. Drain and set aside.

3 Heat oil in a large skillet over medium-high heat. Add broccoli and sauté 5 minutes. Remove from heat. Add sun-dried tomatoes, reserved soaking liquid, penne, shallots, tuna, vinegar, and pepper to the skillet and stir to combine.

4 Store in an airtight container in refrigerator up to 3 days. The salad does not have to be reheated before eating.

CHAPTER 9
Vegan/Vegetarian Entrées

Tofu Vegetable Potpie 162

Black-Eyed Pea Burrito Bowl 164

Crispy Tofu Stir-Fry 165

Southwest Loaded Sweet Potatoes 166

Portobello Mushroom Parmigiana 168

Mushroom Soup with Orzo 169

Roasted Cauliflower Steaks with Creamy Chimichurri 170

Apple Butternut Soup 172

Sesame Tofu with Sautéed Green Beans 173

Falafel with Tzatziki 175

Whole-Grain Penne with Lemony Roasted Asparagus 177

Pesto Rice with Portobello Mushrooms 178

Spicy Chickpea Tacos with Arugula 179

10-Minute Thai Noodles 180

Vegetable Baked Ziti 181

Linguine with Plum Tomatoes, Mushrooms, and Tempeh 182

Coconut Cauliflower Curry 183

Kale-Stuffed Manicotti 184

Black Bean Burgers 186

Sweet Potato and Black Bean Burritos 187

Vegetable Sushi 188

Tofu Vegetable Potpie

SERVES 4

Per Serving

Calories	485
Fat	29g
Sodium	309mg
Carbohydrates	42g
Fiber	4g
Sugar	3g
Protein	13g

LEFTOVER TOFU

To use any leftover tofu, cook it the same way as in this recipe, and then toss it into a stir-fry, add it to a salad, or use it as a topping for a grain bowl.

This comforting potpie is great when reheated and is much lower in calories than most other potpies since it has only a top crust. You can use different vegetables if you prefer, such as asparagus, potatoes, or broccoli.

7 ounces extra-firm tofu

1 tablespoon plus 1 teaspoon olive oil, divided

1½ teaspoons garlic and herb seasoning, divided

⅛ teaspoon salt

1 cup frozen peas and carrots, thawed

½ cup finely diced white onion

¼ cup finely diced celery

½ cup diced white button mushrooms

1 teaspoon dried thyme

1½ cups low-sodium vegetable broth, plus extra as needed

¼ cup all-purpose flour

¼ cup low-fat milk

¼ teaspoon ground black pepper

1 large egg yolk

1 tablespoon water

1 frozen puff pastry sheet, thawed per package directions

1 Place tofu on a small plate or cutting board and wrap a paper towel around it. Press it with your hand to remove excess water. Repeat this a few times. Cut tofu into ½" cubes.

2 Heat 1 tablespoon oil in a large, deep skillet over medium heat. Carefully add tofu cubes in a single layer, making sure there's space between cubes so they don't stick together. Season with ½ teaspoon garlic and herb seasoning and salt. Cook 3 minutes, then turn with a spatula to brown other sides, cooking 2–3 minutes on at least three sides. Transfer tofu to a plate and set aside.

3 Preheat oven to 350°F and adjust oven rack to middle position. In now-empty skillet, heat remaining 1 teaspoon oil. Add peas and carrots, onion, and celery and cook over medium heat 2 minutes. Add mushrooms, thyme, and remaining 1 teaspoon garlic and herb seasoning. Cook 2 minutes. Add broth, stir well, and reduce heat to low.

4 In a small bowl, whisk together flour and milk to create a roux. Add to vegetable mixture, whisking well to prevent flour from clumping. Add pepper and simmer 5 minutes to thicken, whisking occasionally. If mixture looks too thick, add a small amount of extra broth until desired consistency is reached.

5 Remove pan from heat. Place tofu in an 8" pie pan. Pour vegetable mixture over the top. Whisk together egg yolk and water to create an egg wash. Place pastry dough over the pie pan, allowing approximately 1" to hang over edge. Remove any excess dough. Cut four small slits in pastry dough. Brush egg wash over pastry dough.

6 Place pie pan on a baking sheet and place on middle oven rack. Bake 25 minutes or until pastry dough is golden brown.

7 Allow to cool before storing in an airtight container in refrigerator up to 3 days. To reheat, place in a microwave-safe dish and microwave 60–75 seconds.

Black-Eyed Pea Burrito Bowl

SERVES 4	
Per Serving	
Calories	270
Fat	5g
Sodium	318mg
Carbohydrates	48g
Fiber	7g
Sugar	4g
Protein	9g

Black-eyed peas are often underrated, but they're delicious, especially when used in this burrito bowl! You can use leftovers of this recipe to make the Vegetable Burgers in Chapter 10. Use some shredded cheese, cilantro, avocado, or low-fat sour cream as optional toppings.

1 tablespoon olive oil

1 cup diced yellow bell pepper

¾ cup finely diced onion

1 clove garlic, peeled and minced

½ teaspoon ground cumin

½ teaspoon chili powder

¼ teaspoon cayenne pepper

1 (15-ounce) can black-eyed peas, drained and rinsed

1 (10-ounce) can diced tomatoes with green chilies, drained

1 cup roughly chopped white button mushrooms

3 cups chopped kale

2 cups cooked brown rice

1. Heat oil in a large skillet over medium heat. Add bell pepper, onion, garlic, and spices. Cook 3 minutes.
2. Add black-eyed peas, tomatoes, and mushrooms and cook 5 minutes. Add kale and cook 2 minutes, just until kale is softened.
3. Store rice and black-eyed pea mixture in separate containers in refrigerator up to 4 days. To reheat, place in a microwave-safe dish and microwave 60–75 seconds. Place vegetable mixture over rice to serve.

Crispy Tofu Stir-Fry

Make the crispy tofu ahead of time and reheat in a toaster oven for a super-quick dinner option! Pair it with a cooked grain, like rice or quinoa, that you prepared earlier in the week.

14 ounces extra-firm tofu

1 tablespoon sesame oil

½ teaspoon garlic powder

¼ teaspoon salt

1 cup sugar snap peas

¾ cup (¼"-thick) carrot slices

1 small head broccoli, cut into florets

¼ cup Asian-Inspired Low-Sodium Marinade (see recipe in Chapter 3)

2 cups cooked brown rice

¼ cup sliced green onions

SERVES 4

Per Serving

Calories	316
Fat	10g
Sodium	345mg
Carbohydrates	41g
Fiber	4g
Sugar	7g
Protein	15g

1 Place tofu on a small plate or cutting board and wrap a paper towel around it. Press it with your hand to remove excess water. Repeat this a few times. Cut tofu into ½" cubes.

2 Heat oil in a large, deep skillet over medium heat. Carefully add tofu cubes in a single layer, making sure there's space in between cubes so they don't stick together. Season with garlic powder and salt. Cook 3 minutes, then turn with a spatula to brown other sides, cooking 2–3 minutes on at least 3 sides. Once cooked, turn off heat and leave tofu in skillet. If prepping in advance, store cooked tofu in an airtight container in refrigerator up to 3 days.

3 To blanch vegetables, bring 4 cups water to a boil in a medium saucepan over high heat. Carefully add sugar snap peas and carrots. Cook 2 minutes. Add broccoli and cook 3 minutes. Use a strainer to drain vegetables and run under cold water for 30 seconds.

4 Adjust heat under tofu skillet to medium-low and add marinade to skillet. Toss tofu to coat in marinade and heat 30 seconds. Add vegetables, toss to coat, and cook 30 seconds.

5 Store cooked tofu and vegetable mixture in an airtight container in refrigerator up to 3 days. Keep separate from cooked grains. To reheat, place in a microwave-safe dish and microwave 60–90 seconds until heated through. Serve tofu and vegetables over rice. Garnish with green onion.

BLANCHING FOODS

Blanching is a preparation method where food is briefly cooked in hot liquid, usually water, and then submerged in cold water to halt the cooking process. This method helps preserve nutrient quality and color. It's great when making stir-fry dishes so that vegetables are perfectly crisp yet cooked through.

Southwest Loaded Sweet Potatoes

SERVES 2

Per Serving

Calories	375
Fat	12g
Sodium	542mg
Carbohydrates	49g
Fiber	15g
Sugar	7g
Protein	16g

BRING ON THE PROTEIN!

To add extra protein to these loaded sweet potatoes, cook extra-firm tofu in a skillet with chipotle powder and garlic, breaking it up with a spatula as it cooks like you would ground meat. This crumbled tofu can be stored for up to 3 days in the refrigerator and used on salads, mixed into scrambled eggs, or served in tortillas for tacos.

The sweetness from the potatoes and savory flavor from the toppings make for the most satisfying weeknight vegetarian meal! Cook the sweet potatoes ahead of time so they're ready to go for this meal. Make your own salsa at home using the Roasted Tomato Salsa from Chapter 11.

2 large sweet potatoes

⅛ teaspoon cayenne pepper

½ cup shredded Mexican cheese

8 ounces canned black beans, drained and rinsed

½ medium avocado, peeled, pitted, and diced

2 tablespoons salsa

2 tablespoons chopped cilantro leaves and stems

1 Preheat oven to 400°F. Line a baking sheet with aluminum foil. Pierce sweet potatoes several times with a knife and place on the prepared sheet. Bake 45–60 minutes or until fork-tender. Allow sweet potatoes to cool slightly before cutting down the middle lengthwise.

2 Store cooked sweet potatoes in an airtight container in refrigerator up to 4 days. To reheat sweet potatoes, place in a microwave-safe dish and microwave 75–90 seconds.

3 When ready to serve, evenly divide cayenne, cheese, beans, avocado, salsa, and cilantro between sweet potatoes.

Portobello Mushroom Parmigiana

SERVES 4

Per Serving

Calories	174
Fat	8g
Sodium	295mg
Carbohydrates	14g
Fiber	3g
Sugar	6g
Protein	9g

You won't miss the meat in this savory and satisfying vegetarian dish! You can make the vegetable filling in advance and fill the mushroom caps when ready to make the dish for dinner.

4 medium portobello mushrooms

3 tablespoons water

1 tablespoon olive oil

½ cup diced onion

⅔ cup diced zucchini

3 cloves garlic, peeled and minced

1 teaspoon dried oregano

½ cup plus ¼ cup low-sodium tomato-basil marinara sauce, divided

4 teaspoons Italian-style bread crumbs

⅔ cup shredded reduced-fat mozzarella cheese

¼ cup chopped basil leaves

¼ cup grated vegetarian Parmesan cheese

1 Preheat oven to 425°F. Prep mushrooms by removing dirt with a dry paper towel. Remove stem from each mushroom and set aside. Place mushroom caps with gills facing down in a casserole dish. Add water to dish. Bake mushrooms 10 minutes.

2 Meanwhile, heat oil in a medium skillet over medium heat. Add onion and cook 3 minutes. Dice reserved mushroom stems. Add zucchini, diced mushrooms, garlic, and oregano to skillet and cook 3 minutes. Remove pan from heat and stir in ½ cup marinara sauce.

3 Remove mushroom caps from oven and carefully turn over with tongs. Using a spoon, carefully divide cooked vegetables among mushroom caps. Top each mushroom with 1 tablespoon of remaining marinara sauce and 1 teaspoon bread crumbs, then divide mozzarella among mushrooms.

4 Return mushrooms to oven and bake 15 minutes or until tender. Top mushrooms with basil and Parmesan cheese.

5 Store stuffed mushrooms in an airtight container in refrigerator up to 2 days. To reheat, place in a microwave-safe dish covered with a lid and microwave 45–60 seconds.

Mushroom Soup with Orzo

A warming dish for a nippy day, this soup is filled with the earthy flavors of mushrooms and garlic.

24 ounces fresh mushrooms

1 teaspoon olive oil

1 medium onion, peeled and diced

1 medium stalk celery, diced

6 cloves garlic, peeled and minced

6 cups low-sodium vegetable broth

½ teaspoon dried rosemary, crumbled

½ teaspoon dried sage, crumbled

½ teaspoon dried thyme

¼ teaspoon ground black pepper

⅔ cup orzo

1 Slice half of mushrooms, chop the rest, and set aside.

2 Heat oil in a medium stockpot over medium heat. Add onion, celery, and garlic and sauté 3 minutes. Add mushrooms and cook, stirring occasionally, 7 minutes. Add broth, rosemary, sage, thyme, and pepper. Increase heat to high and bring to a boil.

3 Reduce heat to low and stir in orzo. Cover and simmer 20 minutes.

4 Remove from heat. Allow to cool before storing in an airtight container in refrigerator up to 3 days. To reheat, place in a microwave-safe dish and microwave 75–90 seconds.

SERVES 6

Per Serving

Calories	131
Fat	1g
Sodium	152mg
Carbohydrates	25g
Fiber	3g
Sugar	7g
Protein	7g

WHAT IS ORZO?

Orzo is a small pasta with an appearance similar to rice. It's made from semolina flour, a type of wheat flour, which makes it an unacceptable choice for those with celiac disease. For a gluten-free alternative, try substituting cooked brown rice.

Roasted Cauliflower Steaks with Creamy Chimichurri

SERVES 4

Per Serving

Calories	266
Fat	19g
Sodium	541mg
Carbohydrates	19g
Fiber	7g
Sugar	7g
Protein	8g

SAY CHEESE!

Want a different topping option for the Roasted Cauliflower Steaks? In place of the chimichurri, try adding about 2 tablespoons of vegetarian Parmesan cheese or Asiago cheese to each steak when they come out of the oven.

This is a delicious dish that you can enjoy as an entrée or a side dish! When you're making this recipe, you'll end up with leftover cauliflower florets that can easily be roasted for another use.

Roasted Cauliflower Steaks

2 medium heads cauliflower

¼ cup olive oil

½ teaspoon salt

Creamy Chimichurri

2 cups packed fresh cilantro

1 cup packed fresh parsley

1 medium jalapeño pepper, seeded and cut into large pieces

1 medium shallot, peeled and quartered

2 cloves garlic, peeled

2 tablespoons lime juice

1½ tablespoons extra-virgin olive oil

¼ teaspoon salt

¼ cup low-fat plain Greek yogurt

1 For the cauliflower steaks: Preheat oven to 475°F.

2 Remove green leaves from 1 head of cauliflower and trim stem. Set head of cauliflower with stem side down and use a large knife to cut cauliflower in half. Slice 1½" thick to make steaks. Repeat with second head of cauliflower until you have 4 slices. Reserve any remaining cauliflower for another use.

3 Place cauliflower steaks on a rimmed baking sheet. Brush 1 tablespoon oil onto each cauliflower steak, then season each steak with ⅛ teaspoon salt on one side, using less if desired.

4 Cover sheet tightly with aluminum foil and place on rack in upper third of oven. Roast 8 minutes. Uncover sheet, then return to oven and roast another 8 minutes. Carefully flip cauliflower steaks over and roast another 4 minutes.

5 For the chimichurri: Add all ingredients except yogurt to a food processor and process until finely minced. Pour into a small bowl and mix in yogurt.

6 Store chimichurri in an airtight container in refrigerator up to 5 days. Store cauliflower steaks in an airtight container in refrigerator up to 2 days. To reheat, place steaks in a microwave-safe dish and microwave 60 seconds. Top each cauliflower steak with 1 tablespoon creamy chimichurri and serve.

Apple Butternut Soup

SERVES 6

Per Serving

Calories	123
Fat	0g
Sodium	9mg
Carbohydrates	32g
Fiber	4g
Sugar	15g
Protein	2g

APPLE FACTS

Apples are one of the most widely consumed fruits in the world. They can be eaten raw, cooked, dried, juiced, or fermented without diminishing their nutritional value. For your health, buy organic apples, wash them, and consume them with their fibrous, nutrient-rich skin. Apples contain vitamins C and K and flavonoids, substances that may help prevent cancer.

Apples draw out the natural sweetness of butternut squash, delivering a smooth, irresistibly delicious, fat-free soup. Serve your bowl of soup with the Simple Autumn Salad from Chapter 5 or with the Sheet Pan Pork Roast and Vegetables in Chapter 6.

6 cups diced butternut squash

2 cups diced apple

6 cups water

2 cups unsweetened apple juice

½ teaspoon ground cinnamon

⅛ teaspoon ground allspice

1 Place squash, apple, water, and apple juice in a large stockpot and bring to a boil over high heat. Reduce heat to medium-low, cover, and simmer 20 minutes.

2 Remove pot from heat and transfer contents to a blender or food processor. Purée until smooth. Return soup to the pot, add cinnamon and allspice, and stir to combine.

3 Allow to cool before storing in an airtight container in refrigerator up to 3 days. To reheat, place in a microwave-safe dish and microwave 75–90 seconds.

Sesame Tofu with Sautéed Green Beans

This fantastic vegetarian dish is a great choice for those wanting something meaty. The baked tofu is delicious and dense, and the sautéed green beans have an irresistible crunch. Serve it with brown rice for a balanced meal.

1 pound extra-firm tofu

3 teaspoons sesame oil, divided

2 tablespoons toasted sesame seeds

¼ teaspoon ground black pepper

1 medium red onion, peeled and diced

3 cloves garlic, peeled and minced

1 tablespoon minced fresh ginger

1 pound fresh green beans, trimmed and cut into 2" pieces

SERVES 4

Per Serving

Calories	212
Fat	11g
Sodium	11mg
Carbohydrates	15g
Fiber	5g
Sugar	5g
Protein	15g

1 Preheat oven to 425°F and adjust oven rack to middle position. Spray a baking sheet lightly with nonstick cooking spray and set aside.

2 Place tofu on a small plate or cutting board and wrap a paper towel around it. Press it with your hand to remove excess water. Repeat this a few times. Cut tofu crosswise into 6 equal sections, then turn each section over to lay flat. Slice each section in half lengthwise, leaving 12 (1" × 3½") pieces. Cut each piece in half crosswise; you will now have 24 (1" × 1¾") pieces.

3 Place tofu in a medium bowl, add 2 teaspoons oil, and gently toss to coat. Arrange tofu on the prepared sheet and sprinkle evenly with sesame seeds and pepper.

4 Place sheet on middle oven rack and bake 25–30 minutes, turning tofu halfway through.

5 While tofu is baking, heat remaining 1 teaspoon oil in a large skillet over medium heat. Add onion, garlic, and ginger and sauté 2 minutes. Add green beans and sauté 5–8 minutes.

6 Remove tofu from the oven and add to the skillet. Stir to coat. Allow to cool before storing in an airtight container in refrigerator up to 3 days. To reheat, place in a microwave-safe dish and microwave 75–90 seconds.

Falafel with Tzatziki

These little vegetarian chickpea patties are such a nice change from the everyday, they'll feel like a special treat. Wrap them in low-sodium pita or lavash flatbread or enjoy them plain. Garnish with some fresh dill before serving for additional subtle flavor.

SERVES 4

Per Serving

Calories	168
Fat	2g
Sodium	64mg
Carbohydrates	27g
Fiber	6g
Sugar	4g
Protein	11g

Falafel

3 cloves garlic, peeled

1 (15-ounce) can no-salt-added chickpeas, drained and rinsed

1 small onion, peeled and roughly chopped

¼ cup fresh parsley leaves

2 teaspoons ground cumin

1 teaspoon ground coriander

¼ teaspoon dried red pepper flakes

¼ teaspoon ground black pepper

Tzatziki

1 small cucumber, peeled

2 cloves garlic, peeled and minced

1 tablespoon chopped fresh dill

1 teaspoon lemon juice

¾ cup low-fat plain Greek yogurt

⅛ teaspoon ground white pepper

1. For the falafel: Preheat oven to 400°F and adjust oven rack to middle position. Spray a baking sheet lightly with nonstick cooking spray and set aside.
2. Place garlic, chickpeas, onion, parsley, cumin, coriander, red pepper flakes, and black pepper in a food processor. Pulse until smooth.
3. Spoon mixture by tablespoonfuls onto the prepared sheet. Place sheet on middle oven rack and bake 10 minutes. Remove from oven and gently flip falafel patties, then return to oven and bake another 5–10 minutes.

continued on next page

continued

4 For the tzatziki: While falafel is baking, halve cucumber length-wise and gently scrape out seeds with a spoon. Grate cucumber, then place in a clean towel and squeeze to remove excess liquid.

5 Transfer cucumber to a medium bowl and add minced garlic, dill, lemon juice, yogurt, and white pepper. Stir to combine.

6 Remove falafel from oven and allow to cool before storing in refrigerator up to 3 days. Store falafel and tzatziki in refrigerator in separate airtight containers. Use tzatziki within 3 days. To reheat falafel, place in a microwave-safe dish and microwave 75–90 seconds, then top with tzatziki to serve.

Whole-Grain Penne with Lemony Roasted Asparagus

Looking for a simple dish to impress the family, your friends, or even yourself? You won't believe that this dish has such fabulous flavor with so few ingredients! Oven roasting draws out depth in the vegetables, punctuated by the citrus burst.

1½ pounds fresh asparagus, trimmed and cut into 2" pieces

8 ounces white button mushrooms, sliced

1 medium red onion, peeled and diced

1 tablespoon olive oil

3 tablespoons lemon juice, divided

¼ teaspoon ground black pepper

1 (16-ounce) package whole-grain penne

1 tablespoon grated lemon zest

2 tablespoons chopped fresh dill

1 Preheat oven to 450°F and adjust oven rack to middle position. Line a large baking sheet with foil and set aside.

2 Place asparagus, mushrooms, and onion in a medium bowl. Add oil, 2 tablespoons lemon juice, and pepper and toss to coat. Spread on the prepared sheet. Place on middle oven rack and bake 20 minutes.

3 Meanwhile, cook penne according to package directions, omitting salt. Drain and transfer to a large bowl.

4 Add roasted vegetables to pasta, along with all the cooking juices. Add lemon zest, dill, and remaining 1 tablespoon lemon juice and toss to coat.

5 Allow to cool before storing in an airtight container in refrigerator up to 3 days. To reheat, place in a microwave-safe dish and microwave 75–90 seconds.

SERVES 6	
Per Serving	
Calories	277
Fat	3g
Sodium	8mg
Carbohydrates	55g
Fiber	10g
Sugar	4g
Protein	12g

ROASTING FOR FLAVOR

Roasting is cooking food at a very high temperature. You can roast over an open flame, but oven roasting allows for convenience and control of food's placement in relation to the heat source. Roasting allows a food's natural sugars to caramelize, leaving the cooked food sweeter and more complex than when it was raw.

Pesto Rice with Portobello Mushrooms

SERVES 6

Per Serving

Calories	343
Fat	10g
Sodium	28mg
Carbohydrates	54g
Fiber	1g
Sugar	2g
Protein	7g

RICE TIP

If you have time, soak the basmati rice for 30 minutes before cooking to enhance its flavor and texture. Measure rice into a fine-mesh strainer and rinse repeatedly under cool running water. Place rice into cooking pot, add water, and let sit. The soaking water can be used to cook the rice, with no draining necessary.

This one-pot vegetarian meal is perfect for potluck parties. It's best made with white basmati rice, but it's also delicious with your choice of whole-grain pasta.

2 cups basmati rice

3 cups water

1 tablespoon olive oil

1 medium onion, peeled and chopped

2 cloves garlic, peeled and minced

8 ounces baby bella mushrooms

6 tablespoons Basil Pesto (see recipe in Chapter 3)

¼ teaspoon ground black pepper

1 Measure rice into a fine-mesh strainer and rinse under cold running water. Transfer rice to a medium saucepan and add water. Place pan over medium-high heat and bring to a boil. As soon as water begins to boil, reduce heat to low, cover, and simmer 15 minutes.

2 Remove pan from heat and fluff rice with a fork. Set aside.

3 Heat oil in a medium skillet over medium heat. Add onion and garlic and cook, stirring occasionally, 2 minutes.

4 Add mushrooms and sauté until tender, about 4 minutes. Remove from heat.

5 Add rice, pesto, and pepper to the pan. Stir to combine. Allow to cool before storing in an airtight container in refrigerator up to 3 days. To reheat, place in a microwave-safe dish and microwave 75–90 seconds.

Spicy Chickpea Tacos with Arugula

A thick and spicy sauce, meaty chickpeas, the peppery coolness of arugula, and the crunchy bite of taco shells add up to super-tasty tacos! If you're trying to broaden your meatless horizons—or a friend's—these tacos are sure to be a hit.

3 cups canned no-salt-added chickpeas, drained and rinsed

4 tablespoons no-salt-added tomato paste

1 (8-ounce) can no-salt-added tomato sauce

1 tablespoon apple cider vinegar

1 tablespoon packed light brown sugar

2 teaspoons Salt-Free Chili Seasoning (see recipe in Chapter 3)

1 teaspoon ground mustard

1 teaspoon onion powder

½ teaspoon garlic powder

¼ teaspoon ground black pepper

⅛ teaspoon dried red pepper flakes

1 (5.8-ounce) package low-sodium taco shells

6 cups baby arugula

SERVES 6	
Per Serving	
Calories	300
Fat	10g
Sodium	75mg
Carbohydrates	46g
Fiber	8g
Sugar	6g
Protein	9g

1 In a medium saucepan, combine chickpeas, tomato paste, tomato sauce, vinegar, brown sugar, chili seasoning, mustard, onion powder, garlic powder, black pepper, and red pepper flakes and stir.

2 Place pan over medium heat and simmer 10 minutes, stirring frequently. Remove from heat.

3 Allow to cool before storing cooked chickpea mixture in an airtight container in refrigerator up to 4 days. To reheat, place in a microwave-safe dish and microwave 60–75 seconds. Heat taco shells according to package directions. Fill warm taco shells with arugula and chickpea mixture.

10-Minute Thai Noodles

SERVES 6

Per Serving

Calories	435
Fat	9g
Sodium	71mg
Carbohydrates	78g
Fiber	5g
Sugar	3g
Protein	8g

UNSALTED PEANUT BUTTER

Many supermarkets as well as natural food stores sell unsalted peanut butter. Some stores are even installing their own grinding machines, so you can get the freshest salt-free peanut butter imaginable. If you cannot find any locally, you can order unsalted peanut butter online.

These spicy noodles will satisfy your hunger for something healthy and filling. Unsalted chunky peanut butter is specified, but feel free to substitute creamy peanut butter and a tablespoon of chopped unsalted peanuts if you prefer.

1 pound rice noodles

3 teaspoons sesame oil, divided

1 small red onion, peeled and diced

4 cloves garlic, peeled and minced

1 tablespoon minced fresh ginger

1 medium red bell pepper, seeded and diced

½ cup low-sodium vegetable broth

2 tablespoons unsalted chunky peanut butter

2 tablespoons lime juice

½ teaspoon dried red pepper flakes

3 green onions, sliced

1 Cook noodles according to package directions, omitting salt. Drain. Add 1 teaspoon oil to cooked noodles and toss to coat. Set aside.

2 Heat remaining 2 teaspoons oil in a large skillet over medium heat. Add onion, garlic, and ginger and sauté 2 minutes. Add bell pepper and sauté 3 minutes. Remove from heat.

3 Stir in broth, peanut butter, lime juice, red pepper flakes, and green onions.

4 Add noodles and toss to coat. Allow to cool before storing in an airtight container in refrigerator up to 3 days. Noodles can be served cold or reheated in microwave in a microwave-safe dish for 60 seconds.

Vegetable Baked Ziti

Delicious comfort food at its low-sodium best, this version of baked ziti is packed with fresh vegetables. Water-packed mozzarella is often sold in the specialty cheese section of supermarkets. If you can't find it, substitute shredded Swiss cheese.

1 pound whole-grain ziti

1 tablespoon olive oil

1 medium onion, peeled and diced

4 cloves garlic, peeled and minced

1 medium red bell pepper, seeded and diced

1 medium yellow squash, trimmed and diced

1 medium zucchini, trimmed and diced

1 (15-ounce) can no-salt-added diced tomatoes

2 (8-ounce) cans no-salt-added tomato sauce

2 tablespoons no-salt-added tomato paste

1 teaspoon packed light brown sugar

1 teaspoon dried basil

½ teaspoon dried marjoram

½ teaspoon dried oregano

½ teaspoon ground black pepper

¼ teaspoon dried savory

¼ teaspoon dried thyme

4 ounces fresh water-packed mozzarella cheese, shredded

2 tablespoons grated vegetarian Parmesan cheese

SERVES 6	
Per Serving	
Calories	381
Fat	6g
Sodium	110mg
Carbohydrates	68g
Fiber	13g
Sugar	12g
Protein	16g

1 Preheat oven to 400°F and adjust oven rack to middle position.

2 Cook ziti according to package directions, omitting salt. Drain and return pasta to the pot. Set aside.

3 Meanwhile, heat oil in a large skillet over medium heat. Add onion and garlic and sauté 2 minutes. Add bell pepper, squash, zucchini, tomatoes with juice, tomato sauce, tomato paste, sugar, basil, marjoram, oregano, black pepper, savory, and thyme and cook, stirring occasionally, 10 minutes. Remove from heat.

4 Pour sauce into the pot of pasta. Add mozzarella and Parmesan and stir to combine. Pour mixture into a 9" × 13" baking dish and cover tightly with foil. Place dish on middle oven rack and bake 20 minutes.

5 Remove from oven. Allow to cool before storing in an airtight container in refrigerator up to 3 days. To reheat, place in a microwave-safe dish and microwave 75–90 seconds.

Linguine with Plum Tomatoes, Mushrooms, and Tempeh

SERVES 6

Per Serving

Calories	377
Fat	6g
Sodium	39mg
Carbohydrates	64g
Fiber	10g
Sugar	7g
Protein	20g

WHAT IS TEMPEH?

Tempeh is a fermented soybean product sold in firm rectangular cakes. It has a rugged texture and nutty flavor that melds well with many types of food. Tempeh is stocked in most supermarkets beside the tofu and refrigerated imitation meat products. Tempeh is cholesterol-free and a good source of protein, calcium, and iron.

Pasta is always an easy and filling dinner. The slight acidity of the tomatoes provides a wonderful contrast to the nutty, earthy flavors of the mushrooms and tempeh.

1 pound whole-grain linguine

1 (28-ounce) can no-salt-added plum tomatoes, drained, with juice reserved

1 tablespoon olive oil

1 large onion, peeled and diced

8 ounces white button mushrooms, sliced

1 (8-ounce) package organic tempeh, diced

3 cloves garlic, peeled and minced

1 teaspoon salt-free Italian seasoning

½ teaspoon ground black pepper

⅛ teaspoon dried red pepper flakes

1 Cook linguine according to package directions, omitting salt. Drain and set aside.

2 Chop tomatoes and set aside.

3 Heat oil in a medium skillet over medium heat. Add onion, mushrooms, tempeh, and garlic and cook, stirring frequently, 5 minutes. Add tomatoes with juice, Italian seasoning, black pepper, and red pepper flakes. Cook, stirring occasionally, 10 minutes.

4 Spoon sauce over pasta. Allow to cool before storing in an airtight container in refrigerator up to 3 days. To reheat, place in a microwave-safe dish and microwave 60–75 seconds.

Coconut Cauliflower Curry

The intoxicating array of coconut, garlic, and ginger makes this a heavenly vegetarian meal. If you don't have garam masala, substitute salt-free curry powder. Serve the curry with steamed brown or basmati rice. If you want a sweeter flavor, substitute sweet potatoes for the regular potatoes.

1 tablespoon canola oil

1 medium onion, peeled and diced

6 cloves garlic, peeled and minced

1 tablespoon minced fresh ginger

1 tablespoon garam masala

1 teaspoon ground turmeric

2 tablespoons no-salt-added tomato paste

2 cups low-sodium vegetable broth

1 cup light coconut milk

1 medium head cauliflower, cored and cut into florets

3 medium Yukon Gold potatoes, peeled and diced

2 medium carrots, peeled and sliced

1 (15-ounce) can no-salt-added diced tomatoes

1½ cups fresh peas

½ teaspoon ground black pepper

¼ cup chopped fresh cilantro

1 Heat oil in a large stockpot over medium heat. Add onion, garlic, and ginger and cook, stirring frequently, 5 minutes. Add garam masala and turmeric and sauté until fragrant, 30 seconds to 1 minute.

2 Stir in tomato paste, broth, coconut milk, cauliflower, potatoes, carrots, and tomatoes with juice. Increase heat to medium-high and bring to a boil.

3 Reduce heat to medium-low, cover, and simmer 20 minutes.

4 Stir in peas and pepper and cook another 2–3 minutes.

5 Remove from heat and stir in cilantro. Allow to cool before storing in an airtight container in refrigerator up to 3 days.

6 To reheat, place curry in a microwave-safe dish and microwave 75–90 seconds.

SERVES 6

Per Serving

Calories	281
Fat	5g
Sodium	144mg
Carbohydrates	51g
Fiber	11g
Sugar	11g
Protein	9g

WHAT IS GARAM MASALA?

Garam masala is a ground spice blend used extensively in Indian cooking. Although blends may differ, garam masala typically includes cinnamon, cumin, coriander, cloves, ginger, nutmeg, pepper, mace, star anise, and/or bay leaves. Garam masala is potent in terms of fragrance and flavor, but unlike many curry powders, it is usually not spicy.

Kale-Stuffed Manicotti

Spinach, Swiss chard, or another dark leafy green may be substituted for the kale in this vegan version of the classic Italian dish.

SERVES 6

Per Serving

Calories	253
Fat	4g
Sodium	49mg
Carbohydrates	43g
Fiber	8g
Sugar	9g
Protein	14g

NUTRITIONAL YEAST FLAKES

Nutritional yeast is an inactive yeast with a zingy, cheese-like flavor that makes it a delicious choice for low-sodium and vegan diets. The yeast can be sprinkled on popcorn, pasta, or anything you'd like to perk up. Nutritional yeast contains important vitamins, such as vitamin B_{12}, which is often found in meat, so it's an especially nutritious supplement for vegetarians and vegans.

1 (8-ounce) package manicotti

1 medium onion, peeled and chopped

3 cloves garlic, peeled and minced

7 cups chopped kale

1 pound firm tofu, drained

1 teaspoon salt-free Italian seasoning

¼ teaspoon ground black pepper

⅛ teaspoon dried red pepper flakes

3 cups no-salt-added pasta sauce, divided

2 tablespoons nutritional yeast flakes

2 tablespoons chopped fresh parsley

1 Preheat oven to 400°F and adjust oven rack to middle position.

2 Cook manicotti according to package directions, omitting salt. Drain and set aside.

3 Meanwhile, spray a medium stockpot with nonstick cooking spray and place over medium heat. Add onion and garlic and sauté until soft, about 3 minutes. Add kale and cook, stirring occasionally, another 4–5 minutes.

4 Remove pot from heat and transfer contents to a food processor. Pulse until smooth. Add tofu, Italian seasoning, black pepper, and red pepper flakes and pulse until smooth.

5 Spread a thin layer of pasta sauce in the bottom of a 9" × 13" baking dish. Fill manicotti with kale mixture and arrange in the dish. Pour remaining pasta sauce over manicotti and sprinkle with nutritional yeast.

6 Cover dish with foil, place on middle oven rack, and bake until hot and bubbly, 20–30 minutes.

7 Allow to cool before storing in an airtight container in refrigerator up to 3 days. To reheat, place in a microwave-safe dish and microwave 75–90 seconds. Garnish with parsley.

Black Bean Burgers

SERVES 4	
Per Serving	
Calories	276
Fat	1g
Sodium	25mg
Carbohydrates	53g
Fiber	13g
Sugar	2g
Protein	14g

Garnish these hearty Southwestern-flavored vegetable burgers with homemade guacamole and salsa. To create a balanced meal, serve alongside the Southwestern Beet Slaw or Arugula with Pears and Red Wine Vinaigrette (see both recipes in Chapter 5).

2 (15-ounce) cans no-salt-added black beans, drained and rinsed

1 small shallot, peeled and minced

3 cloves garlic, peeled and minced

1 medium red bell pepper, seeded and chopped

¼ cup chopped fresh cilantro

1 tablespoon lime juice

2 teaspoons Salt-Free Chili Seasoning (see recipe in Chapter 3)

¼ teaspoon ground black pepper

½ cup salt-free bread crumbs

1 Preheat oven to 425°F and adjust oven rack to middle position. Spray a baking sheet lightly with nonstick cooking spray and set aside.

2 Place beans in a food processor and purée until smooth. Transfer beans to a large bowl, then add all remaining ingredients and mix together. Form into 4 large patties.

3 Place patties on the prepared sheet. Place sheet on middle oven rack and bake 10 minutes. Remove from oven and gently flip patties, then return to oven and bake another 5 minutes.

4 Remove from oven and allow to cool before storing in an airtight container in refrigerator up to 4 days. To reheat, place on a microwave-safe plate and microwave 60–75 seconds.

Sweet Potato and Black Bean Burritos

The filling of these Sweet Potato and Black Bean Burritos is an irresistible combination of flavors and textures, both sweet and savory. Keep the cooked burrito filling in the refrigerator as a quick lunch option!

1 tablespoon olive oil

½ medium onion, peeled and diced

1 (15-ounce) can cut sweet potatoes, drained

1 (15-ounce) can no-salt-added black beans, drained and rinsed

1½ teaspoons Salt-Free Chili Seasoning (see recipe in Chapter 3)

¼ teaspoon salt

4 (6") whole-wheat tortillas

¼ cup low-sodium salsa

1 small avocado, peeled, pitted, and quartered

¼ cup low-fat sour cream

¼ cup chopped fresh cilantro

SERVES 4	
Per Serving	
Calories	443
Fat	12g
Sodium	339mg
Carbohydrates	71g
Fiber	14g
Sugar	10g
Protein	12g

1 Heat oil in a large skillet over medium heat. Add onion and sauté 3 minutes. Add sweet potatoes, beans, chili seasoning, and salt. Cook 5 minutes, using a rubber spatula or wooden spoon to stir and mash beans and sweet potatoes together. About half of beans should be mashed and sweet potatoes should be broken into smaller pieces once mixture is cooked. Allow mixture to cool before storing in an airtight container in refrigerator up to 3 days.

2 When ready to serve, warm tortillas in microwave or toaster oven. To reheat sweet potato mixture, place in a microwave-safe dish and microwave 90 seconds. Top each tortilla with sweet potato and bean mixture, salsa, avocado, sour cream, and cilantro. Fold ends toward the center, then roll up from the other side, into a cylinder.

Vegetable Sushi

Although it looks complicated, sushi is simple and inexpensive to make, requiring nothing more than the ingredients, a flexible bamboo sushi mat, and a sharp knife. Dry sheets of nori seaweed are sold in the Asian aisle of most supermarkets. Sushi rice should also be there.

SERVES 6

Per Serving

Calories	259
Fat	0g
Sodium	13mg
Carbohydrates	57g
Fiber	2g
Sugar	1g
Protein	6g

SUSHI TIP

When making sushi, position a bowl of water nearby on the counter. Dip your sticky fingers into the water to make rice arrangement easier, and use the water to rinse your knife for clean slicing.

2 cups sushi rice

3 cups water

1 medium cucumber, peeled

1 medium carrot, peeled

2 tablespoons unflavored rice vinegar

6 sheets unflavored nori

1 Place rice and water in a medium saucepan and bring to a boil over high heat. Reduce heat to low, cover, and simmer 20 minutes.

2 While rice is cooking, halve cucumber lengthwise, then gently scrape out seeds with a spoon. Slice carrot and cucumber into thin matchsticks or strips and set aside.

3 When rice is done cooking, remove from heat. Stir in vinegar.

4 Take out 1 sheet of nori. One side should be shinier than the other; place the shiny side down on a bamboo mat. Spread a thin layer of rice (about ¼" thick) over the top, leaving a 1" bare lip near you and about 2" bare on the far edge.

5 Place a few strips of cucumber and carrot on top of rice, 2"–3" from bare edge closest to you. Lightly wet bare edges, then carefully roll nori away from you, pressing firmly to seal. Continue rolling to far edge, then roll back and forth to seal completely.

6 Using a very sharp knife, slice the roll into 6 equal segments, dipping the knife into water and cleaning off the blade between cuts to prevent sticking. Repeat with remaining ingredients.

7 Store in an airtight container in refrigerator up to 2 days.

CHAPTER 10

Freezer Meals

Spicy Lime Chicken 190

Chili-Rubbed Seared Salmon 191

Turkey Meatballs 192

Mediterranean Turkey Burgers 193

Vegetarian Lasagna 195

Greek Lemon Chicken Orzo Soup 197

Black Bean Vegetable Soup 198

White Bean and Vegetable Soup 199

Tandoori Masala Chicken 200

Chili-Spiced Ground Beef 202

Slow Cooker Squash and Chickpea Curry 203

Vegetable Burgers 204

Baked Pumpkin Oatmeal 205

Lemon Blueberry Quinoa Breakfast Bars 207

Breakfast Burritos 208

Spicy Lime Chicken

SERVES 6

Per Serving

Calories	160
Fat	4g
Sodium	349mg
Carbohydrates	5g
Fiber	1g
Sugar	2g
Protein	26g

This flavorful chicken is so easy to make and comes in handy when the mood for tacos or burritos hits! Always keep this stocked in your freezer to feed a pesky craving with a healthy alternative. Make your own salsa at home using the Roasted Tomato Salsa from Chapter 11.

1½ **pounds boneless, skinless chicken breast**

½ **cup Spicy Lime, Cilantro, and Garlic Marinade (see recipe in Chapter 3)**

½ **medium yellow onion, peeled and cut into wedges**

1 **cup refrigerated mild salsa**

1 Place chicken in a medium bowl and pour marinade over chicken. Cover and place in refrigerator to marinate 2 hours.

2 Place onion wedges in a slow cooker. Place chicken on top of onion. Pour salsa over chicken. Cook on low 4 hours or until chicken can easily be shredded with a fork. Use tongs to remove chicken and onion. Place chicken on a plate or in a bowl and shred.

3 Once cool, transfer shredded chicken and onion to a freezer-safe resealable bag or container. Keep in freezer up to 3 months.

4 To thaw, place in refrigerator 24 hours. To reheat, place in a microwave-safe dish and microwave 90 seconds or until internal temperature reaches 165°F.

Chili-Rubbed Seared Salmon

Surprised to see salmon as part of a freezer meal? This Chili-Rubbed Seared Salmon turns out perfectly flaky and requires very little cooking time. Pair it with Brown Rice and the Roasted Broccoli and Cauliflower (see recipes in Chapter 3) and you have a delicious, spicy meal in a bowl.

1 pound salmon fillets, about 1" thick with skin on

1 teaspoon Salt-Free Chili Seasoning (see recipe in Chapter 3)

1 tablespoon olive oil

SERVES 3	
Per Serving	
Calories	231
Fat	9g
Sodium	117mg
Carbohydrates	0g
Fiber	0g
Sugar	0g
Protein	31g

1 Preheat oven to 350°F. Place salmon skin-side down and evenly sprinkle chili seasoning over each fillet. Set aside.

2 Once oven is preheated, heat oil in a large oven-safe skillet over medium-high heat. Place salmon skin-side up in skillet. Cook 3 minutes. Using tongs, carefully turn salmon fillets over. Place skillet in oven and cook 4 minutes. Salmon should be slightly undercooked at this point so that it does not become overcooked once reheated.

3 Remove skillet from oven and allow salmon to cool completely in the skillet. Once cool, place fillets in an airtight, freezer-safe container in a single layer. If you need to stack salmon fillets, use parchment paper to separate them. Freeze up to 1 month.

4 To thaw, place salmon in refrigerator 8 hours before serving. To reheat, place in a microwave-safe dish covered with a lid and microwave 2–3 minutes or until internal temperature reaches 145°F.

Turkey Meatballs

SERVES 6

Per Serving

Calories	157
Fat	7g
Sodium	172mg
Carbohydrates	3g
Fiber	0g
Sugar	0g
Protein	18g

Frozen meatballs can be such a lifesaver on a busy weeknight! You don't have to defrost these before using, which saves time, and they go well with marinara sauce. Pair them with the Spicy and Tangy Barbecue Sauce from Chapter 3 for a fun twist.

1 pound 93 percent lean ground turkey

1 large egg

⅓ cup panko bread crumbs

¼ cup finely diced white onion

2 teaspoons salt-free garlic and herb seasoning

¼ teaspoon salt

1 Preheat oven to 375°F. Line an 11" × 17" baking sheet with aluminum foil.
2 Place all ingredients in a large bowl. Mix well with a spoon until egg is incorporated and ingredients are evenly combined.
3 Use a spoon or cookie dough scoop to portion out meat mixture. Roll into 1" meatballs and place about 1" apart on the prepared sheet.
4 Bake 20 minutes or until internal temperature reaches 165°F.
5 Allow to cool to room temperature. Place in a single layer in a freezer-safe bag and store flat in freezer. Use within 3 months. When ready to use, place in a microwave-safe bowl and microwave for 60 seconds at a time until internal temperature reaches 165°F.

Mediterranean Turkey Burgers

These flavorful, juicy Mediterranean Turkey Burgers are great cooked in a skillet or outdoors on the grill. Double or triple the recipe to make more burgers to have on hand for meal prep or your next cookout!

1 pound 93 percent lean ground turkey
¼ cup finely diced red onion
¼ cup finely chopped parsley leaves
¼ cup crumbled feta cheese
½ teaspoon dried oregano
½ teaspoon garlic powder

1 Line a small baking sheet with parchment paper. Set aside.

2 In a medium mixing bowl, combine all ingredients and mix with a metal spoon or your hands until just combined. Divide mixture into 4 equal portions and pat each into a patty shape. Place on the prepared sheet.

3 Place sheet in freezer 4–6 hours. Once patties are frozen, transfer them to a freezer-safe resealable bag or container, placing parchment paper in between patties.

4 To thaw, place patties in refrigerator 24 hours before preparing on the grill or in a skillet. Cook burgers to an internal temperature of 165°F.

SERVES 4

Per Serving

Calories	224
Fat	11g
Sodium	169mg
Carbohydrates	2g
Fiber	0g
Sugar	1g
Protein	26g

Vegetarian Lasagna

A good lasagna is hard to beat, and this freezer-friendly version makes it easy to feed a large family or to enjoy slice by slice as desired. The lasagna goes into the freezer uncooked to maintain the best quality.

1 tablespoon olive oil

¾ cup diced white onion

4 cloves garlic, peeled and minced

8 ounces baby bella mushrooms, roughly chopped

2 cups quartered, sliced zucchini

1½ teaspoons dried oregano

¼ teaspoon ground black pepper

⅛ teaspoon dried red pepper flakes

3 cups baby spinach

1 large egg

15 ounces part-skim ricotta cheese

¼ teaspoon salt

¼ teaspoon garlic powder

1 (24-ounce) jar reduced-sodium marinara sauce, divided

9 oven-ready lasagna noodles

1½ cups shredded low-fat mozzarella cheese

3 ounces shredded vegetarian Parmesan cheese

SERVES 8	
Per Serving	
Calories	352
Fat	16g
Sodium	575mg
Carbohydrates	30g
Fiber	3g
Sugar	6g
Protein	21g

1 Heat oil in a large, deep skillet over medium-high heat. Add onion and sauté 2 minutes. Add garlic, mushrooms, zucchini, oregano, black pepper, and red pepper flakes. Cook 4 minutes, stirring occasionally. Remove skillet from heat, stir in spinach, and mix until wilted.

2 In a small bowl, combine egg and ricotta. Add salt and garlic powder.

3 Spread ½ cup marinara sauce on the bottom of a 11" × 7" freezer-safe dish. Place 3 lasagna noodles side by side. Spoon one-third of ricotta mixture on top of lasagna noodles, followed by one-third of mozzarella and one-third of Parmesan. Top with half of cooked vegetables. Repeat layers, finishing top layer with remaining marinara sauce and cheese.

4 Allow lasagna fillings to cool completely. Place plastic wrap directly on top of lasagna surface to keep as much air out as possible, then wrap entire pan in plastic wrap. Cover dish with aluminum foil. Place in freezer up to 1 month.

continued on next page

continued

5 To thaw, place in refrigerator 24 hours before baking. Preheat oven to 375°F and allow lasagna to sit at room temperature while oven preheats. Remove foil and plastic wrap, then re-cover pan with foil before baking lasagna 60–70 minutes, until internal temperature reaches 165°F. Remove foil and bake another 10 minutes to brown top of lasagna. Remove from oven and let sit 5 minutes before slicing.

6 To reheat individual portions of lasagna, thaw and bring to room temperature as directed above. Preheat oven to 350°F and bake lasagna in an oven-safe dish 30 minutes until internal temperature reaches 165°F.

Greek Lemon Chicken Orzo Soup

This bright and flavorful soup makes use of leftover shredded chicken or a rotisserie chicken from the store. If you prefer a lower-carb version of the soup, leave out the orzo. Try garnishing this soup with chopped chives or green onions!

1 tablespoon olive oil

¾ cup diced white onion

⅔ cup sliced carrots

2 cloves garlic, peeled and minced

⅓ cup orzo

3 cups shredded cooked chicken

64 ounces low-sodium chicken broth

1 tablespoon lemon zest

1 tablespoon lemon juice

1 cup crumbled feta cheese

1 Heat oil in a large stockpot or Dutch oven over medium-high heat. Add onion and carrots. Sauté 5 minutes. Add garlic and sauté 1 minute.

2 Stir in orzo and allow it to get golden brown, stirring occasionally and cooking about 1 minute. Add chicken, broth, lemon zest, and lemon juice.

3 Bring soup to a boil over high heat, then reduce heat to low and simmer 10 minutes, making sure orzo is cooked. Turn off heat and remove pan from burner.

4 Allow soup to cool before storing in a freezer-safe container in freezer up to 1 month.

5 Thaw soup in refrigerator for 48 hours. To reheat, place in a microwave-safe dish and microwave 60–90 seconds until heated through. Top with feta cheese before serving.

SERVES 4

Per Serving	
Calories	385
Fat	14g
Sodium	717mg
Carbohydrates	19g
Fiber	2g
Sugar	5g
Protein	42g

ORZO

Orzo is a pasta, but it looks very similar to rice because it's cut very short. You can find it with all the other pasta in the grocery store. If you prefer using rice in the soup, follow the same cooking method as with the orzo.

Black Bean Vegetable Soup

SERVES 4

Per Serving

Calories	197
Fat	1g
Sodium	149mg
Carbohydrates	38g
Fiber	9g
Sugar	9g
Protein	9g

Thick and hearty, with a deep, rich taste, this vegetarian soup is ready in less than 30 minutes. Don't drain the canned tomatoes or beans; the liquid becomes part of the flavorful broth.

1 small red onion, peeled and diced

3 cloves garlic, peeled and minced

2½ cups low-sodium vegetable broth, divided

1 small carrot, peeled and diced

1 medium stalk celery, diced

1 small sweet potato, peeled and diced

1 (15-ounce) can no-salt-added diced tomatoes

1 (15-ounce) can no-salt-added black beans

¼ cup red wine

1 tablespoon no-salt-added tomato paste

1½ teaspoons ground cumin

1 teaspoon dried oregano

½ teaspoon ground coriander

¼ teaspoon dried red pepper flakes

¼ teaspoon ground black pepper

2 tablespoons chopped fresh cilantro

1 Place a medium stockpot over medium heat. Add onion, garlic, and ¼ cup broth and sauté 2 minutes. Add another ¼ cup broth, carrot, celery, sweet potato, and tomatoes with juice. Sauté 3 minutes.

2 Add remaining 2 cups broth, beans, wine, tomato paste, cumin, oregano, coriander, red pepper flakes, and black pepper. Bring to a boil, then reduce heat to low, cover, and simmer 15–20 minutes, until vegetables are tender.

3 Remove from heat and stir in cilantro. Allow to cool before storing in a freezer-safe container or resealable bag in the freezer up to 1 month.

4 To thaw, place in refrigerator for 48 hours. To reheat, place in a microwave-safe dish and microwave 60–90 seconds at a time until heated through.

White Bean and Vegetable Soup

This is an easy and hearty vegetarian soup made partly with nutritious pantry staples like canned beans and vegetables! This is a great vegetarian option for the fall. Serve with toasted bread or a side salad for a filling meal.

1 (27-ounce) can collard greens, drained

1 (15-ounce) can Great Northern beans, drained and rinsed

1½ cups fresh green beans, cut into 1" pieces

¾ cup diced carrots

½ cup diced green bell pepper

¼ cup finely diced white onion

4 cups low-sodium tomato juice

2 cups vegetable broth

1 Combine all ingredients in a slow cooker, adding liquids last. Stir. Cook 4 hours on low.

2 Allow soup to cool before storing in freezer-safe containers or freezer-safe resealable bags in freezer up to 3 months.

3 To thaw, place in refrigerator for 48 hours. To reheat, place in a microwave-safe dish and microwave 60–90 seconds at a time until heated through.

SERVES 10

Per Serving

Calories	114
Fat	1g
Sodium	567mg
Carbohydrates	22g
Fiber	5g
Sugar	7g
Protein	7g

Tandoori Masala Chicken

SERVES 4

Per Serving

Calories	208
Fat	8g
Sodium	474mg
Carbohydrates	8g
Fiber	1g
Sugar	4g
Protein	28g

SUBSTITUTE FOR TANDOORI MASALA SEASONING

If you cannot find tandoori masala seasoning, try this blend instead: 1 tablespoon garam masala, 1 teaspoon Kashmiri chili powder, and ¼ teaspoon cayenne pepper. Mix them well in a bowl.

Creamy and full of warming spice, this Tandoori Masala Chicken is a go-to comfort meal. To make this even more meal prep–friendly, use leftover Brown Rice or Quinoa (see recipes in Chapter 3). You can garnish with fresh cilantro.

1 cup finely chopped white onion

½ cup finely chopped cilantro leaves and stems

1½ tablespoons tandoori masala seasoning

1 tablespoon lemon juice

1 tablespoon olive oil, divided

1" piece fresh ginger, grated

3 cloves garlic, peeled and minced

¼ teaspoon salt

1 pound boneless, skinless chicken breast

½ cup tomato sauce

6 ounces canned light coconut milk

⅓ cup low-fat plain Greek yogurt

1 To make tandoori masala marinade, combine onion, cilantro, tandoori masala seasoning, lemon juice, ½ tablespoon oil, ginger, garlic, and salt in a medium bowl and mix well. Spoon mixture into a freezer-safe resealable bag.

2 Cut chicken into 1" pieces. Add chicken to bag with marinade. Remove air from bag and seal. Massage bag of chicken (with clean hands) and marinade using your hands. Flatten bag and place in freezer up to 3 months.

3 To thaw, place in refrigerator 24 hours. When ready to cook, heat a large skillet over medium heat with remaining ½ tablespoon olive oil. Remove chicken from marinade using tongs, leaving as much juice in bag as you can, and place in skillet. Add tomato sauce and coconut milk, stirring to combine. Cook on medium-low 18–20 minutes. Sauce should bubble slightly. Chicken should reach an internal temperature of 165°F.

4 Remove pan from heat and stir in yogurt.

Chili-Spiced Ground Beef

SERVES 4

Per Serving

Calories	160
Fat	6g
Sodium	303mg
Carbohydrates	1g
Fiber	0g
Sugar	1g
Protein	23g

KEEPING IT LEAN

When it comes to ground beef, choose lean when you can to save on calories and saturated fat. Any ground beef that is 93 percent lean (or leaner) qualifies. This will also save you from having to drain a lot of grease after cooking the ground beef!

Here's a great option the whole family will love! You can easily double this recipe to freeze if you'd like to keep more on hand for busy weeknights. Make the Creamy Chimichurri (see the Roasted Cauliflower Steaks with Creamy Chimichurri recipe in Chapter 9) if you plan to make tacos with this ground beef. Serve in tacos, quesadillas, or lettuce wraps. Make your own salsa at home using the Roasted Tomato Salsa from Chapter 11.

1 pound 93 percent lean ground beef

1½ teaspoons Salt-Free Chili Seasoning (see recipe in Chapter 3)

¼ teaspoon salt

3 tablespoons salsa

1 Place a large skillet over medium-high heat and add beef, chili seasoning, and salt. Break beef into smaller pieces using a spatula. Cook beef until no longer pink or until internal temperature reaches 160°F.

2 Allow beef to cool completely before placing in freezer-safe storage bags or containers; keep in freezer up to 1 month.

3 To thaw, place in refrigerator at least 24 hours. To reheat, place in a skillet over medium heat and add salsa. Cover and heat 5 minutes, stirring occasionally.

Slow Cooker Squash and Chickpea Curry

Add this easy curry dish to your list of comforting weeknight meals! Using frozen diced butternut squash saves on prep time. This dish has a nice amount of heat, but you can leave out the red pepper flakes if you have a more delicate spice tolerance.

12 ounces frozen diced butternut squash

1 teaspoon olive oil

½ cup diced yellow onion

1½ tablespoons curry powder

¼ teaspoon dried red pepper flakes

½ teaspoon ground turmeric

¼ teaspoon salt

2 cloves garlic, peeled

1 (15-ounce) can chickpeas, drained and rinsed

2 cups chopped kale

1 (14-ounce) can light coconut milk

8 ounces vegetable broth

½ cup frozen peas, thawed

1 small bunch cilantro, chopped

1 Thaw squash according to package directions.

2 Heat oil in large skillet over medium-high heat. Add onion and cook 3 minutes before adding squash, curry powder, red pepper flakes, turmeric, salt, and garlic. Mix with a spatula and cook 3 minutes.

3 Pour squash mixture into a slow cooker, then add chickpeas, kale, coconut milk, and broth. Cook 3 hours on low. About 30 minutes before cook time ends, add peas and allow to heat through. Top with cilantro.

4 Store in an airtight container in refrigerator up to 3 days. To freeze, allow curry to cool for 1 hour before placing in freezer-safe glass storage containers or freezer-safe resealable bags, and store in freezer up to 1 month. To thaw, place in refrigerator overnight. Reheat in a slow cooker, microwave, or saucepan to a minimum temperature of 165°F.

SERVES 6

Per Serving

Calories	165
Fat	5g
Sodium	336mg
Carbohydrates	24g
Fiber	5g
Sugar	5g
Protein	5g

CHICKPEAS OR GARBANZOS?

They're the same thing! No matter what you call them, these little legumes are a good source of protein, vitamin B_6, fiber, and folate. They are commonly used in hummus and are a popular plant-based protein source.

Vegetable Burgers

SERVES 4

Per Serving

Calories	259
Fat	4g
Sodium	490mg
Carbohydrates	59g
Fiber	8g
Sugar	4g
Protein	11g

This recipe makes use of leftovers from the Black-Eyed Pea Burrito Bowl in Chapter 9. You can enjoy these burgers on a bun, with a salad, or alongside your favorite side dish.

2 cups cooked brown rice, cooled to room temperature

2 cups leftover Black-Eyed Pea Burrito Bowl (without the rice from the recipe in Chapter 9 included in the mixture), at room temperature

4 whole-wheat burger buns

1 Add rice and burrito bowl mixture to food processor and pulse until mixture begins to hold together. Use a spatula to transfer mixture to a medium bowl.

2 Line a small baking sheet with parchment paper. Evenly divide mixture to form 4 patties. Place baking sheet in freezer and let sit for 8 hours. Store frozen patties in a freezer-safe container or freezer-safe resealable bag up to 1 month.

3 Thaw patties in refrigerator 24 hours before cooking. Heat a medium skillet over medium-high heat and lightly coat with non-stick cooking spray. Add patties and cook 3 minutes on each side, carefully flipping with a spatula.

4 Serve on burger buns.

Baked Pumpkin Oatmeal

Try oatmeal in a new way by baking it into oatmeal muffins! These are easy to reheat, and you can add any toppings you like for a quick breakfast or snack.

3 cups old-fashioned oats

1 teaspoon sodium-free baking powder

½ teaspoon ground cinnamon

¼ teaspoon ground cardamom

¾ cup low-fat vanilla Greek yogurt

½ cup pumpkin purée

½ cup low-fat milk

1 large egg

2 tablespoons packed light brown sugar

½ teaspoon vanilla extract

1   Preheat oven to 350°F and adjust oven rack to middle position. Line a twelve-cup muffin tin with paper liners or spray with non-stick cooking spray.

2   In a large bowl, combine oats, baking powder, cinnamon, and cardamom. Stir well.

3   In a small bowl, mix yogurt, pumpkin purée, milk, egg, sugar, and vanilla. Pour wet mixture into dry mixture and stir until just combined.

4   Use a spoon to divide mixture among the prepared muffin cups, filling each one about three-quarters full. Place muffin tin on middle oven rack and bake 18–20 minutes, until oatmeal is set.

5   Allow baked oatmeal cups to cool in muffin tin before storing in a freezer-safe resealable bag or container in freezer up to 2 weeks. To serve, place in a microwave-safe dish and microwave 60 seconds.

SERVES 6

Per Serving

Calories	229
Fat	5g
Sodium	36mg
Carbohydrates	39g
Fiber	5g
Sugar	10g
Protein	9g

TOPPINGS TO TRY

Once you've reheated the Baked Pumpkin Oatmeal, top it with blueberries, banana slices, or pecans. For a sweet treat, add mini chocolate chips or a drizzle of 100 percent grade A maple syrup.

Lemon Blueberry Quinoa Breakfast Bars

Enjoy the sweetness of blueberry and the sour taste of lemon paired with hearty quinoa in these breakfast bars. Melt and drizzle 3 ounces of white chocolate chips on top for added sweetness.

½ cup quinoa

1 cup water

½ teaspoon ground cinnamon

¼ cup granulated sugar

¼ cup low-fat vanilla Greek yogurt

2 large eggs

1 tablespoon lemon juice

1 teaspoon lemon zest

½ teaspoon vanilla extract

1¼ cups oats

1¼ cups shredded sweetened coconut

½ teaspoon sodium-free baking powder

¾ cup fresh blueberries

SERVES 9

Per Serving

Calories	194
Fat	7g
Sodium	53mg
Carbohydrates	29g
Fiber	3g
Sugar	13g
Protein	5g

1 In a small saucepan, combine quinoa, water, and cinnamon. Bring to a boil, then reduce heat to low, cover, and simmer 15–20 minutes or until water is absorbed. Pour quinoa into a large glass bowl and allow to cool slightly.

2 Line an 8" × 8" baking dish with parchment paper, allowing it to hang over the edges. Preheat oven to 350°F.

3 In a small bowl, mix sugar, yogurt, eggs, lemon juice, lemon zest, and vanilla.

4 Add oats, coconut, and baking powder to quinoa. Mix well. Pour yogurt mixture into quinoa mixture and stir until just combined. Fold in blueberries. Mixture should be moist but not runny.

5 Pour mixture into the prepared dish and bake 25 minutes.

6 Remove dish from oven and allow bars to cool completely before removing from dish and cutting into squares.

7 Transfer to a freezer-safe resealable bag or container, placing parchment paper between breakfast bars. Store in freezer up to 1 month. To serve, place on a microwave-safe dish and microwave 60 seconds.

Breakfast Burritos

Per Serving

Calories	285
Fat	12g
Sodium	403mg
Carbohydrates	28g
Fiber	4g
Sugar	4g
Protein	16g

These burritos are a satisfying breakfast option for those on the go! They reheat quickly, and you can pair them with a banana, an apple, or other fresh fruit for a balanced breakfast.

6 large eggs

2 tablespoons low-fat milk

¼ teaspoon garlic powder

⅛ teaspoon salt

1 tablespoon unsalted butter, divided

3 cups spinach leaves

½ cup diced red bell pepper

6 (8") 100 percent whole-wheat tortillas

4 ounces shredded mozzarella cheese

1 Whisk together eggs, milk, garlic powder, and salt in a medium bowl. Melt ½ tablespoon butter in a large skillet over medium-high heat. Pour in egg mixture and cook, stirring occasionally, until eggs are cooked through. Transfer to a large plate to cool.

2 Rinse or wipe out skillet and place over medium heat. Melt remaining ½ tablespoon butter in skillet, then add spinach and bell pepper. Cook 3 minutes, stirring frequently, until spinach is wilted. Transfer to a large plate to cool completely.

3 Arrange a workstation to assemble burritos. Heat tortillas before assembling burritos by microwaving 20 seconds on a microwave-safe plate. Evenly divide mozzarella among tortillas, placing it slightly below the center of the tortilla. Next, divide eggs among tortillas, placing on top of cheese. Top with spinach and bell pepper. To roll, fold in sides of each tortilla so they nearly touch. Once sides are folded in, use your thumbs to bring up the bottom over the fillings. Tuck in sides while bringing in the bottom and tightly roll the tortilla. Place burritos seam side down in a gallon-sized freezer-safe resealable bag so burritos do not unroll.

4 Store in freezer up to 1 week. If freezing longer, wrap burritos in aluminum foil to prevent freezer burn. Use within 1 month.

5 To reheat, remove foil, place burritos on a microwave-safe plate covered with a slightly dampened paper towel, and microwave 2 minutes.

CHAPTER 11

Snacks

Summer Fruit Salsa with Cinnamon Pita Chips 210

Cranberry Almond Energy Bites. 211

Avocado "Hummus" 212

Healthier 7-Layer Dip 213

Blueberry Cottage Cheese Parfait 214

Zucchini Sticks 215

Homemade Soft Pretzels. 216

Crunchy Coated Nuts 218

"Cheesy" Seasoned Popcorn 219

Seasoned Sesame Kale Chips 220

Sweet Potato Crisps 221

Chewy Granola Bars. 222

Whole-Grain Crackers with Rosemary, Garlic, and Parmesan. 223

Roasted Red Pepper Hummus 225

Holy Guacamole 226

Garlic Lovers' Hummus 227

Pineapple Salsa. 227

Roasted Tomato Salsa 228

Summer Fruit Salsa with Cinnamon Pita Chips

This Summer Fruit Salsa with Cinnamon Pita Chips is a fun and sweet twist on traditional chips and salsa. This dish is not only visually appealing but provides a healthy dose of vitamin C and potassium as well!

SERVES 8

Per Serving

Calories	174
Fat	4g
Sodium	144mg
Carbohydrates	34g
Fiber	5g
Sugar	12g
Protein	4g

KIWI FRUIT QUICK PREP TIP

Instead of peeling the kiwi fruit, cut them in half widthwise and then slip a spoon between the fruit's flesh and the skin. Carefully turn the fruit as you run the spoon around and scoop out the flesh in one piece. Prep the fruit as needed or enjoy it as a snack!

Cinnamon Pita Chips

1 tablespoon granulated sugar

1 teaspoon ground cinnamon

4 whole-wheat pitas

2 tablespoons unsalted butter, melted

Fruit Salsa

3 medium kiwi fruit, skin removed and diced into ¼" pieces

2 cups strawberries, diced into ¼" pieces

1 medium dragon fruit, peeled and diced into ¼" pieces

½ medium mango, peeled and diced into ¼" pieces

1 teaspoon lime zest

1 tablespoon lime juice

1 tablespoon honey

1 For the pita chips: Preheat oven to 400°F. Mix sugar and cinnamon in a small bowl. Set aside.

2 Cut each pita into 4 equal triangles, then split each triangle in half to get a thinner piece. Place triangles on a large baking sheet, being sure to not overlap them. Brush triangles with butter and sprinkle cinnamon sugar on top. Place sheet in oven and bake 5–6 minutes. If chips aren't quite crispy yet, bake another 1–2 minutes. Allow chips to cool before storing at room temperature in an airtight container up to 3 days.

3 For the fruit salsa: Combine all diced fruits in a medium bowl. Add lime zest, lime juice, and honey. Mix well. Keep refrigerated until ready to serve. Use within 2 days.

Cranberry Almond Energy Bites

No baking is required for these nutrient-packed energy bites! Cranberry Almond Energy Bites make a great post-workout snack to help refuel. They're a balanced combination of quality carbohydrates and protein.

1 cup rolled oats

½ cup dried cranberries, chopped

½ cup almond butter

¼ cup raw almonds, chopped

1 tablespoon 100 percent grade A maple syrup

½ tablespoon chia seeds

1 In a large mixing bowl, mix all ingredients until thoroughly combined.

2 Form 1" balls of oat mixture using your hands and place balls on a small baking sheet. Place sheet in refrigerator for 15 minutes to allow bites to harden. Store energy bites in an airtight container in refrigerator up to 5 days.

SERVES 6

Per Serving

Calories	248
Fat	14g
Sodium	1mg
Carbohydrates	25g
Fiber	5g
Sugar	10g
Protein	7g

NUT BUTTER SWAPS

The almond butter in this recipe can be swapped for peanut butter or cashew butter, but the consistency may differ. If you have trouble getting the energy bites to stick together, use additional nut butter.

Avocado "Hummus"

SERVES 8

Per Serving

Calories	185
Fat	12g
Sodium	169mg
Carbohydrates	14g
Fiber	4g
Sugar	1g
Protein	5g

KEEP AVOCADO FRESH

Once you cut into an avocado, oxidation begins, and the flesh will start to brown soon after. To minimize oxidation, reduce exposure to oxygen by sprinkling lemon or lime juice over the cut avocado. Wrap in plastic wrap so the plastic clings to the avocado. Store in refrigerator.

Avocado makes everything better—even this hummus-inspired dip! There's lots of flavor in this dip thanks to the addition of lemon juice, cilantro, and jalapeño. Serve with multigrain tortilla chips or fresh vegetables.

¼ cup plus 2 tablespoons extra-virgin olive oil

1 (15.5-ounce) can Great Northern beans, rinsed

1 large avocado, peeled and pitted

¼ cup fresh cilantro leaves

2½ tablespoons lemon juice

1 large clove garlic, peeled

½ medium jalapeño pepper, seeds and ribs removed

½ teaspoon ground cumin

⅛ teaspoon salt

⅛ teaspoon cayenne pepper

Water

1 Combine all ingredients except water in a food processor or blender and process until smooth. If more liquid is needed to make the hummus smooth, add 1 tablespoon water at a time until desired consistency is achieved.

2 Store hummus in an airtight container in refrigerator up to 2 days.

Healthier 7-Layer Dip

A lightened-up, healthier version of a classic get-together dish, this seven-layer dip is a true crowd-pleaser! It's a great way to use up any leftover bell pepper, green onion, and cilantro.

2 medium ripe avocados, peeled and pitted

½ cup packed baby spinach leaves

1 teaspoon lime juice

¼ teaspoon salt

½ cup low-fat plain Greek yogurt

¼ teaspoon ground cumin

16 ounces refried beans

½ cup salsa

½ cup diced green bell pepper

¼ cup sliced green onions

¼ cup chopped cilantro leaves

1 In a blender or food processor, combine avocado, spinach, lime juice, and salt. Process until smooth.

2 In a small bowl, mix yogurt and cumin.

3 Evenly spread avocado mixture on the bottom of a 5" × 9" loaf pan or 1.5-quart baking dish. Spread yogurt mixture on top of avocado mixture. Next, spread refried beans into an even layer. Add a layer of salsa, followed by bell pepper, green onions, and cilantro. Store in an airtight container in refrigerator up to 3 days. Keep refrigerated until ready to serve.

SERVES 8

Per Serving

Calories	121
Fat	5g
Sodium	440mg
Carbohydrates	13g
Fiber	6g
Sugar	2g
Protein	5g

DITCH SOUR CREAM FOR GREEK YOGURT!

Low-fat plain Greek yogurt is a great substitute for sour cream. It contains more protein per serving and less fat, and no one will even taste the difference.

Blueberry Cottage Cheese Parfait

SERVES 2

Per Serving

Calories	353
Fat	11g
Sodium	464mg
Carbohydrates	45g
Fiber	10g
Sugar	14g
Protein	21g

When you need a satisfying snack, try a parfait made with cottage cheese! You will love adding frozen wild blueberries to cottage cheese for a protein-rich midday energy boost.

1⅓ cups low-fat cottage cheese

2 teaspoons ground cinnamon

1 cup frozen blueberries, thawed

1 cup shredded wheat cereal

4 tablespoons shredded unsweetened coconut

4 teaspoons chia seeds

1 In a small bowl, mix cottage cheese and cinnamon. Store in refrigerator up to 3 days until ready to assemble parfait.
2 When ready to serve, spoon ⅓ cup cottage cheese mixture into the bottom of a Mason jar or a wide glass. Top with ¼ cup blueberries followed by ¼ cup cereal, 1 tablespoon coconut, and 1 teaspoon chia seeds. Repeat layers with same amounts of ingredients.

Zucchini Sticks

Modeled after fried mozzarella, these yummy Zucchini Sticks are crisp and golden on the outside and tender inside. Pair with the Seasoned Turkey Burgers with Sautéed Mushrooms and Swiss from Chapter 7.

1 large egg white

1 tablespoon water

3 tablespoons salt-free bread crumbs

1 tablespoon grated Parmesan cheese

1 teaspoon salt-free Italian seasoning

½ teaspoon garlic powder

½ teaspoon onion powder

¼ teaspoon ground black pepper

⅛ teaspoon ground paprika

2 medium zucchini, trimmed and cut into long wedges

½ cup no-salt-added pasta sauce

1 Preheat oven to 450°F and adjust oven rack to middle position. Spray a baking sheet lightly with nonstick cooking spray and set aside.

2 Beat egg white and water in a small shallow bowl. Set aside. Place bread crumbs, Parmesan, Italian seasoning, garlic powder, onion powder, pepper, and paprika in a medium shallow bowl and whisk to combine.

3 Dip each piece of zucchini into egg white mixture, then roll in bread crumb mixture. Place on the prepared sheet. Place sheet on middle oven rack and bake 15 minutes.

4 Remove zucchini from oven. Allow to cool before storing in an airtight container in refrigerator up to 2 days. To reheat, place zucchini sticks in an air-fryer or convection toaster oven at 400°F for 8 minutes. While reheating zucchini, gently warm pasta sauce in a small saucepan over medium-low heat for 5 minutes. Pour into a small bowl and use to dip.

SERVES 6

Per Serving

Calories	39
Fat	0g
Sodium	34mg
Carbohydrates	7g
Fiber	2g
Sugar	3g
Protein	2g

FOR THE LOVE OF ZUCCHINI

Easy to grow and notoriously prolific, zucchini is a garden favorite. When planting, leave plenty of space for the specimens to spread. The leaves and vegetables may grow very large. Zucchini is best harvested when young and tender. The flowers of the plant are also edible.

Homemade Soft Pretzels

Per Serving

Calories	206
Fat	1g
Sodium	8mg
Carbohydrates	42g
Fiber	3g
Sugar	4g
Protein	7g

Delicious, hot-from-the-oven soft pretzels are easier to make than you'd think. After baking, spray them lightly with nonstick cooking spray or olive oil and sprinkle them with your choice of seasoning. Enjoy the pretzels plain or serve them with salt-free mustard.

4½ teaspoons active dry yeast

1½ cups warm water

2 tablespoons honey

3 cups unbleached all-purpose flour

1 cup white whole-wheat flour

1 large egg, beaten

1 Preheat oven to 425°F and adjust oven rack to middle position.

2 Place yeast in a large bowl. Add water, honey, and both flours and stir to combine. Turn dough out onto a lightly floured surface and knead 5 minutes.

3 Divide dough into 10 equal pieces. Roll each piece into a long snakelike tube, then twist to form a pretzel. Place pretzels on a large baking sheet and brush lightly with beaten egg.

4 Place sheet on middle oven rack and bake 15 minutes, until golden brown. Remove from oven and place pretzels on a wire rack to cool. Store in an airtight container at room temperature up to 2 days or in a freezer-safe bag in freezer up to 1 month. Thaw at room temperature.

Crunchy Coated Nuts

SERVES 8

Per Serving

Calories	227
Fat	17g
Sodium	12mg
Carbohydrates	14g
Fiber	3g
Sugar	5g
Protein	6g

HEALTHY HOMEMADE GIFTS

The most thoughtful gifts are often those you make yourself. Packaging unsalted nuts and other salt-free snacks in tins or glass containers is a tasty way of showing you care. Homemade salt-free seasonings and condiments are practical as well as delicious. When placed in a pretty jar or squeeze bottle, they're a delicious gift.

Slightly sweet, with a spicy kick from the cayenne, these crunchy nuts are the life of any party. If you prefer less heat, reduce the amount of cayenne pepper. This recipe is adapted from Food Network Kitchens Favorite Recipes.

1 large egg white

3 tablespoons packed light brown sugar

2 teaspoons dried oregano

¾ teaspoon ground coriander

½ teaspoon ground cumin

¼ teaspoon ground cayenne pepper

⅛ teaspoon ground cloves

2 cups unsalted mixed nuts

1 Preheat oven to 300°F and adjust oven rack to middle position. Line a rimmed baking sheet with parchment paper or foil.

2 Place egg white, sugar, oregano, coriander, cumin, cayenne, and cloves in a medium bowl and whisk until combined.

3 Add nuts and toss until evenly coated.

4 Arrange nuts in a single layer on the prepared sheet.

5 Place sheet on middle oven rack and bake 30 minutes. Halfway through baking time, remove sheet from the oven and stir nuts, then return to oven.

6 Remove sheet from oven and set on a wire rack to cool. Nuts will crisp as they dry and cool, so let them cool completely before removing from the sheet. Store in an airtight container at room temperature up to 5 days.

"Cheesy" Seasoned Popcorn

This seasoned popcorn will satisfy salty snack cravings anytime. Experiment with different herbs or try a sugar and spice blend.

2 tablespoons nutritional yeast flakes

1½ teaspoons dried dill

1 teaspoon dried parsley

¾ teaspoon garlic powder

¾ teaspoon onion powder

½ teaspoon ground paprika

¼ teaspoon dried thyme

¼ teaspoon ground black pepper

⅓ cup popcorn kernels

2 teaspoons extra-virgin olive oil

MAKES 10 CUPS	
Per Serving (1 cup)	
Calories	43
Fat	1g
Sodium	2mg
Carbohydrates	7g
Fiber	1g
Sugar	0g
Protein	2g

1 Combine nutritional yeast, dill, parsley, garlic powder, onion powder, paprika, thyme, and pepper in a small bowl and stir. Set aside.

2 Place popcorn kernels in an air popper. Place a large stockpot beneath the popcorn dispenser, turn on the popper, and wait until all kernels have popped. Turn off popper and set aside.

3 Drizzle oil over popcorn and toss to coat. Sprinkle with the nutritional yeast mixture and stir vigorously for several minutes, until completely coated.

4 Store in an airtight container at room temperature up to 2 days.

Seasoned Sesame Kale Chips

SERVES 4

Per Serving

Calories	36
Fat	1g
Sodium	162mg
Carbohydrates	6g
Fiber	4g
Sugar	1g
Protein	2g

WHAT IS KELP?

Kelp is a type of harvested salty-tasting seaweed. Kelp is low in sodium, fat, and calories; aids metabolism with its high concentration of iodine; and is a great source of vitamin K and folate. Kelp is sold in dried form, either alone or as part of a seasoning blend.

Light as air, crisp, and irresistible, these chips get their salty taste from low-sodium kelp seasoning. You can substitute another salt-free seasoning if you prefer.

1 bunch fresh kale

2½ teaspoons Bragg Organic Sea Kelp Delight Seasoning

2 teaspoons toasted sesame seeds

1 Preheat oven to 325°F and adjust oven rack to middle position. Lightly spray a baking sheet with nonstick cooking spray and set aside.

2 Wash kale and pat dry. Make sure kale is dried after washing, then remove leaves from tough stalks, cut or tear leaves into pieces, and arrange in a single layer on the prepared sheet (two batches may be needed if kale doesn't fit on one sheet).

3 Spray kale lightly with nonstick cooking spray and sprinkle with seasoning and sesame seeds.

4 Place sheet on middle oven rack and bake 12 minutes. Remove from oven and transfer chips to a sheet of wax paper or foil to cool. Repeat process with any remaining ingredients.

5 Store in an airtight container at room temperature up to 3 days.

Sweet Potato Crisps

Love sweet potato chips? This homemade version is so good, you may never settle for buying them from the grocery store again. They pair well with sandwiches, including the Mediterranean Turkey Burgers from Chapter 10. This recipe is adapted from Chowhound.com.

1 medium sweet potato, peeled

2 teaspoons olive oil

½ teaspoon ground paprika

1 Position two oven racks in the middle of the oven. Preheat oven to 350°F.

2 Slice sweet potato into paper-thin rounds using a mandoline or very sharp knife.

3 Place slices in a medium bowl, add oil and paprika, and toss to coat. Arrange slices in a single layer on two large baking sheets. Do not overlap.

4 Place sheets on middle two oven racks and bake 8 minutes. Switch the sheets' positions and bake another 7–8 minutes, until edges of slices begin to curl, and centers are golden brown and dry to the touch.

5 Remove sheets from oven and place on wire racks. Allow crisps to cool a few minutes before transferring to a bowl. Store in an airtight container at room temperature up to 3 days.

SERVES 2

Per Serving

Calories	92
Fat	5g
Sodium	20mg
Carbohydrates	12g
Fiber	2g
Sugar	4g
Protein	1g

Chewy Granola Bars

SERVES 8

Per Serving

Calories	235
Fat	10g
Sodium	38mg
Carbohydrates	33g
Fiber	3g
Sugar	19g
Protein	4g

DIFFERENCES IN OATS

Oats come in three main types. Quick or instant oats are precooked and dried. They cook quickly and are great for oatmeal or baked goods. Old-fashioned rolled oats are specially steamed to speed cooking and are all-purpose. Steel-cut oats are cut, not rolled. They have the longest cooking time but have a chewy texture that makes them good for oatmeal.

These soft and chewy granola bars make a healthy, less sweet alternative to their commercial counterparts. They're perfect for a quick energy boost or a go-to snack anytime. Kids will love them!

1¾ cups old-fashioned oats

½ cup pecan halves, finely chopped

½ cup dried cherries

3 tablespoons raw, unsalted pumpkin seeds

⅛ teaspoon salt

⅓ cup honey

2 tablespoons melted coconut oil

½ teaspoon vanilla extract

½ teaspoon ground cinnamon

¼ teaspoon ground cardamom

1 Line an 8" × 8" baking pan with parchment paper, allowing some paper to hang over the sides so it can easily be pulled out later. Set aside.

2 Place oats, pecans, cherries, pumpkin seeds, and salt in a large bowl and whisk to combine.

3 In a small bowl, whisk together honey, oil, vanilla, cinnamon, and cardamom. Pour liquid mixture over dry mixture and use a spoon to mix well to coat all the ingredients.

4 Pour mixture into the prepared pan. Using the flat bottom of a measuring cup or spatula sprayed with nonstick cooking spray, flatten granola into pan, pressing hard to make it compact. Place pan in refrigerator to chill at least 2 hours.

5 Preheat oven to 350°F. Place pan in oven and bake 25 minutes or until bars are golden brown around the edges. Remove from oven and place on a wire rack to cool about 5 minutes. Remove parchment paper from pan by lifting the sides and place on wire rack to cool completely. Place on cutting board and cut into 8 equal-sized bars. Store in an airtight container at room temperature up to 7 days, or wrap individually and freeze up to 3 months. Thaw overnight in refrigerator or at room temperature.

Whole-Grain Crackers with Rosemary, Garlic, and Parmesan

These crisp crackers make super snacks. Partner them with soup, sliced Swiss cheese, and crunchy grapes for a wonderful light meal.

1⅔ cups white whole-wheat flour

½ teaspoon sodium-free baking powder

1 tablespoon salt-free all-purpose seasoning

1 teaspoon ground rosemary

1 teaspoon garlic powder

½ cup low-fat milk

¼ cup grated Parmesan cheese

3 tablespoons olive oil

1 large egg white

1–2 tablespoons water (if needed)

1 Preheat oven to 400°F and adjust oven rack to middle position. Spray a baking sheet lightly with nonstick cooking spray and set aside.

2 Place flour, baking powder, seasoning, rosemary, and garlic powder in a medium bowl and whisk to combine.

3 Add milk, Parmesan, oil, and egg white and stir to make a stiff dough. Add water as needed if dough is too dry.

4 Turn dough out onto a lightly floured surface and knead several minutes, until dough is smooth and intact. Roll out to about ⅛" thick.

5 Cut into 1½" squares and transfer to the prepared sheet.

6 Place sheet on middle oven rack and bake 10 minutes. Remove from oven and transfer crackers to a wire rack to cool. Store in an airtight container at room temperature up to 7 days.

MAKES 6½ DOZEN

Per Serving (6 crackers)	
Calories	99
Fat	4g
Sodium	43mg
Carbohydrates	12g
Fiber	2g
Sugar	0g
Protein	3g

PARMESAN CHEESE

Parmesan cheese can add a lot of flavor, but it can also add unwanted fat and sodium. When selecting a cheese, check nutrition facts carefully.

Roasted Red Pepper Hummus

Flavored by succulent roasted red pepper, this colorful dip is great with chips or vegetables and makes a wonderful low-sodium sandwich spread.

1 (15-ounce) can no-salt-added chickpeas, drained and rinsed

⅓ cup jarred roasted red peppers

2 cloves garlic, peeled

2 tablespoons lemon juice

2 tablespoons tahini

1 Place all ingredients in a food processor and pulse until smooth.
2 Transfer to a small bowl, then cover and refrigerate until serving. Keeps for 4 days in the refrigerator.

MAKES 1½ CUPS

**Per Serving
(2 tablespoons)**

Calories	52
Fat	1g
Sodium	69mg
Carbohydrates	8g
Fiber	2g
Sugar	0g
Protein	2g

Holy Guacamole

MAKES 1 CUP

**Per Serving
(2 tablespoons)**

Calories	32
Fat	2g
Sodium	2mg
Carbohydrates	3g
Fiber	2g
Sugar	0g
Protein	1g

AVOCADO FACTS

Avocados are a fruit native to South and Central America. Ripe avocados have a leathery skin that yields gently to pressure. Prepare a ripe avocado by cutting it lengthwise to the core, gently breaking it open, removing the pit, and peeling off the skin. Avocados are high in vitamins B_6, C, E, and K and may help prevent prostate cancer.

Vibrant in color and flavor, this simple dip makes any meal more special. Serve it with everything from chips to tacos to rice and beans. You'll love the water trick to keep guac fresh!

1 large avocado, peeled, pitted, and diced

1 small tomato, chopped

2 tablespoons lime juice

2 cloves garlic, peeled and minced

1 tablespoon chopped fresh cilantro

½ teaspoon ground cumin

⅛ teaspoon ground cayenne pepper

1 Place avocado in a deep bowl and mash with a fork, as smoothly or coarsely as desired. Stir in all remaining ingredients.

2 Place guacamole in a bowl with a tight-fitting lid. Using a spoon, press guacamole down to remove any air bubbles. Slowly add lukewarm water over top of guacamole, ensuring that the water covers the entire surface and reaches about ½" up the sides of the bowl. Cover the bowl with a lid and store in refrigerator up to 3 days. When ready to serve, remove lid, gently pour out water, and stir guacamole.

Garlic Lovers' Hummus

Hummus is the ultimate vegetarian dip and sandwich filling. This version calls for tahini, a smooth sesame butter sold in many supermarkets. If you can't find it, try substituting low-sodium vegetable broth. For a milder flavor, reduce the amount of garlic.

1 (15-ounce) can no-salt-added chickpeas, drained and rinsed

3 tablespoons tahini

3 tablespoons lemon juice

2 tablespoons extra-virgin olive oil

4 cloves garlic, peeled

1 Place all ingredients in a food processor and pulse until smooth.
2 Transfer to a small bowl, then cover and refrigerate at least 1 hour before serving. Store in an airtight container in refrigerator up to 4 days.

MAKES 1½ CUPS	
Per Serving **(2 tablespoons)**	
Calories	78
Fat	4g
Sodium	17mg
Carbohydrates	8g
Fiber	2g
Sugar	0g
Protein	2g

Pineapple Salsa

Ripe fresh fruits make delicious salsas, and juicy pineapple is among the best options. Add an extra jalapeño or two for fire. Pair this salsa with the Black Bean Burgers from Chapter 9 or serve with some tortilla chips.

½ medium pineapple, peeled, cored, and finely diced

1 small jalapeño pepper, seeded and minced

1 small red bell pepper, seeded and diced

3 cloves garlic, peeled and minced

2 tablespoons lime juice

¼ cup chopped fresh cilantro

1 Place all ingredients in a medium bowl and stir to combine.
2 Cover and refrigerate until ready to serve. Use within 3 days.

MAKES 3 CUPS	
Per Serving **(2 tablespoons)**	
Calories	11
Fat	0g
Sodium	0mg
Carbohydrates	3g
Fiber	0g
Sugar	2g
Protein	0g

Roasted Tomato Salsa

MAKES 2 CUPS

**Per Serving
(2 tablespoons)**

Calories	13
Fat	0g
Sodium	2mg
Carbohydrates	3g
Fiber	1g
Sugar	2g
Protein	1g

This delicious, flavorful salsa with roasted tomato, bell pepper, and onion is fairly mild; to increase the heat, leave the jalapeño seeds in or add more hot peppers.

5 medium tomatoes, halved

1 medium green bell pepper, halved and seeded

1 medium onion, peeled, trimmed, and halved

3 cloves garlic, peeled and minced

1 small jalapeño pepper, seeded and minced

1 tablespoon chopped fresh cilantro

3 tablespoons apple cider vinegar

1 teaspoon ground cumin

⅛ teaspoon liquid smoke

1 Preheat oven to 450°F and adjust oven rack to middle position. Spray a baking sheet lightly with nonstick cooking spray.
2 Place tomatoes, bell pepper, and onion (cut sides down) on the prepared sheet. Place sheet on middle oven rack and roast 15 minutes.
3 Remove sheet from oven and let rest until cool enough to touch. Gently peel skins from tomatoes and bell pepper. Lift tomatoes from sheet (they will be very soft) and gently squeeze out and discard seeds. Transfer tomato pulp to a medium bowl.
4 Chop roasted bell pepper and onion and add to bowl.
5 Add garlic, jalapeño, cilantro, vinegar, cumin, and liquid smoke to the bowl and stir to combine.
6 Cover and refrigerate until ready to serve. Use within 3 days.

CHAPTER 12

Desserts

Zucchini Oatmeal Cookies. 230

Coconut Chia Pudding. 231

Lemon White Chocolate Popcorn 232

Cinnamon Peanut Butter Cookies 233

Vegan Lemon Drops. 234

Cinnamon Apple Pear Sauce. 236

Roasted Plantain Boats 237

Banana Walnut Scones 238

Gingersnaps 240

Carrot Cake Cookies. 241

Coconut Chocolate Chip Blondies 243

Mini Cornmeal Rhubarb Crisps 244

Mango Crumble 245

Vegan Chocolate Cupcakes. 246

Pound Cake Minis 247

Jumbo Pumpkin Chocolate Chip Muffins 248

Crumb-Topped Mango Muffins 249

Peach Cobbler. 250

Lemon Coconut Scones. 252

Zucchini Oatmeal Cookies

MAKES 18

Per Serving (2 cookies)

Calories	140
Fat	2g
Sodium	210mg
Carbohydrates	26g
Fiber	3g
Sugar	8g
Protein	5g

PUMPKIN SEEDS

Pumpkin seeds are high in fiber, healthy fats, and magnesium. Be sure to purchase shelled pumpkin seeds so they're ready to use! They add a nice crunch to these tender cookies, but you can substitute sunflower seeds for pumpkin seeds if you prefer.

When summer hits and zucchini is in season, make these cookies as a unique option for breakfast. That's right—your inner child will rejoice with dessert for breakfast. They're soft, satisfying, and not too sweet.

1¼ cups whole-wheat flour

1 cup quick-cooking oats

2 tablespoons unsalted shelled pumpkin seeds

½ teaspoon baking soda

½ teaspoon salt

½ teaspoon ground cinnamon

1 cup shredded zucchini

½ cup unsweetened applesauce

1 large egg

¼ cup packed brown sugar

½ teaspoon vanilla extract

1 Preheat oven to 375°F. Line a baking sheet with parchment paper.

2 In a large bowl, combine flour, oats, pumpkin seeds, baking soda, salt, and cinnamon. Mix until combined, then make a well in the center. Set aside.

3 In a medium bowl, mix zucchini, applesauce, egg, sugar, and vanilla. Pour liquid mixture into dry mixture and stir until combined.

4 Using a ¼-cup measuring cup, scoop mixture onto the prepared sheet. Bake 12–14 minutes until golden and an inserted toothpick comes out clean. Remove cookies from sheet and allow to cool on a wire rack before storing in an airtight container at room temperature up to 3 days.

Coconut Chia Pudding

This easy pudding is a perfect healthy breakfast or snack! It tastes like a dessert but is full of protein and fiber from the chia seeds. The shredded coconut and unsalted pistachios are optional.

¼ cup chia seeds

16 ounces canned coconut milk

1 tablespoon agave nectar

¼ teaspoon ground cardamom

½ tablespoon shredded sweetened coconut

1 tablespoon chopped unsalted shelled pistachios

⅓ cup blueberries

1   In a small bowl, combine chia seeds, coconut milk, agave nectar, and cardamom. Mix well. Pour into an airtight container and refrigerate at least 8 hours, stirring well after 4 hours. Store chia pudding in an airtight container in refrigerator up to 2 days.

2   When ready to serve, toast coconut and pistachios in a small skillet over medium-low heat 5 minutes. Place ½ cup chia pudding in a bowl and top with coconut, pistachios, and blueberries.

SERVES 3

Per Serving

Calories	398
Fat	35g
Sodium	23mg
Carbohydrates	17g
Fiber	5g
Sugar	5g
Protein	6g

TASTY TOPPINGS

The sky's the limit when it comes to topping this chia seed pudding! Try fresh mango, pineapple, and toasted coconut for a tropical twist, or chopped strawberries, hazelnuts, and cacao nibs for a chocolaty treat!

Lemon White Chocolate Popcorn

SERVES 4

Per Serving	
Calories	280
Fat	17g
Sodium	303mg
Carbohydrates	30g
Fiber	2g
Sugar	19g
Protein	3g

When you need to satisfy a sweet tooth, this Lemon White Chocolate Popcorn will hit the spot! It will last up to 3 days, so you'll have an easy sweet treat on hand when the craving strikes.

1 (3-ounce) bag lightly salted microwave popcorn

¾ cup white chocolate chips

¼ teaspoon canola oil

1 tablespoon grated lemon zest

1 Pop microwave popcorn according to package directions. Place popcorn into a large mixing bowl, removing any unpopped kernels.

2 Place white chocolate chips in a small microwave-safe bowl and microwave 25–30 seconds at a time, stirring in between. Be careful to not overheat chocolate. Stir in oil, mixing well.

3 Pour one-third of melted chocolate over popcorn and mix. Repeat this two more times until all chocolate is used.

4 Once popcorn is coated, pour onto a large baking sheet. Sprinkle lemon zest over popcorn, distributing evenly.

5 Spread popcorn out into a single layer and allow to dry about 2 hours. Store in an airtight container at room temperature up to 3 days.

Cinnamon Peanut Butter Cookies

This vegan version of peanut butter cookies is a melt-in-your-mouth experience! Applesauce is used in place of butter or egg to help the cookie dough bind together.

1 cup low-sodium natural creamy peanut butter

¼ cup applesauce

⅓ cup white whole-wheat flour

¼ cup packed brown sugar

1 teaspoon baking soda

½ teaspoon ground cinnamon

¼ teaspoon salt

1 Preheat oven to 350°F and adjust oven rack to middle position. Line a baking sheet with parchment paper.

2 In a medium bowl, combine peanut butter and applesauce until smooth.

3 In a small bowl, mix flour, sugar, baking soda, cinnamon, and salt. Combine until no more lumps of sugar remain. Pour dry ingredients into peanut butter–applesauce mixture. Mix well. Refrigerate dough 30 minutes.

4 Using a tablespoon measure, spoon out dough and roll between your hands to form balls. Place dough balls on the prepared sheet, leaving an inch between them. Use a fork to make a crisscross pattern and to flatten each dough ball.

5 Place sheet on middle oven rack and bake 8 minutes. Remove sheet from oven and allow cookies to cool 2 minutes on sheet before transferring to a wire rack to cool completely. Store in an airtight container at room temperature up to 5 days.

SERVES 8

Per Serving

Calories	236
Fat	15g
Sodium	296mg
Carbohydrates	18g
Fiber	3g
Sugar	10g
Protein	8g

WHY WHITE WHOLE-WHEAT FLOUR?

White whole wheat is a type of wheat, and it's 100 percent whole wheat, which means it's a whole grain! It's packed with fiber, mild in flavor, and light in color. You can often sub in white whole-wheat flour for all-purpose flour, except in cakes and some breads.

Vegan Lemon Drops

SERVES 36

Per Serving

Calories	80
Fat	4g
Sodium	0mg
Carbohydrates	10g
Fiber	0g
Sugar	3g
Protein	1g

VEGAN WHITE CHOCOLATE

Vegan white chocolate chips are sold at some supermarkets and natural food stores, as well as online. Although they may be more difficult to find, they're worth the effort. In addition to their sweet, creamy taste, some white vegan chips aren't just low in sodium—they're sodium-free!

These vegan cookies pack a huge puckery punch that's softened by the sweetness of white chocolate chips. For another great taste, swap the lemon juice and zest for lime.

1¼ cups unbleached all-purpose flour

¾ cup white whole-wheat flour

⅓ cup canola oil

⅓ cup 100 percent grade A maple syrup

3 tablespoons lemon juice

1 tablespoon grated lemon zest

¾ cup vegan white chocolate chips

1 Preheat oven to 375°F and adjust oven rack to middle position. Take out two baking sheets and set aside.

2 Place both flours, oil, maple syrup, lemon juice, and zest in a large bowl and stir to combine. Mixture will be quite dry and crumbly. Stir in white chocolate chips.

3 Scoop dough ½ tablespoon at a time and shape into cookies. Place cookies on the baking sheets and bake on middle oven rack 10 minutes.

4 Remove from oven and transfer cookies to a wire rack to cool. Store cookies in an airtight container at room temperature up to 5 days.

Cinnamon Apple Pear Sauce

SERVES 6	
Per Serving	
Calories	92
Fat	0g
Sodium	2mg
Carbohydrates	24g
Fiber	2g
Sugar	20g
Protein	0g

If you like a sweet and tart applesauce, this recipe is for you. Braeburn apples or Pink Lady apples, also sometimes referred to as Cripps Pink, have a great sweet-tart taste that makes them good options for this recipe. The pear adds a unique texture.

3 medium Pink Lady apples, peeled, cored, and diced
1 medium Bartlett pear, cored and diced
¾ cup water
¼ cup packed light brown sugar
1 teaspoon ground cinnamon

1 Combine all ingredients in a large saucepan. Bring to a boil over medium heat, then reduce heat to low, cover, and cook 20 minutes.
2 Remove saucepan from stovetop. Using an immersion blender or a food processor, blend to the desired consistency, chunky or smooth. If using a food processor, use caution when removing the lid because the contents will be hot.
3 Store in an airtight container in refrigerator up to 7 days. Serve warm or cold.

Roasted Plantain Boats

A simple yet fun and unusual treat you can be creative with! These Roasted Plantain Boats are filled with Greek yogurt, shredded coconut, and pistachios for a satisfyingly sweet and healthy way to either begin or end your day.

2 medium ripe plantains, peels removed

½ teaspoon melted coconut oil

¼ cup low-fat vanilla Greek yogurt

¼ cup shredded unsweetened coconut

2 tablespoons unsalted shelled pistachios

1 Preheat oven to 400°F. Line a baking sheet with parchment paper and place plantains on sheet.

2 Drizzle oil over plantains. Place in oven and bake 15 minutes. Remove from oven and flip plantains, then return to oven and bake another 10 minutes.

3 Remove pan from oven and allow plantains to cool 10 minutes. Set plantains up so you can cut them open down the middle (do not cut all the way through). Do not add toppings until ready to serve. Store cooked plantains in an airtight container in refrigerator up to 3 days.

4 To reheat, place a plantain on a microwave-safe plate and microwave 30–45 seconds. Gently spread plantains open and top with yogurt, coconut, and pistachios.

SERVES 2

Per Serving

Calories	359
Fat	9g
Sodium	49mg
Carbohydrates	69g
Fiber	5g
Sugar	36g
Protein	6g

TOPPING OPTIONS

These plantain boats would be delicious topped with cacao nibs, cinnamon, nut butter such as almond butter, or seeds such as chia seeds or sunflower kernels for a nutrient boost.

Banana Walnut Scones

SERVES 8

Per Serving

Calories	397
Fat	20g
Sodium	148mg
Carbohydrates	50g
Fiber	5g
Sugar	20g
Protein	7g

These slightly sweet and nutty scones are a great make-ahead option that can be eaten for dessert or breakfast. They pair well with a cup of black coffee or tea!

2 medium ripe bananas, peeled

¼ cup 100 percent grade A maple syrup

¼ cup low-fat plain Greek yogurt

½ cup walnut halves

1 cup all-purpose flour

1 cup whole-wheat flour

⅓ cup plus 1 tablespoon granulated sugar, divided

1¾ teaspoons ground cinnamon, divided

1 teaspoon sodium-free baking powder

½ teaspoon salt

4 tablespoons unsalted butter, cold and cut into small cubes

½ cup finely chopped walnuts, divided

1 Preheat oven to 350°F. Line a baking sheet with parchment paper and lightly dust with flour.

2 In a small bowl, mash bananas with a fork. Add maple syrup and yogurt. Mix well and set aside.

3 In a food processor, pulse walnut halves until finely ground. Pour into a large bowl and add both flours. Mix together and add ⅓ cup sugar, 1½ teaspoons cinnamon, baking powder, and salt. Mix well.

4 Add butter to flour mixture, then, using a pastry cutter or your hands, cut in butter until mixture starts to resemble coarse crumbs. Add 6 tablespoons chopped walnuts to flour mixture and stir in liquid mixture until just combined, being careful not to overmix dough. Form dough into a 9" circle about 1" thick on the prepared baking sheet. Place baking sheet in the freezer for 20 minutes.

5 Remove sheet from freezer and cut dough into 8 equal triangles. Top with the following remaining ingredients: 1 tablespoon sugar, ¼ teaspoon cinnamon, and 2 tablespoons chopped walnuts. Separate pieces from one another before baking 20–22 minutes, until scones are golden in color and an inserted toothpick comes out clean.

6 Allow scones to sit 5 minutes on sheet before placing on a wire rack to cool completely. Store in an airtight container at room temperature up to 4 days.

Gingersnaps

SERVES 18

Per Serving

Calories	81
Fat	3g
Sodium	5mg
Carbohydrates	14g
Fiber	0g
Sugar	8g
Protein	1g

COOKIE BAKING TIP

Never place cookie dough on a hot baking sheet; the cookies will precook before reaching the oven and end up overly dark. For perfect results, use multiple baking sheets. Measure the dough onto a cool baking sheet, bake, then move the cookies to a wire rack. Use a second baking sheet while allowing the hot sheet to cool.

Fans of classic gingersnaps will love these dark, aromatic cookies with a crisp bite. And they're not just low in sodium; they're low in fat too!

4 tablespoons unsalted butter

½ cup packed light brown sugar

2 tablespoons molasses

1 large egg white

2½ teaspoons ground ginger

¼ teaspoon ground allspice

1 teaspoon sodium-free baking soda

½ cup white whole-wheat flour

½ cup unbleached all-purpose flour

1 tablespoon demerara sugar

1 Preheat oven to 375°F and adjust oven rack to middle position. Line a large baking sheet with parchment paper and set aside.

2 Beat together butter, brown sugar, and molasses in a large bowl using an electric mixer on medium speed. Add egg white, ginger, and allspice and mix well. Stir in baking soda, then gradually add both flours. Beat until combined, scraping down the sides of the bowl as necessary.

3 Scoop dough by tablespoonfuls and roll into small balls. Place balls on the prepared sheet and press down using a glass dipped in demerara sugar.

4 Place sheet on middle oven rack and bake 10 minutes.

5 Remove from oven and transfer cookies to a wire rack to cool. Store in an airtight container at room temperature up to 5 days.

Carrot Cake Cookies

These soft whole-grain cookies have the taste and texture of carrot cake! To make the oat flour, measure rolled oats into a food processor and pulse until fine.

3 medium carrots, peeled and shredded

1½ cups unbleached all-purpose flour

¾ cup oat flour

¾ cup packed light brown sugar

1 large egg white

⅓ cup canola oil

1 tablespoon vanilla extract

1 teaspoon sodium-free baking powder

1½ teaspoons ground cinnamon

½ teaspoon ground nutmeg

¼ teaspoon ground ginger

⅛ teaspoon ground cloves

1 Preheat oven to 375°F and adjust oven rack to middle position. Line two large baking sheets with parchment paper and set aside.

2 Place all ingredients in a large bowl and stir to combine. Dough will be quite sticky.

3 Drop by tablespoonfuls onto the prepared sheets. Place one sheet on middle oven rack and bake 12 minutes.

4 Remove from oven and transfer cookies to a wire rack to cool. Repeat with the remaining sheet. Store in an airtight container at room temperature up to 4 days.

SERVES 36

Per Serving

Calories	68
Fat	2g
Sodium	9mg
Carbohydrates	11g
Fiber	1g
Sugar	5g
Protein	1g

ICE CREAM SCOOPS MAKE PERFECT COOKIES!

Instead of fumbling with tablespoons, scoop out cookie dough using a small retractable ice cream scoop. Ice cream scoops produce uniform, picture-perfect cookies and reduce hassle and mess. Small scoops are sold at kitchenware shops and other stores as well as online.

Coconut Chocolate Chip Blondies

Use dark, semisweet, or milk chocolate chips in these irresistibly delicious cookie bars. Add chopped almonds, too, if you like some crunch in your blondies.

5 tablespoons unsalted butter, softened

⅔ cup packed light brown sugar

2 large egg whites

2 teaspoons vanilla extract

½ teaspoon sodium-free baking powder

¾ cup white whole-wheat flour

½ cup unbleached all-purpose flour

¼ cup unsweetened shredded coconut

½ cup semisweet chocolate chips

SERVES 16	
Per Serving	
Calories	140
Fat	6g
Sodium	10mg
Carbohydrates	20g
Fiber	1g
Sugar	12g
Protein	2g

1 Preheat oven to 350°F and adjust oven rack to middle position. Grease and flour an 8" × 8" baking pan and set aside.

2 Place butter and sugar in a large bowl and beat using an electric mixer on medium speed to combine. Stir in egg whites and vanilla. Add baking powder and mix.

3 Gradually add both flours and coconut, then fold in chocolate chips.

4 Transfer batter to the prepared pan and smooth the top. Place on middle oven rack and bake 30 minutes.

5 Remove from oven and place pan on a wire rack to cool completely before cutting into 16 squares. Store in an airtight container at room temperature up to 5 days.

Mini Cornmeal Rhubarb Crisps

SERVES 4

Per Serving

Calories	189
Fat	7g
Sodium	9mg
Carbohydrates	32g
Fiber	3g
Sugar	21g
Protein	2g

RHUBARB FACTS

Rhubarb is an easy-to-grow perennial vegetable with poisonous green leaves and edible pink or red stalks. Rhubarb has a very tart flavor that can be offset by sugar, so it's often used in baked goods and desserts. Rhubarb's high acidity reacts badly with some metal cookware, so cook or bake rhubarb in stainless steel or nonstick pans whenever possible.

With soft lemon-flavored fruit blanketed by a crunchy, sweet cornmeal crust, these little crisps make a sensational spring dessert for company.

3 cups sliced fresh rhubarb

3 tablespoons granulated sugar

2 tablespoons lemon juice

¼ cup cornmeal

1 tablespoon grated lemon zest

3 tablespoons packed light brown sugar

2 tablespoons old-fashioned rolled oats

2 tablespoons nonhydrogenated vegetable shortening

1 Preheat oven to 375°F and adjust oven rack to middle position.

2 Place rhubarb, granulated sugar, and lemon juice in a large bowl and toss to coat. Divide mixture evenly among four (4") ramekins.

3 Place cornmeal, lemon zest, brown sugar, and oats in a medium bowl and whisk to combine. Add shortening and work it into the mixture using your fingers. When a sturdy crumb has been achieved, sprinkle mixture over rhubarb, dividing evenly.

4 Place ramekins on middle oven rack and bake 20 minutes. Remove from oven and set aside to cool a few minutes.

5 Store in an airtight container in refrigerator up to 4 days. To reheat, microwave 25–30 seconds (make sure ramekins are microwave-safe). Serve warm.

Mango Crumble

Sink your teeth into tender chunks of mango with a cinnamon-scented crust. For a juicier filling, omit the cornstarch.

2 medium barely ripe mangoes, peeled, pitted, and cut into 1" chunks

2 tablespoons packed light brown sugar

1 tablespoon cornstarch

1½ teaspoons minced fresh ginger

½ cup unbleached all-purpose flour

½ cup white whole-wheat flour

½ cup granulated sugar

1 teaspoon ground cinnamon

¼ teaspoon ground ginger

3 tablespoons unsalted butter

1 Preheat oven to 350°F and adjust oven rack to middle position.

2 Place mangoes, brown sugar, cornstarch, and minced ginger in a medium bowl and toss to coat. Pour mixture into an 8" square baking dish and spread evenly.

3 In another medium bowl, whisk together both flours, granulated sugar, cinnamon, and ground ginger.

4 Cut butter into small pieces and add to the bowl. Using your fingers, work butter into the mixture until it resembles damp sand and sticks together when squeezed. Sprinkle mixture evenly over the fruit.

5 Place pan on middle oven rack and bake 25–30 minutes, until tender. Remove from oven and place on a wire rack to cool. Store in an airtight container at room temperature up to 3 days. Crumble can be served warm or cool. To reheat, place in a microwave-safe dish and microwave 25–30 seconds.

SERVES 8

Per Serving	
Calories	210
Fat	5g
Sodium	2mg
Carbohydrates	41g
Fiber	3g
Sugar	27g
Protein	3g

Vegan Chocolate Cupcakes

SERVES 16

Per Serving

Calories	119
Fat	2g
Sodium	3mg
Carbohydrates	25g
Fiber	2g
Sugar	14g
Protein	2g

These vegan, whole-grain cupcakes are low in fat and sodium, so you can indulge in moist, dense, chocolate-laden pleasure without the extra calories!

1⅔ cups white whole-wheat flour

¾ cup packed light brown sugar

¼ cup unsweetened cocoa powder

2 teaspoons sodium-free baking soda

1 cup water

½ cup unsweetened applesauce

1 teaspoon vanilla extract

½ cup vegan semisweet chocolate chips

1 Preheat oven to 350°F and adjust oven rack to middle position. Line sixteen cups in two twelve-cup muffin tins with paper liners, or spray with nonstick cooking spray, and set aside.

2 Place flour, sugar, cocoa, and baking soda in a large bowl and whisk together. Add water, applesauce, and vanilla and stir until combined.

3 Spoon batter into the prepared muffin cups, filling each one roughly two-thirds full. Sprinkle chocolate chips evenly over batter.

4 Place muffin tins on middle oven rack and bake 20 minutes. Remove from oven and place on a wire rack to cool for 10 minutes. Then remove cupcakes from muffin tins and cool completely on wire rack. Store in an airtight container at room temperature up to 3 days.

Pound Cake Minis

Save these rich little cakes for a seriously special occasion.
Although healthier than classic pound cake, they're still decadent.

½ cup unsalted butter

¼ cup nonhydrogenated vegetable shortening

1 cup granulated sugar

2 large egg whites

2 teaspoons vanilla extract

¼ teaspoon almond extract

½ teaspoon sodium-free baking powder

1¼ cups unbleached all-purpose flour

½ cup low-fat milk

SERVES 18

Per Serving	
Calories	151
Fat	8g
Sodium	10mg
Carbohydrates	18g
Fiber	0g
Sugar	11g
Protein	2g

1 Preheat oven to 350°F and adjust oven rack to middle position. Line eighteen cups in two twelve-cup muffin tins with paper liners, or spray with nonstick cooking spray, and set aside.

2 Place butter and shortening in a large bowl. Add sugar and beat with an electric mixer on medium speed until fluffy. Beat in egg whites and extracts. Stir in baking powder. Gradually add flour, alternating with small additions of milk, and stir until combined.

3 Spoon batter into the prepared muffin cups, filling each one roughly two-thirds full. Place muffin tins on middle oven rack and bake 20 minutes.

4 Remove from oven and place pan on a wire rack to cool for 10 minutes. Then remove pound cakes from muffin tins and cool completely on wire rack. Store in an airtight container at room temperature up to 3 days.

Jumbo Pumpkin Chocolate Chip Muffins

SERVES 6	
Per Serving	
Calories	280
Fat	8g
Sodium	21mg
Carbohydrates	49g
Fiber	4g
Sugar	31g
Protein	4g

Moist, dense, and pumpkin-rich, these jumbo muffins are a meal in themselves. Substitute chopped nuts or dried fruit for the chocolate chips if you like.

1 cup pumpkin purée

⅔ cup packed light brown sugar

1 large egg white

2 tablespoons canola oil

1 teaspoon vanilla extract

1 tablespoon sodium-free baking powder

½ teaspoon ground cinnamon

1 cup white whole-wheat flour

2 tablespoons low-fat milk

⅓ cup semisweet chocolate chips

1 Preheat oven to 400°F and adjust oven rack to middle position. Line a six-cup muffin tin with paper liners or spray with nonstick cooking spray. Set aside.

2 Place pumpkin purée, sugar, egg white, oil, and vanilla in a large bowl and stir to combine. Add all remaining ingredients and mix until incorporated.

3 Spoon the batter into the prepared muffin cups, filling each one about two-thirds full. Place muffin tin on middle oven rack and bake 20–25 minutes.

4 Remove from oven and transfer muffins to a wire rack to cool. Store in an airtight container at room temperature up to 4 days. If freezing, store muffins in a freezer-safe resealable bag up to 3 months.

Crumb-Topped Mango Muffins

Let these tropical muffins remind you that paradise isn't just a state of mind. These soft vanilla-lemon muffins are dotted with juicy chunks of mango, and the tops are complemented by the sweet crunch of macadamia nut crumbs.

¼ cup packed light brown sugar

¼ cup finely chopped unsalted macadamia nuts

1½ tablespoons plus 1½ cups unbleached all-purpose flour, divided

½ teaspoon ground cinnamon

1 tablespoon unsalted butter

½ cup white whole-wheat flour

1 tablespoon sodium-free baking powder

½ cup granulated sugar

1 large egg white

1 cup low-fat milk

3 tablespoons canola oil

1 teaspoon vanilla extract

1 tablespoon grated lemon zest

1 medium mango, peeled, pitted, and finely diced

SERVES 6

Per Serving

Calories	434
Fat	14g
Sodium	34mg
Carbohydrates	70g
Fiber	3g
Sugar	34g
Protein	8g

1 Preheat oven to 400°F and adjust oven rack to middle position. Line a six-cup muffin tin with paper liners or spray with nonstick cooking spray. Set aside.

2 Combine brown sugar, nuts, 1½ tablespoons all-purpose flour, and cinnamon in a small bowl. Cut the butter in with your fingertips, processing until mixture has the consistency of wet sand. Set aside.

3 Place remaining 1½ cups all-purpose flour, whole-wheat flour, baking powder, and granulated sugar in a large bowl and whisk to combine. Add egg white, milk, oil, vanilla, and lemon zest and stir just until moist. Gently fold in mango.

4 Spoon batter into the prepared muffin cups, filling each one about three-quarters full, then top with crumb mixture, dividing evenly among the cups (about 2 tablespoons each).

5 Place muffin tin on middle oven rack and bake 25–30 minutes. Remove from oven and gently transfer muffins to a wire rack to cool completely. Store in an airtight container at room temperature up to 3 days. If freezing, store muffins in a freezer-safe resealable bag up to 3 months.

Peach Cobbler

SERVES 8

Per Serving

Calories	291
Fat	6g
Sodium	16mg
Carbohydrates	54g
Fiber	3g
Sugar	31g
Protein	5g

This version of the classic dessert with heart-healthy whole grain and ripe, juicy fruit can be topped with whipped cream or nonfat frozen yogurt.

6 medium peaches, peeled, pitted, and sliced

3 tablespoons ⅔ cup plus granulated sugar, divided

3 tablespoons lemon juice

1¼ cups unbleached all-purpose flour

½ cup white whole-wheat flour

1 teaspoon sodium-free baking powder

4 tablespoons unsalted butter, melted and cooled

1 large egg white

½ cup low-fat milk

1 tablespoon vanilla extract

1 Preheat oven to 400°F and adjust oven rack to middle position.
2 Place peaches, 3 tablespoons sugar, and lemon juice in a medium bowl and toss to coat peaches. Transfer to a 9" × 13" baking dish. Set aside.
3 Place both flours, remaining ⅔ cup sugar, and baking powder in a large bowl and whisk to combine. Add butter, egg white, milk, and vanilla and stir to combine. Batter will be thick. Spoon batter over peaches.
4 Place dish on middle oven rack and bake 30 minutes. Remove dish from oven and place on a wire rack to cool.
5 Cover dish with plastic wrap or aluminum foil and store in refrigerator up to 3 days. Cobbler can be served warm or cool. To reheat, place in a microwave-safe dish and microwave 30–45 seconds.

Lemon Coconut Scones

SERVES 8

Per Serving

Calories	254
Fat	8g
Sodium	2mg
Carbohydrates	41g
Fiber	1g
Sugar	17g
Protein	3g

Light and sweet, these lovely lemon-scented scones are made for an afternoon tea, book club meeting, or fancy brunch party.

2 cups unbleached all-purpose flour

⅔ cup granulated sugar

1 tablespoon sodium-free baking powder

5 tablespoons unsalted butter

5 ounces light coconut milk

3 tablespoons lemon juice

1 tablespoon grated lemon zest

1 Preheat oven to 425°F and adjust oven rack to middle position. Line a baking sheet with parchment paper and set aside.

2 Place flour, sugar, and baking powder in a large bowl and whisk to combine. Add butter and, using a pastry cutter or your hands, cut in butter until mixture resembles coarse crumbs. Stir in coconut milk, lemon juice, and lemon zest.

3 Turn dough out onto a lightly floured surface and pat into a 9" round. Using a long, sharp knife, cut dough into 8 equal wedges. Transfer wedges to the prepared sheet.

4 Place sheet on middle oven rack and bake 12 minutes. Remove from oven and transfer scones to a wire rack to cool. Store in an airtight container at room temperature up to 4 days. If freezing, store in a freezer-safe resealable bag up to 3 months.

CHAPTER 13

Beverages/Smoothies

Chocolate Strawberry Power Smoothie 254

Thin Mint Cocoa 254

Chocolate Banana Smoothie 255

Almond Butter Jelly Smoothie 255

Mango Coconut Water Slush 256

Watermelon Refresher 256

Mango Mint Smoothie 257

Wild Blueberry Edamame Smoothie 257

Green Mango Smoothie 259

Gingered Wheatgrass Tea 260

Ruby Red Grapefruit Spritzer 260

Orange Banana Smoothie 261

Maple Iced Mocha 261

Piña Colada Smoothies 262

Chocolate Strawberry Power Smoothie

SERVES 2	
Per Serving	
Calories	265
Fat	4g
Sodium	205mg
Carbohydrates	46g
Fiber	8g
Sugar	18g
Protein	11g

This smoothie is creamy, lightly sweetened with dates, and a delicious way to start the day. The chickpeas add little flavor to the smoothie but pack in the protein!

2 cups frozen strawberries

4 pitted dates

⅔ cup canned chickpeas, drained and rinsed

1½ cups low-fat milk, divided

1 tablespoon dark cocoa powder, divided

1 To prep smoothie packs, evenly divide strawberries, dates, and chickpeas between two freezer-safe storage bags or reusable containers. Keep in freezer up to 1 month.

2 To make smoothie, add ¾ cup milk, ½ tablespoon cocoa, and 1 frozen smoothie pack to a blender. Blend until smooth. Repeat with remaining milk, cocoa, and smoothie pack.

Thin Mint Cocoa

SERVES 4	
Per Serving	
Calories	145
Fat	2g
Sodium	137mg
Carbohydrates	30g
Fiber	3g
Sugar	27g
Protein	2g

This vegan version of the traditional hot cocoa is perfectly minty and soothing! Serve it with some freshly made Gingersnaps from Chapter 12 for a delicious winter treat.

¼ cup unsweetened cocoa powder

¼ cup packed light brown sugar

3½ cups unsweetened vanilla almond milk

¼ teaspoon peppermint extract

1 Prepare powder mixture in advance by whisking cocoa powder and sugar together in a small bowl. Store in an airtight container in a cool, dry place up to 3 months.

2 Measure milk into a medium saucepan and place over medium-high heat until milk begins to steam, 3–5 minutes. Whisk in cocoa mixture until no clumps remain.

3 Remove from heat. Stir in peppermint extract.

Chocolate Banana Smoothie

A creamy, chocolaty treat that also makes a great post-workout snack! There's oatmeal added to this smoothie for a boost of fiber.

1 large banana, peeled and cut in half

½ medium avocado, peeled, pitted, and cubed

2 tablespoons rolled oats

1 cup low-fat milk, divided

2 cups ice cubes, divided

2 tablespoons low-sodium natural peanut butter, divided

2 teaspoons cocoa powder, divided

SERVES 2	
Per Serving	
Calories	295
Fat	15g
Sodium	98mg
Carbohydrates	32g
Fiber	6g
Sugar	10g
Protein	10g

1 To prep smoothie packs, evenly divide banana, avocado, and oats between two freezer-safe storage bags or reusable containers. Keep in freezer up to 1 month.

2 To make smoothie, add ½ cup milk, 1 cup ice, 1 tablespoon peanut butter, 1 teaspoon cocoa, and 1 frozen smoothie pack to a blender. Blend until smooth. Repeat with remaining milk, ice cubes, peanut butter, cocoa, and smoothie pack.

Almond Butter Jelly Smoothie

A sweet, heart-healthy smoothie made with 100 percent Concord grape juice and almond butter, this Almond Butter Jelly Smoothie is a classic food pairing in smoothie form, sure to satisfy any sweet tooth!

1 cup frozen dark sweet cherries

½ cup frozen wild blueberries

1 cup 100 percent Concord grape juice, divided

¼ cup vanilla kefir, divided

2 tablespoons almond butter, divided

2 tablespoons chia seeds, divided

SERVES 2	
Per Serving	
Calories	299
Fat	12g
Sodium	27mg
Carbohydrates	43g
Fiber	8g
Sugar	32g
Protein	8g

1 To prep smoothie packs, evenly divide cherries and blueberries between two freezer-safe storage bags or reusable containers. Keep in freezer up to 1 month.

2 To make smoothie, add ½ cup grape juice, 2 tablespoons kefir, 1 tablespoon almond butter, 1 tablespoon chia seeds, and 1 frozen smoothie pack to a blender. Blend until smooth. Repeat with remaining juice, kefir, almond butter, chia seeds, and smoothie pack.

Mango Coconut Water Slush

SERVES 2

Per Serving

Calories	167
Fat	1g
Sodium	127mg
Carbohydrates	42g
Fiber	5g
Sugar	28g
Protein	3g

A refreshing, tropical slushy that's perfect for sipping in the summertime! Rehydrate and satisfy your sweet tooth with this Mango Coconut Water Slush.

4 ice cubes

1 cup frozen mango chunks

2 small bananas, peeled and cut into 1" pieces

6 fresh mint leaves

1 cup unflavored coconut water, divided

½ teaspoon honey, divided

1 To prep smoothie packs, evenly divide ice, mango, bananas, and mint between two freezer-safe storage bags or reusable containers. Keep in freezer up to 1 month.

2 To make slushy, add ½ cup coconut water, ¼ teaspoon honey, and 1 frozen smoothie pack to a blender. Blend until smooth. Repeat with remaining coconut water, honey, and smoothie pack.

Watermelon Refresher

SERVES 4

Per Serving

Calories	69
Fat	1g
Sodium	252mg
Carbohydrates	15g
Fiber	3g
Sugar	11g
Protein	2g

On a hot summer day, this should be your go-to beverage to rehydrate! Coconut water is great for replenishing electrolytes after physical activity because it contains potassium, sodium, and magnesium.

2 cups watermelon cubes

2 teaspoons lime juice

1 teaspoon minced fresh ginger

1 teaspoon chopped fresh basil leaves

4 cups chilled unflavored coconut water

1 In a blender, combine watermelon, lime juice, ginger, and basil. Blend until liquefied. Keep in refrigerator up to 2 days.

2 Pour one-fourth of the watermelon mixture into a serving glass. Top with 1 cup coconut water and stir. Repeat with remaining ingredients.

Mango Mint Smoothie

This smoothie will add some pep to your step in the morning with a burst of fresh mint! Frozen mango and banana make for a deliciously creamy smoothie.

2 cups frozen mango chunks

1 large banana, peeled and cut in half

½ cup fresh mint leaves

1 cup low-fat milk, divided

1 To prep smoothie packs, evenly divide mango, banana, and mint between two freezer-safe storage bags or reusable containers. Keep in freezer up to 1 month.

2 To make smoothie, add ½ cup milk and 1 frozen smoothie pack to a blender. Blend until smooth. Repeat with remaining milk and smoothie pack.

SERVES 2	
Per Serving	
Calories	225
Fat	3g
Sodium	67mg
Carbohydrates	47g
Fiber	5g
Sugar	31g
Protein	7g

Wild Blueberry Edamame Smoothie

The edamame in this smoothie adds a boost of protein without compromising the sweet flavor of the blueberries. Plus, wild blueberries are tiny but super flavorful and packed with antioxidants.

1½ cups frozen wild blueberries

1 cup frozen whole strawberries

⅔ cup frozen shelled edamame, thawed

1 cup low-fat milk, divided

2 tablespoons hemp seeds, divided

1 To prep smoothie packs, evenly divide blueberries, strawberries, and edamame between two freezer-safe storage bags or reusable containers. Keep in freezer up to 1 month.

2 To make smoothie, add ½ cup milk, 1 tablespoon hemp seeds, and 1 frozen smoothie pack to a blender. Blend until smooth. Repeat with remaining milk, seeds, and smoothie pack.

SERVES 2	
Per Serving	
Calories	270
Fat	10g
Sodium	75mg
Carbohydrates	33g
Fiber	9g
Sugar	14g
Protein	15g

Green Mango Smoothie

Tender baby spinach gives this smoothie its bright color and nutrient boost. The sweet and fruity flavor hides the spinach well; close your eyes and you'd never guess it's in there!

1 cup baby spinach

1 medium kiwi fruit, peeled and cut into 4 equal pieces

1 small banana, peeled and sliced into 4 equal pieces

1 cup mango juice, divided

½ cup low-fat vanilla Greek yogurt, divided

1 To prep smoothie packs, evenly divide spinach, kiwi fruit, and banana among four freezer-safe storage bags or reusable containers. Keep in freezer up to 1 month.

2 To make smoothie, add ¼ cup mango juice, 2 tablespoons yogurt, and 1 frozen smoothie pack to a blender. Blend until smooth. Repeat three times with remaining juice, yogurt, and smoothie packs.

SERVES 4

Per Serving

Calories	83
Fat	1g
Sodium	19mg
Carbohydrates	17g
Fiber	1g
Sugar	13g
Protein	4g

Gingered Wheatgrass Tea

SERVES 1	
Per Serving	
Calories	135
Fat	0g
Sodium	1mg
Carbohydrates	36g
Fiber	0g
Sugar	35g
Protein	1g

If you want to swap out your daily cup of coffee for a caffeine-free beverage, try this tea for an energy boost. Mix a larger batch of the ground ginger and honey together in advance to easily scoop from when you'd like a mug.

1 teaspoon ground ginger

2 tablespoons honey

¼ teaspoon wheatgrass powder

8 ounces boiling water

1 In a small airtight container, whisk together ginger and honey to make a syrup. Seal container and store at room temperature up to 10 days.

2 To make tea, add wheatgrass powder to a mug, then add water. Mix in ginger syrup, about 1 teaspoon at a time, to desired sweetness.

Ruby Red Grapefruit Spritzer

SERVES 4	
Per Serving	
Calories	19
Fat	0g
Sodium	12mg
Carbohydrates	5g
Fiber	0g
Sugar	5g
Protein	0g

An irresistibly rosy hue and mint freshness make this cocktail a satisfying nonalcoholic alternative to champagne.

¾ cup ruby red grapefruit juice

12 ounces unflavored seltzer water

4 teaspoons chopped fresh mint, divided

1 Combine grapefruit juice and seltzer water. Keep in refrigerator until ready to serve, up to 2 days.

2 To serve, add 1 teaspoon mint to a glass and top with one-fourth grapefruit juice mixture. Repeat with remaining ingredients.

Orange Banana Smoothie

With its deliciously decadent taste, this Orange Banana Smoothie is sure to add brightness to your morning.

1 cup frozen mango chunks

1 small banana, peeled and cut into 2 pieces

1 cup spinach

½ medium avocado, peeled, pitted, and cubed

1 cup orange juice, divided

2 cups low-fat vanilla Greek yogurt, divided

SERVES 2	
Per Serving	
Calories	421
Fat	13g
Sodium	94mg
Carbohydrates	52g
Fiber	7g
Sugar	37g
Protein	27g

1 To prep smoothie packs, evenly divide mango, banana, spinach, and avocado between two freezer-safe storage bags or reusable containers. Keep in freezer up to 1 month.

2 To make smoothie, add ½ cup orange juice, 1 cup yogurt, and 1 frozen smoothie pack to a blender. Blend until smooth. Repeat with remaining juice, yogurt, and smoothie pack.

Maple Iced Mocha

A sippable iced concoction of coffee, cocoa, and milk that's sweetened with a touch of maple syrup, this is perfect as a ready-to-go specialty coffee beverage for breakfast or an anytime pick-me-up.

1 small banana, peeled

½ cup brewed coffee

½ cup low-fat milk

½ cup low-fat plain Greek yogurt

1 tablespoon unsweetened cocoa powder

½ teaspoon ground cinnamon

1 tablespoon 100 percent grade A maple syrup

SERVES 2	
Per Serving	
Calories	152
Fat	3g
Sodium	53mg
Carbohydrates	26g
Fiber	3g
Sugar	15g
Protein	9g

Place all ingredients in a blender and blend until smooth. Store in an airtight container in refrigerator up to 2 days. Shake well before serving.

Piña Colada Smoothies

SERVES 4

Per Serving

Calories	128
Fat	1g
Sodium	145mg
Carbohydrates	23g
Fiber	3g
Sugar	17g
Protein	7g

COCONUT WATER

Coconut water is sold in cans and disposable juice boxes, often in the international aisle of grocery stores. Coconut water has the same great flavor as fresh coconut but is low in fat. Drink cold coconut water as pure refreshment, freeze it as ice cubes to subtly flavor cocktails, or add it to recipes for coconut nuance.

In these nonalcoholic coladas, coconut water adds the same great flavor as coconut milk without the fat.

2 cups diced fresh pineapple

1 small banana, peeled and cut into 4 pieces

2 cups unflavored coconut water, divided

1 cup low-fat vanilla Greek yogurt, divided

1 To prep smoothie packs, evenly divide pineapple and banana among four freezer-safe storage bags or reusable containers. Keep in freezer up to 1 month.

2 To make smoothie, add ½ cup coconut water, ¼ cup yogurt, and 1 frozen smoothie pack to blender. Blend until smooth. Repeat three times with remaining coconut water, yogurt, and smoothie packs.

Two-Week Meal Plan

Week 1			
	Breakfast	**Lunch**	**Snack**
Monday	ABC Muffins + 1 hard-cooked egg + Maple Turkey Sausage	Salmon Cakes with Roasted Red Potatoes, Carrots, and Brussels Sprouts	Chewy Granola Bars
Tuesday	Maple Turkey Sausage + whole-wheat bread + Grapefruit and Orange Yogurt Parfait	Greek Lemon Chicken Orzo Soup with toasted whole-wheat bread	ABC Muffins
Wednesday	ABC Muffins + 1 hard-cooked egg + Maple Turkey Sausage	Southwest Loaded Sweet Potatoes	Grapefruit and Orange Yogurt Parfait
Thursday	Maple Turkey Sausage + whole-wheat bread + Grapefruit and Orange Yogurt Parfait	Greek Lemon Chicken Orzo Soup (from freezer) with toasted whole-wheat bread	ABC Muffins
Friday	Breakfast Burritos	Crispy Tofu Stir-Fry	Chocolate Strawberry Power Smoothie
Saturday	Breakfast Burritos	Tuscan Kale Salad	Cranberry Almond Energy Bites
Sunday	Sunday Morning Waffles	Tuscan Kale Salad	Cranberry Almond Energy Bites

	Week 1		
	Dinner	**Dessert**	**Prep Ahead**
Monday	30-Minute Ground Beef Pizza		Make Coconut Chia Pudding
Tuesday	Southwest Loaded Sweet Potatoes	Coconut Chia Pudding	Breakfast Burritos
Wednesday	Greek Lemon Chicken Orzo Soup with side salad and toasted bread	Coconut Chia Pudding	Turkey Meatballs
Thursday	Crispy Tofu Stir-Fry		
Friday	Pesto Rice with Portobello Mushrooms		
Saturday	Pesto Rice with Portobello Mushrooms		Peach Cobbler
Sunday	Turkey Meatballs served with whole-wheat pasta or over cooked Quinoa and low-sodium marinara sauce	Peach Cobbler	Vegetable Egg Muffins, tuna salad from Zesty Tuna Lettuce Wraps, Vegetable Burgers

Week 2

	Breakfast	Lunch	Snack
Monday	2 Vegetable Egg Muffins + 1 leftover Sunday Morning Waffle	Zesty Tuna Lettuce Wraps	Blueberry Cottage Cheese Parfait
Tuesday	2 Vegetable Egg Muffins + whole-wheat bread	Sheet Pan Pork Roast and Vegetables	Chocolate Banana Smoothie
Wednesday	Breakfast Burritos	Zesty Tuna Lettuce Wraps + fresh fruit	Blueberry Cottage Cheese Parfait
Thursday	Raspberry Almond Overnight Oats	Greek Chicken and Cauliflower Rice Bowl	Green Mango Smoothie
Friday	Raspberry Almond Overnight Oats	Sesame Shrimp Stir-Fry	Crunchy Coated Nuts
Saturday	Breakfast Burritos	Turkey Meatballs with whole-wheat pasta and low-sodium marinara sauce	Chewy Granola Bars
Sunday	Sweet Potato Breakfast Pie	Seared Sirloin Steaks with Garlicky Greens + side salad	Chewy Granola Bars

	Week 2		
	Dinner	**Dessert**	**Prep Ahead**
Monday	Sheet Pan Pork Roast and Vegetables	Peach Cobbler	
Tuesday	Vegetable Burger with Zucchini Sticks		
Wednesday	Greek Chicken and Cauliflower Rice Bowl		Make Overnight Oats
Thursday	Sesame Shrimp Stir-Fry		Make Overnight Oats, Crunchy Coated Nuts
Friday	Vegetable Burger with Zucchini Sticks		
Saturday	Seared Sirloin Steaks with Garlicky Greens + roasted sweet potatoes	Cinnamon Peanut Butter Cookies	Greek Lemon Chicken Orzo Soup
Sunday	Salmon Cakes w/ Roasted Red Potatoes, Carrots, and Brussels Sprouts	Cinnamon Peanut Butter Cookies	Prep ground beef for pizza, roast sweet potatoes, ABC Muffins, Maple Turkey Sausage

STANDARD US/METRIC
MEASUREMENT CONVERSIONS

VOLUME CONVERSIONS

US Volume Measure	Metric Equivalent
⅛ teaspoon	0.5 milliliter
¼ teaspoon	1 milliliter
½ teaspoon	2 milliliters
1 teaspoon	5 milliliters
½ tablespoon	7 milliliters
1 tablespoon (3 teaspoons)	15 milliliters
2 tablespoons (1 fluid ounce)	30 milliliters
¼ cup (4 tablespoons)	60 milliliters
⅓ cup	90 milliliters
½ cup (4 fluid ounces)	125 milliliters
⅔ cup	160 milliliters
¾ cup (6 fluid ounces)	180 milliliters
1 cup (16 tablespoons)	250 milliliters
1 pint (2 cups)	500 milliliters
1 quart (4 cups)	1 liter (about)

WEIGHT CONVERSIONS

US Weight Measure	Metric Equivalent
½ ounce	15 grams
1 ounce	30 grams
2 ounces	60 grams
3 ounces	85 grams
¼ pound (4 ounces)	115 grams
½ pound (8 ounces)	225 grams
¾ pound (12 ounces)	340 grams
1 pound (16 ounces)	454 grams

OVEN TEMPERATURE CONVERSIONS

Degrees Fahrenheit	Degrees Celsius
200 degrees F	95 degrees C
250 degrees F	120 degrees C
275 degrees F	135 degrees C
300 degrees F	150 degrees C
325 degrees F	160 degrees C
350 degrees F	180 degrees C
375 degrees F	190 degrees C
400 degrees F	205 degrees C
425 degrees F	220 degrees C
450 degrees F	230 degrees C

BAKING PAN SIZES

American	Metric
8 × 1½ inch round baking pan	20 × 4 cm cake tin
9 × 1½ inch round baking pan	23 × 3.5 cm cake tin
11 × 7 × 1½ inch baking pan	28 × 18 × 4 cm baking tin
13 × 9 × 2 inch baking pan	30 × 20 × 5 cm baking tin
2 quart rectangular baking dish	30 × 20 × 3 cm baking tin
15 × 10 × 2 inch baking pan	30 × 25 × 2 cm baking tin (Swiss roll tin)
9 inch pie plate	22 × 4 or 23 × 4 cm pie plate
7 or 8 inch springform pan	18 or 20 cm springform or loose bottom cake tin
9 × 5 × 3 inch loaf pan	23 × 13 × 7 cm or 2 lb narrow loaf or pate tin
1½ quart casserole	1.5 liter casserole
2 quart casserole	2 liter casserole

Index

Note: Page numbers in **bold** indicate recipe category lists.

Apples
    Apple Butternut Soup, 172
    Cinnamon Apple Pear Sauce, 236
    pancakes and muffins with, 59, 66, 68
    Pork Chops with Sautéed Apples and Shallots, 117
    Tart Apple Salad with Fennel and Honey Yogurt Dressing, 84
Asparagus, 34, 56, 177
Avocado, 72–73, 212, 213, 226

Bacon, 80, 106
Bananas
    desserts with plantains and, 237, 238–39
    muffins and pancakes with, 44, 61, 66
    smoothies/slush with, 255, 256, 257, 259, 261, 262–63
Beans and other legumes. *See also* Green beans

about: chickpeas/garbanzos, 203
Black Bean Burgers, 186
Black Bean Vegetable Soup, 198
Black-Eyed Pea Burrito Bowl, 164
Chicken, Black Bean, and Vegetable Soft Tacos, 127
Chicken, Corn, and Black Bean Chili, 128
Falafel with Tzatziki, 175–76
Healthier 7-Layer Dip, 213
hummus dishes, 225, 227
other recipes with, 70–71, 137, 166–67, 254
Red Lentil Soup with Bacon, 106
Slow Cooker Squash and Chickpea Curry, 203
Spicy Chickpea Tacos with Arugula, 170
Sweet Potato and Black Bean Burritos, 187
White Bean and Vegetable Soup, 199

Wild Blueberry Edamame Smoothie, 257–58
Beef entrées, **101**, 104–5, 107–11, 114, 202
Beets, 70–71, 82
Berries
    muffins with, 44, 67
    smoothies with, 254, 255, 257–58
    snacks with, 207, 210, 211, 214
Beverages/smoothies, **253**–62
Breakfast, **43**–68, 207, 208
Broccoli, 38, 139, 148, 160, 165
Broth, basic low-sodium, 29
Brussels sprouts, 37, 102
Burgers
    Black Bean Burgers, 186
    Mediterranean Turkey Burgers, 193
    Seasoned Turkey Burgers with Sautéed Mushrooms and Swiss, 142
    Vegetable Burgers, 204
Burritos and burrito bowl, 164, 187, 208

Cabbage, 80, 144
Carrot Cake Cookies, 241
Carrots, Roasted in Red Potatoes, Carrots, and Brussels Sprouts, 37
Cauliflower
Coconut Cauliflower Curry, 183
Greek Chicken and Cauliflower Rice Bowl, 122
Homemade Cauliflower Rice, 33
Roasted Broccoli and Cauliflower, 38
Roasted Cauliflower Steaks with Creamy Chimichurri, 170–71
Cheese
Blueberry Cottage Cheese Parfait, 214
eggs with (See Eggs)
Honey-Sweetened Fruit and Ricotta Toast, 45
pasta with (See Pasta)
Chicken
entrées, 119, 120–22, 124–37, 190, 200–201
Greek Chicken and Cauliflower Rice Bowl, 122
Greek Lemon Chicken Orzo Soup, 197
Homemade Chicken Stock, 28
Whole Roasted Chicken, 26–27
Chili, 128
Chili seasoning, salt-free, 42
Chocolate, hot cocoa and smoothie with, 254, 255

Chocolate and white chocolate, desserts with, 232, 234–35, 243, 246, 248
Citrus
desserts with, 234, 252
Grapefruit and Orange Yogurt Parfait, 54
Grapefruit Salmon Salad, 77–78
Grapefruit Sauce, 152–53
Lemon Blueberry Quinoa Breakfast Bars, 207
spritzer and smoothie with, 260, 261
Coconut, desserts with, 231, 237, 243, 252
Coconut and coconut water, drinks/smoothie with, 256, 262–63
Coffee, in Maple Iced Mocha, 261
Cooking spray, 149
Corn and cornmeal, 62, 67, 72–73, 128, 244. See also Popcorn
Corn bread, 100
Couscous, 86, 88–89, 93, 97, 99
Crackers, whole-grain, 223

DASH diet
about: definition and overview, 13, 14–15; this book and, 10–11; weight loss and, 16
fitting into your lifestyle, 18
foods to choose and to limit, 16–18
helping with hypertension, 15–16
meal prepping, 19–23

sodium-free baking powder and, 66
two-week meal plan, 264–67
Desserts, **229**–52
Drinks/smoothies, **253**–62

Eggs
about: liquid substitutes, 41
Asparagus, Swiss, and Ricotta Frittata, 56
Breakfast Burritos, 208
Butternut Squash and Fajita Vegetable Frittata, 51–52
Swiss Cheese and Chive Mini Quiches, 55
Vegetable Egg Muffins, 45

Freezer meals, **189**–208

Garam masala, about, 183
Gingered Wheatgrass Tea, 260
Gingersnaps, 240
Granola and granola bars, 48, 53, 222
Green beans, 79, 83, 173, 199
Grocery shopping tips, 22–23

Herbes de Provence, 159
Hummus, 212, 225, 227

Kale, other dishes with, 114, 135, 164, 184, 203, 220
Kale, salads with, 70–71, 75, 77–78, 80
Kebabs, chicken, 120–21

Mango, 137, 245, 249, 256, 257, 259, 261
Meal plan, two-week, 264–67
Meal prep components, **25**–42
Meal prepping, 19–23

Meatloaf minis, 140
Muffins and toast, 44–47, 66–68, 205, 248, 249
Mushrooms
    Linguine with Plum Tomatoes, Mushrooms, and Tempeh, 182
    Mushroom Soup with Orzo, 169
    Pesto Rice with Portobello Mushrooms, 178
    Portobello Mushroom Parmigiana, 168
    Sautéed Asparagus and Mushrooms, 34
    Scrambled Tofu with Mushrooms and Zucchini, 58

Nutritional yeast flakes, about, 184
Nuts and seeds
    about: pistachios, 48; pumpkin seeds, 230; unsalted peanut butter, 180
    Almond Butter Jelly Smoothie, 255
    Cranberry Almond Energy Bites, 211
    Crunchy Coated Nuts, 218
    desserts with, 230, 231, 233, 238–39
    granola and granola bars, 48, 53, 222

Oats
    Baked Pumpkin Oatmeal, 205
    bars and bites with, 207, 211, 222
    granolas with, 48, 53, 222

muffins with, 44, 68
Overnight Oats, 34
Raspberry Almond Overnight Oats, 54
Zucchini Oatmeal Cookies, 230

Pancakes and waffles, 59–62, 64–65
Pasta
    about: orzo, 197
    Kale-Stuffed Manicotti, 184–85
    Linguine with Plum Tomatoes, Mushrooms, and Tempeh, 182
    soups with, 103, 125, 144, 169
    10-Minute Thai Noodles, 180
    Thai-Inspired Pasta Salad, 85
    Tuna Pasta Salad with Broccoli and Sun-Dried Tomatoes, 160
    Vegetable Baked Ziti, 181
    Vegetarian Lasagna, 195–96
    Whole-Grain Pasta with Meat Sauce, 108
    Whole-Grain Penne with Lemony Roasted Asparagus, 177
    Whole-Grain Rotini with Pork, Pumpkin, and Sage, 115
Peaches and peach cobbler, 46–47, 250–51
Pears, 65, 87, 90, 236
Peppers, stuffed, 141
Pineapple, 156, 227, 262–63
Pizza, 107, 139
Popcorn, 219, 232

Pork entrées, **101**, 102, 103, 106, 113, 115–17
Potatoes
    Cheesy Potato Chowder, 124
    Garlic Rosemary Mashed Potatoes, 98
    Healthy Fish and Chips, 150–51
    Roasted Red Potatoes, Carrots, and Brussels Sprouts, 37
    salads with, 81, 83
Pound Cake Minis, 247
Pretzels, homemade soft, 216–17
Pumpkin, 53, 115, 205, 248

Quinoa, 30, 32, 49, 207

Rhubarb, in Mini Cornmeal Rhubarb Crisps, 244
Rice
    about: soaking before cooking, 178
    Brown Rice, 31
    Homemade Cauliflower Rice, 33
    Lemon Parmesan Rice with Fresh Parsley, 92
    Pesto Rice with Portobello Mushrooms, 178
    Rice-Quinoa Blend, 30
    Saucy Barbecued Chicken with Rice, 130
Roasting for flavor, 177

Salads and sides, 49, **69–100**, 160
Sandwiches. *See* Burgers; Burritos and burrito bowl; Tacos; Wraps

Sauces, dressings, and dips. *See also* Hummus
  about: how vinegar is made, 160; low-sodium tartar sauce, 150; mayonnaise substitute, 157
  Asian-Inspired Low-Sodium Marinade, 42
  Basil Pesto, 40
  Cinnamon Apple Pear Sauce, 236
  Creamy Chimichurri, 170–71
  Fruit Salsa, 210
  Grapefruit Sauce, 152–53
  Grape Tomato Salsa, 155
  Healthier 7-Layer Dip, 213
  Holy Guacamole, 226
  Honey Yogurt Dressing, 84
  Italian Vinaigrette, 84
  Pineapple Relish, 156
  Pineapple Salsa, 227
  Roasted Tomato Salsa, 228
  Salt-Free Mayonnaise, 41
  Spicy and Tangy Barbecue Sauce, 39
  Spicy Lime, Cilantro, and Garlic Marinade, 40
  Tzatziki, 175–76
Scones, 238–39, 252
Seafood, 77–78, **143**–60, 191
Smoothies/beverages, **253**–62
Snacks, **209**–28
Soups, 103, 106, 124, 125, 128, 144, 169, 172, 197–99
Spinach, 93, 96, 195–96, 208, 259, 261
Squash. *See also* Pumpkin
  about: zucchini, 215
  Apple Butternut Soup, 172
  Butternut Squash and Fajita Vegetable Frittata, 51–52

Curry-Roasted Butternut Squash, 39
Scrambled Tofu with Mushrooms and Zucchini, 58
Slow Cooker Squash and Chickpea Curry, 203
Zucchini Cakes, 91
Zucchini Oatmeal Cookies, 230
Zucchini Sticks, 215
Stock and broth, 28, 29
Storing prepared meals, 23
Sushi, vegetable, 188
Sweet potatoes
  meat and vegetable dishes with, 102, 127
  Roasted Sweet Potatoes, 35
  Sheet Pan Pork Roast and Vegetables, 102
  Southwest Loaded Sweet Potatoes, 166–67
  Sweet Potato and Black Bean Burritos, 187
  Sweet Potato Breakfast Pie, 63
  Sweet Potato Crisps, 221

Tabbouleh Salad, 88–89
Tacos, 127, 179
Tempeh, 182
Tofu
  about: adding protein with, 166; leftover uses, 162
  Crispy Tofu Stir-Fry, 165
  Kale-Stuffed Manicotti, 184–85
  Scrambled Tofu with Mushrooms and Zucchini, 58

Sesame Tofu with Sautéed Green Beans, 173
Tofu Vegetable Potpie, 162–63
Tools for meal prepping, 21–22
Turkey
  Asian Turkey Lettuce Wraps, 123
  Broccoli, Ground Turkey, and Pesto Pizza, 139
  Ground Turkey Meatloaf Minis, 140
  Maple Turkey Sausage, 57
  Mediterranean Turkey Burgers, 193
  Seasoned Turkey Burgers with Sautéed Mushrooms and Swiss, 142
  Turkey and Brown Rice–Stuffed Peppers, 141
  Turkey Meatballs, 192
Turmeric, about, 58

Vegan/vegetarian Entrées, **161**–88, 195–96

Watermelon Refresher, 256
Wheat Berry Pilaf with Roasted Vegetables, 95
Wheatgrass tea, gingered, 260
Wraps, 123, 137, 146–47, 208. *See also* Burritos and burrito bowl; Tacos